HERO OF THE UPHOLDER

Hero of the Upholder

The Story of Lieutenant Commander
M. D. Wanklyn VC, DSO**

Jim Allaway

Airlife
England

To A. E. Bullock DSM, and Lieutenant A. E. Bullock RN, submariners in two world wars — and to all those 'still on patrol'.

Their feats, their fortunes and their fames
Are hidden from their nearest kin;
No eager public backs or blames,
No journal prints the yarns they spin
(The Censor would not let it in!)
When they return from run or raid.
Unheard they work, unseen they win.
That is the custom of 'The Trade'.

Rudyard Kipling
The Trade

Copyright © Jim Allaway, 1991

First published in the UK in 1991 by
Airlife Publishing Ltd.

British Library Cataloguing in Publication Data
Allaway, Jim, *1950-*
Hero of the *Upholder*
   1.   World War 2. Naval operations by Great Britain. Royal Navy
   I.   Title
   940.5451
   ISBN 1 85310 218 0

Printed in England by Livesey Ltd., Shrewsbury.

Airlife Publishing Ltd.
101 Longden Road, Shrewsbury, England.

Contents

Foreword

by Admiral of the Fleet Lord Fieldhouse of Gosport GCB, GBE — Flag Officer Submarines, 1976-78

It is somewhat surprising that, until this book, so little has been written about David Wanklyn, an officer who played such a major part in the last war. For, as the Commanding Officer of the Submarine *Upholder*, in only just over one year, early 1941 to April 1942, operating out of Malta, he sank the greatest tonnage of enemy shipping of any of our submariners. He has been held by successive generations of submariners as the archetypal CO whose bravery and high professionalism have never been in doubt.

For my generation of post-war submarine officers he has been almost a mythical figure, and this immensely readable and well researched book of Jim Allaway's has given us an insight into the man and his family which I found utterly fascinating.

David Wanklyn will always be, by definition, a legendary figure, but with this book the legend is brought to life, springing out of the pages. I wholeheartedly recommend it to anyone, old or young, with an interest in the immense contribution of the British Submarine Service towards victory in the Second World War.

Author's Preface
and Acknowledgements

Within the Submarine Service the name of Wanklyn is spoken in awe; outside the Royal Navy it is hardly known. Yet he was the leading British ace of World War II — and in terms of awards for valour the VC and three DSOs he earned in command of HMS *Upholder* make him the most highly decorated of all RN personnel to have served in that conflict.

German U-boat men came home to flower garlands and the whirr of cine cameras. Nazi propagandists were quick to present their achievements — which were indeed hugely significant and out of all proportion to their numbers — in the most glowing terms. Tangible rewards in the form of the highest military decorations were swiftly forthcoming. By contrast their Allied counterparts returned from patrol almost unnoticed. State recognition for individuals commended for gallantry only came through after many months — too often posthumously — and promotion was slow. Yet while it is true that they did not have the same opportunity as their German counterparts to chalk up huge tallies of merchant shipping tonnage sunk in the North Atlantic, their record in the Mediterranean in particular, in starving the supply lines to the Afrika Korps, was outstanding and was recognised as one of the most telling contributory factors in the eventual victory over Rommel in the Western Desert. Wanklyn was pre-eminent in this campaign and the record he shared with his fellow COs of the Tenth Flotilla at Malta was achieved in spite of the fact that they began the war quite criminally ill-prepared in the techniques of conducting operations.

Why then, in retrospect, have our submariners been accorded so little in the way of public acclaim? Part of the answer must lie in the then still widely prevalent Admiralty view of the submarine as 'the weapon of the weaker power', of it being somehow 'mean, underhand and damned British'. That attitude, in the context of the modern sea power struggle, has changed. But half a century ago it was strongly held by a nation that had long based the idea of its maritime supremacy in the reputation of the capabilities of a large surface Fleet. At Jutland in 1916 the myth of that Fleet's invincibility was exploded — though not by the U-boats, which were busy elsewhere, wreaking havoc in other strategically much more important areas, the supply routes across the Atlantic and generally, around the coast of the UK. Then as later, Britain's survival depended on the safe passage of every kind of provision; at one point in World War I food stocks alone were expected to run out in six weeks and only the late introduction of the convoy system averted catastrophe.

But the subject of this book grew to manhood in a period in which the British forgot many of the lessons of 1914–18. The role of the submarine was misunderstood — despite the clear example of the enemy's lone-wolf operators — and the interwar years were marked by a series of disastrous experiments with huge, unwieldy submarine cruisers capable of high surface speeds to enable them to keep up with units of the surface Fleet. None of them fired a shot in anger, though they claimed many lives in some of the worst peacetime submarine accidents.

Thus it may be said that Wanklyn, in common with the rest of his contemporaries, had to learn his business virtually from scratch. All who knew him spoke of a consummate professional devoted to his craft. As his fame grew his patrol reports were required reading for his fellow COs. At first sight he was the type who might have inspired G. A. Henty at an earlier period to write a school prize novel — *With Wanklyn at Malta*. Indeed, he possessed many of the preferred attributes of the late Victorian hero — compassion, dedication, simple Christian conviction and apparently unshakeable confidence in his own abilities.

Yet he was also a shy man of considerable sensitivity, and as a leader of men surprisingly vulnerable to feelings of insecurity where personal relationships were concerned. Though much admired by his fellows for his skill and daring, he was seldom disposed to argue his case against the views of senior officers — unlike, for example, the extrovert, emotional 'Tommo' Tompkinson or the abrasive, eccentric Anthony Miers. And while he was able to inspire the love of his fellow men, his character was marked by a reserve that discouraged intimacy. He formed few close friendships.

There will be no room here to recount the exploits of his many distinguished companions in the Tenth Flotilla who comprise the Royal Navy Submarine Service's single most celebrated pantheon. Several of them were as capable and almost as successful — and certainly luck played a part in HMS *Upholder's* extraordinary career. But the impression remains that Wanklyn's celebrity within the close-knit family of what used to be known as 'The Trade' is by no means solely due to his martial prowess. He may just have been, in the words of one submarine skipper who survived the war, 'simply a nicer fellow than the rest of us'. The grief within the Service that followed his passing was profound. He was, and remains, an inspiration — and something of an enigma.

Of the people who have helped me in the preparation of this book, my thanks, first of all, to Mr Gus Britton of the Royal Navy Submarine Museum, for his unrivalled knowledge of the minutiae of submarine history; for introducing me to his wide circle of contacts;

and for deleting from the manuscript the several solecisms I unwittingly committed. He fired my enthusiasm for the project when he suggested that any sort of biography of the Royal Navy's leading submarine ace was a near impossibility. HMS *Upholder* went to the bottom with all hands and all her commander's personal effects followed suit in another ill-fated submarine a few days later — there would be 'no-one to talk to and hardly any archive material to draw on,' he advised.

Yet in the course of nearly two years of research we made contact with a number of his surviving relatives, friends and contemporaries — including several of his antagonists — as well as five men who served with him in *Upholder* and missed, for one reason or another, her last patrol. So I have made the attempt. It is not a work of scholarship, although I have given it some of the trappings — to assist, as I hope, those who may find the means to deliver a more rounded portrait of one of the Submarine Service's most revered and, at the same time, most elusive personalities.

I have relied substantially on first-hand accounts, including Wanklyn's own meticulous patrol reports which are preserved at the Public Records Office and the Submarine Museum. All books consulted are listed in the Bibliography, but I have drawn on only one at length: Rear Admiral G. W. G. Simpson's *Periscope View*, which is likely to remain one of the best histories of the Tenth Flotilla as a whole. For permission to quote from this and from Jill Edwards' *The British Government and the Spanish Civil War* I am indebted to Macmillan Ltd; also to Thames and Hudson Ltd for an extract from Gabriel Jackson's *A Concise History of the Spanish Civil War*; and to the estate of Ernle Bradford and Hamish Hamilton Ltd for a passage from *Siege: Malta 1940/43*.

I am grateful to Mrs Betty Wanklyn for giving me access to her own files relating to her husband's achievements and for the loan of his surviving correspondence; and to the following, for furnishing me with their personal recollections: Capitano di Vascello the Barone Francesco Acton, Mr Bryant Bird, Captain Michael Crawford, Mr George Curnall, Mr William Curtis, Rear Admiral George Gay, Vice Admiral Sir Peter Gretton, Vice Admiral Sir Arthur Hezlet, Mrs Melloney Harris, Mr Fred Matthews, Vice Admiral Sir Hugh Mackenzie, Captain Pat Norman, Commander Dick Raikes, the Rev. Christopher Read, Commander Michael St John, Mrs Stella Danvers, Mr Gordon Selby, Mr George Tuckwood, Mr Jack Wanklyn, Miss Joan Wanklyn, Mr Peter Wanklyn and Lt Colonel Robert Wilson.

Finally, I would like to acknowledge the assistance of Mr David Ashton of the Royal Navy Historical Library; Mr Mario Tortolani of the NATO translation department, HQ Commander-in-Chief Fleet; Fleet Public Relations Officer Mr Geoffrey Palmer; Mr Michael

Smith of Vickers Public Relations Department; Captain W. W. F. Chatterton Dickson, RN, compiler of *Seedie's Roll of Naval Honours and Awards 1939-1959*; Mr Alexander Tulloch of the Academy of Graphology; and my mother, who helped type the final draft.

Old Portsmouth
1990

Chapter 1
'A fitting and a most humbling occasion'

On launch day at Vickers shipyard the children of Barrow-in-Furness turn out en-masse. Many of them — most of them, probably — will one day find employment there; well over half the town's workforce are on the staff. But this particular day, 2 December 1986, was to mark the unveiling of the first conventional diesel-electric submarine built for the Royal Navy in over 20 years and the employees had a big stake in the proceedings. The company had been privatised earlier in the year and over 80 per cent of them had taken up shares in ownership. The management had just announced a healthy profit of £7,700,000 from the first six months of operation; with orders worth £2 billion and ten years' work pretty well guaranteed, unlike many shipbuilding communities of the North they could look to the future with confidence.

Barrow, a bleak, medium-sized town on the Cumbrian coast backed by spectacular rugged scenery on the fringe of the Lake District, is very much a submarine community. In 1986 it was celebrating its centenary as Britain's leading submarine builder for the Royal Navy and fifteen other navies. The new vessel, designed to replace the ageing Oberon patrol boats (submarines are 'boats,' not 'ships') was the 325th to be built by the yard for the Senior Service. It was also to be one of the last to be launched in the old traditional way — sliding swiftly down the slipway to the accompaniment of rousing cheers in a cloud of rust thrown up by the massive coils of the restraining chains. Only one more would begin its career thus; thereafter they would enter their natural element in a more convenient but decidedly less dramatic fashion, gently lowered into the water on a giant electric lift operated by over 100 winches — a process likely to take an hour and a half.

The Union flag was much in evidence as the crowds waited in drizzling rain for the Royal sponsor, Her Royal Highness The Duchess of Kent. Coolly stunning as ever, despite the grey skies and blustering wind, she arrived on Platform One at the town station at 9.40 a.m., the familiar broad sweep of ash blonde hair topped by an emerald green pill box hat, the rest of her outfit set to match with touches of black and white — mimicking, whether by happy accident or design, the Vickers company livery. As her party made its way through the gates to the launch site and mounted the lofty platform in front of the submarine's gleaming black bow, the Works Band voiced their appreciation, striking up with *'Ain't She Sweet?'*[1]

At 10.40 a.m. precisely she swung the bottle — not champagne but a decidedly non-vintage elderberry wine made by the wife of the new vessel's Engineer Officer[2] — with practised ease and announced in ringing tones: 'I name this ship HMS *Upholder* . . .'

And so, as a helicopter whirred overhead, filming the event for a company marketing feature, the most distinguished name in the history of the Submarine Service was born again. So too was laid the keystone of a project that might have seemed an anachronism in the nuclear age. Overall, nuclear submarines have the operational edge over diesel-electric boats, which are considerably more restricted in range. But the Vickers Type 2400, of which *Upholder* was the prototype, had sufficient advantages in silence of operation and economy to make it an attractive buy both to the Royal Navy and their political masters — whoever they might be.

Her predecessor had been the top-scoring British submarine of World War II. In twenty-five patrols over sixteen months in 1941-42 she sank 129,529 tons of enemy shipping, including two U-boats, a destroyer, an armed trawler, fifteen transport and supply ships — and probably a cruiser and another destroyer. Her deeds are recorded at the Royal Navy Submarine Museum at Gosport in Hampshire, traditional home of the Service as the base for the 1st Submarine Squadron at HMS *Dolphin*.

Dolphin had tended in recent years to be overshadowed by the nuclear estalishments at Devonport and Faslane on the Clyde. Now the Government's decision to buy the Vickers 2400 design seemed to have secured its future and £70m was being invested there in building works and equipment, preparing for the arrival of four new *Upholder* class submarines costing close on £100m each that were expected to have entered service by the middle of the next decade. Haslar Creek at the mouth of Portsmouth Harbour was being dredged down to a depth of over 30ft to accommodate the boats, which had a deeper draught reflecting their nuclear-style configuration, and the Submarine School there was starting a package of 70 new courses for the men who would serve in them.

Nearly twice as fast as her World War II predecessor and able to dive much deeper, the new *Upholder* was armed with the Sub Harpoon anti-ship missile, a self-guiding weapon with a range of over 40 miles — quite a contrast to the chancy, pre-set salvo torpedoes her predecessor had to rely on to carry out her attacks — as well as the newly-modified Mk 24 Tigerfish wire-guided torpedo. At the Press conference Vickers Chief Executive Dr Rodney Leach described her multi-role capability. Highly effective in anti-submarine and anti-ship operations, she could also be used for coastal surveillance, reconnaissance missions and secret landings of agents and special forces. Noise reduction techniques, including hull coatings originally developed for the nuclear submarine programme, had been adapted for her.

'This first boat . . . will demonstrate that her stealth and combat systems are superior to any other in the world — or for that matter on any other builder's drawing boards. *Upholder* has the combat capabilities of a nuclear submarine, lacking only the endurance of a nuclear power plant. We are justifiably proud of her.'

Apart from the mass of computerised sensors and sonars with which any modern boat is crammed, the most striking thing about her to any old-time submariner would be the accommodation. The new *Upholder* had two decks forward of the main machinery space occupying the whole of the aft section. Most of the lower deck below the Control Room and the weapons compartment was given over to the crew. Settees in the Wardroom and both ratings' messes, two separate washrooms each with showers and a total of three WCs — such facilities may seem little more than adequate provision for the comfort of 44 men, but to the crew of the old *Upholder* they would have spelled luxury beyond imagination. And while the everyday fare on board was not likely to match up to the fillet of Beef Wellington washed down with 1982 Chateau Lyonnat that the launch guests were shortly to savour, it would be a lot closer to haute cuisine than the old wartime diet of tinned herrings and cheese 'oosh'. The 2400 had a galley with an electric range, deep fryer, oven and grill — and with a high capacity refrigerator to keep the food fresh there was practically no limit to her cooks' invention.

All in all, the living in *Upholder* would be a distinct step up from the class she was to replace. Facing the Press with Dr Leach was her first designated commanding officer, 34-year-old Lt Commander Nick Harris. He was presently 'driving' the venerable HMS *Oberon* and so was shortly to be moving from the first of the old to the first of the new. The Oberons had an enviable reputation for performance and efficiency and had been rated as the best diesel-electric submarines in service in the world, having given sterling service to the navies of Australia, Canada, Brazil and Chile as well as to the Royal Navy over the past 20 years. Harris, however, had done duty in the latest class of nuclear-powered Fleet submarines and in two of the even more spacious Polaris boats, so he already had a taste of the comparatively gracious underwater lifestyle available to submariners in the latter part of the 20th century. Malvern-educated, a tall, openly friendly young man, confidently fast-talking, his responses to the probings of the media were nonetheless well-considered. He appeared to be enjoying himself.

The captain of the earlier *Upholder* probably wouldn't have — big social occasions were definitely not his scene. An hour later, as they watched the glistening black hulk glide down into Walney Channel to be hitched to the waiting tugs and towed round to Buccleuch Dock for outfitting, two of the special guests were remembering a quietly spoken, rather shy individual, fond of the outdoors and his own company.

These two were lucky to be there and they knew it. Forty-four years earlier the first *Upholder* had gone down with all hands off Tripoli. Losses were high at that time for British submarines operating out of Malta; the men who served in them had a less than fifty/fifty chance of survival. Captain Michael 'Tubby' Crawford had been the boat's First Lieutenant for the larger portion of her brilliant career and had only left her to complete his commanding officer's qualifying course. Later he had operated his own successful command, HMS *Unseen*, and had twice earned the award of the Distinguished Service Cross. He had survived the war, he believed, thanks to the lessons he learned from his former skipper — and now he learned that *Unseen* was to be the name given to the second of the Upholder class.

Former Chief Petty Officer Gordon Selby had missed *Upholder's* last patrol by a few weeks, through his transfer on promotion to another boat. He had travelled from Australia to be present at the launch ceremony and planned to return again for the commissioning at a later date.

The hand of fate had intervened to save one or two more 'Upholders' — in curious circumstances, it will be revealed — but by and large the men who died on that final dive to oblivion had been together from the beginning. Crawford and Selby were rarities and were singled out for special mention by the Chairman of Vickers, Sir David Nicolson, in his address over lunch.

'The heroic deeds of HMS *Upholder's* Commanding Officer and crew stand proud in the annals of the British Submarine Service . . . The launch of HMS *Upholder* today is a fitting and a most humbling occasion, on which to remember those who made the supreme sacrifice in the cause of freedom and justice.'

As the wine flowed, the name of one of these came frequently to the lips of the celebrants — Malcolm David Wanklyn.

Chapter 2
Out of Argentina

He liked to think of himself as a Scot — and wanted others to think it, too. Yet his father, though of old English stock, was born in the Argentine, his mother's parents were Irish and he himself first saw light of day in Calcutta.

His father, William Lumb Wanklyn, was brought up in Ayrshire where he early learned to enjoy the outdoor life of a country gentleman, becoming like his son at a later date a proficient shot and an expert dry fly fisherman. David, as he was known in the family, spent much of his own youth in William's childhood haunts. Ever after, he regarded Scotland as his spiritual home; in the temporal sense he can hardly be said to have had one at all.

The Wanklyns trace their family tree back to John Wanklyn of Kimbolton in Herefordshire, whose life spanned the last three-quarters of the 16th century. They spent most of the next at nearby Goodrich and were later to settle around Manchester. Then John Bradshaw Wanklyn moved to the other side of the world to found with his father-in-law a highly successful financial business in the wide-open market of Buenos Aires. His son, Frederick, David's grandfather, was Collecting Clerk of a firm that merged into the Mercantile Bank of the River Plate, of which he was finally Managing Director. The Wanklyn '*quinta*' on the Flores Road at Caballito became one of the best-known properties in the chief city of the Argentine. It was later occupied by General Julio Roca — leader of the so-called 'War of the Desert' campaign in which he ruthlessly exterminated the encroaching indians of Patagonia — who moved in there on his election as President of the Republic of 1880, when Buenos Aires became the nation's capital.

Some time earlier the failure of the Argentine Bank and the financial crisis that followed had brought the Mercantile down. Frederick died of pneumonia in 1875. His estate was so mismanaged that his widow, the former Elizabeth Riestra Lumb, was left virtually destitute. She was forced to take ship for England with all her eight children — the eldest of whom was 15 and the youngest, David Wanklyn's father, only three years old.* (See footnote on page 16).

The family fortunes have had some spectacular ups and downs over the past century or so and this was one of their first major reverses. Worse was soon to follow. The vessel that embarked them was the Royal Mail Steam Packet Company's new iron screw steamer *Boyne*, under the command of Captain R. H. Macaulay — 'an officer experienced in the service.' After stopping off at Lisbon she was running through dense fog on the evening of a particularly unlucky Friday the 13th of August when she struck the rocks off the Isle of Molene near Brest. The 108 passengers — including all the Wanklyns — and 113 crew were safely taken off and landed at Molene where they were, according to the *Illustrated London News* account, 'kindly taken care of by the few inhabitants'.[2]

None of them had saved any of their luggage — and the 'kindly' locals managed to cheat them out of much of what was subsequently recovered. Some of the crew broke open caskets of gold and diamonds — the *Boyne* carried over £20,000 in specie plus a valuable cargo of coffee, tapioca and hides — and were later arrested by the French authorities.

On the Monday after the weekend following the wreck a French warship arrived to bring the survivors to Brest, where the Wanklyns were put up in an hotel. A few days later they made their way to England via Paris and Boulogne. The future looked bleak and it was inevitable that the family should be broken up and divided out to the charity of their relations. Young William was taken up by one of their many connections, one Willie McConnell, a fine-cotton spinner based in Manchester. He had a large house at Knockdolian, Ayrshire, where William was to grow up virtually an adopted member of the family.[3]

Through McConnell's patronage he was educated at Marlborough College and went on to train as an engineer at Crewe Railway Works. By 1906, when he married, he was Colliery Engineer with Partridge Jones and John Paton in Monmouthshire. His bride, Marjorie Josephine Rawson, was a keen horsewoman who rode to hounds whenever she had the opportunity. At 21 she was 14 years William's junior. Her infectious, youthful high spirits, sociability and courage in the chase were in counterpoint to her quietly kindly, hardworking and highly successful husband's maturity. She was to retain these qualities, which might perhaps otherwise have been translated into a wasteful and shallow frivolity, in a later period when her circumstances were suddenly much reduced — and they were shown to be the bedrock of stability.

Shortly after their marriage the couple moved house — the first of

---

* An interesting episode in the continuing history of the Wanklyn family's business interests in Buenos Aires occurred in 1897 when Frederick's nephew — Mr J. B. Wanklyn of Flores, who survived the earlier crisis and went on to build up one of the most important financial agencies on the River Plate — was shot on the steps of his bank ('by a customer to whom he refused to grant an overdraft, I always like to think', says David's sister Joan). He died 34 hours later in the British Hospital and 'The Wanklyn Case' became a cause celebre. The Buenos Aires *Standard*, no doubt reflecting the concern of its largely business-based readership, described it as 'one of the greatest tragedies the city has ever known.'[1]

many moves, as it turned out — to the village of Bricket Wood near St Albans. William was taking the train to his London office one Saturday morning when Sir Andrew Yule, the jute magnate, climbed into the same compartment. Yule knew Wanklyn, was aware of his growing reputation and was looking for someone to expand a new interest in India. By the end of the journey he had offered him the post of Chief Engineer of the Port Engineering Company in Calcutta. Wanklyn was 35. His business had led him round the world and he had already visited Northern India as well as Japan, Singapore and Canada but this was a major opening and he snapped it up. Before long he was a junior partner and by the time his third son David was born, on 28 June 1911* at their house, The Hermitage, Alipore, overlooking the famous Calcutta Zoo, he was the city's Consul General for Sweden — an honorary post, reflecting his standing in the business community, in which he was responsible for the interests of the nationals of that country residing in the port. The day-to-day work in this connection was handled by a salaried consul, so William's duties were mostly social. He acted as host to visiting VIPs — including on one occasion the Crown Prince and Princess of Sweden. To the great delight of his native servants, they were allowed to sport the blue and yellow colours of the Swedish Royal House in their turbans for the duration of the couple's stay. The Hermitage was really not large enough to take a party with a sizeable retinue. There was only one main bedroom and bathroom, so the Wanklyns gave over their suite to the visitors and slept in the conservatory![5]

A few months after David's birth the Wanklyns were invited to participate in the British Empire's most spectacular ceremonial occasion — the great Durbar attended by King George V and Queen Mary. Derived from the Persian 'Darbar', the word means either a governmental meeting of chieftans or, less commonly, a gathering for the sole purpose of paying homage. It was the latter interpretation that was applied to the Imperial Durbars, all held in the ancient city of Delhi in the fleeting epoch of the Raj. The first, in 1877, celebrated Queen Victoria's proclamation as Empress; the second, in 1903, marked the accession of Edward VII; and the third, the last, most impressive, most dignified and most expensive of the series, was designed to follow King George V's coronation as King-Emperor.

It was an awe-inspiring event, never to be forgotten by those privileged to witness it — certainly not by King George, that most assiduous and dutiful of monarchs, in whom it bound an already strong sense of duty with a mystical feeling of mission and purpose that was never to leave him. He was there at his own insistence —

* The first son, Jack, was born in 1907; Peter followed 11 months later; Patrick in 1915; Nancy in 1917 (she died of meningitis on her first birthday); and Joan, the only surviving sister, in 1924.

against the advice of his Prime Minister and Cabinet — and he would be the only British monarch to visit the country in imperial state.

The British may have had their faults as rulers abroad — although their record compares favourably with other imperialists of the 20th century — but they knew how to put on a show. The Durbar of 1911 was the ultimate statement of their achievement and power. Across 45 square miles of the plains beside the Jumna River they built a huge city of luxurious tents and marquees to house a quarter of a million guests and their attendants. Six of the pavilions, naturally the most opulent of all, hung with rose-coloured silks and embroideries and carpeted with priceless oriental rugs, were furnished for the King Emperor and his Consort. Here George V received each and every one of his noble Indian subjects in the run up to the main event on December 12.

This took place within two vast concentric amphitheatres, the larger accommodating a hundred thousand spectators and the smaller notables of the Indian Empire — including William and Marjorie, who had left baby David behind in Calcutta in the care of his English nanny. At centre stage was a lofty dais 200ft across, rising up on decreasing marble platforms, the last of which bore two gilded silver thrones resting on cloth of gold carpet beneath a towering golden cupola. In the morning 50,000 troops paraded to music from massed bands 1600 strong.[6] The timing of the ceremonies was perfect — but no-one could have foreseen how swiftly transient the splendour of all they represented was to be.

As the Wanklyns, at the height of their material and social success, took their turn to be presented to the Gods on Olympus, they could not have known that the apogee of Empire was also its swan song as a family of power and influence in the world — and theirs, too.

Chapter 3
Wanklyn Minimus

When the world went to war in August 1914, William was 42 and not in the best of health. Ill-acclimatised to the enervating heat of India, his medical rating was C3. Yet now he itched to do his bit in the chilly mire of Flanders.

For nearly a year he fretted to be sent home while the authorities pressed him to stay on. He joined the Calcutta Light Horse, nowadays chiefly remembered for a species of Dad's Army derring-do in World War II, when some of its officers gained a whiff of eccentric glory by boarding and setting fire to a German commerce raider berthed in the neutral port of Goa — an incident celebrated in the 1980 feature film *The Sea Wolves*, starring Gregory Peck and Roger Moore. A quarter of a century earlier the Light Horse had been organised as a yeomanry regiment for local defence and was hardly a serious factor in the context of the epic struggle waged far away in Western Europe. Marjorie also played at soldiers, running a small equestrian VAD company with half-a-dozen other wives who could ride. They were drilled by a sergeant from a local mounted unit and once performed a display before the Viceroy.[1]

Eventually William's persistence won through and he came home in 1915 to a commission as a Major in the Royal Engineers. David and his brothers had been sent home to board with their Aunt Cora, William's sister, who had married the Rector of Hitchin at Stowmarket, Suffolk. David's health had been giving cause for concern. He had only recently recovered from diphtheria, an acute infectious disease now practically unknown in civilised communities owing to universal vaccination but which then had a high rate of mortality. Before his departure for England, still convalescent, he had a second lucky escape when the train in which he was travelling was derailed in a tunnel. He was rescued by his nanny, who crawled on all fours carrying him on her back while his mother shepherded the older boys through the smoke and steam.[2]

The outbreak of hostilities injected a new element of danger into the long and tedious voyage to and from India. 'On one of mother's trips back to Calcutta from visiting the children in the UK, her ship was shadowed for several days in the Red Sea area by the notoriously successful German raider *Emden*,' Joan records.

On David's parents' return the family moved back to Monmouthshire, to Moynes Court at Mathern near Chepstow. After a spell at Aldershot, William crossed over to France to the trenches of the

Front Line. He was there for a full year before his own health irretrievably broke down and he was sent home to lighter duties.[3]

About this time David, who was then five or six years old, met a young Naval officer who was to settle his choice of career — his family have always believed the encounter was significant and certainly the boy never deviated from his chosen course, at once announced and frequently reiterated throughout his youth.

Lieutenant Alec Anderson, only son of Marjorie's eldest sister, was a darkly good-looking young man lately invested with the glamour of a clash with the enemy. His destroyer had rammed and sunk a German U-boat off the Irish coast. Her bows were severely damaged as a result and she had limped into Newport for repairs. It was a convenient opportunity for Alec to pay a call on his aunt. He came across David and his mother collecting eggs from the hen-houses in the garden at Moynes Court, by then given over to agriculture as part of the Home Front war effort and managed by Marjorie with characteristic energy.

In his early family photographs David appears as a rather solemn child with an air of concern over 'doing the right thing'. He hung on Alec's every word and was deeply impressed when he and his mother visited his ship at his invitation.*

At the end of the war the Wanklyns shifted their base yet again — to Knockinaam, near Portpatrick, Wigtownshire, close to the beloved Ayrshire of William's youth — a move prompted by his new posting to Scotland as an Inspector of Munitions. Knockinaam Lodge, now a two-star hotel, is still described in the AA Book as 'two miles down an unclassified road.' Joan remembers this as 'a stony track with deep ruts and very steep in places — murder for a car. The place had no electricity and mother had to clean, trim and fill more than a dozen oil lamps each day.'[4] They were there for five years. It was a superb location for a family in love with the wilds, a stone's throw from the sea with opportunities close at hand for trout fishing in the burns and rock climbing expeditions — often led by the irrepressible Marjorie, who would take delight in urging her growing lads on to minor feats of mountaineering. In the mad scramble that followed, David always held back, weighing up the situation before committing himself while his brothers raced ahead, hell for leather. He became, before he was quite 12 years old, a keen angler and was fond of shooting and boating. In good weather the boys rowed round the rocky coast for church service on Sundays and David's eventual robust Christianity secured a healthy, no-nonsense foundation.

The outdoor life went some way to restoring his initially precarious health but he was, withal, a very quiet child, the others nicknamed

---

* Lieutenant Anderson survived the war only to succumb to the influenza epidemic that followed it.

him 'Mouse'. Yet he was no daydreamer — indeed he was observed to be unusually receptive. While still too young to share lessons with Jack and Peter's governess he would sit in a corner, seemingly giving all his attention to his toys — and suddenly pipe up with the answer to some problem that had stumped the older boys.[5]

At the time of the move to Knockinaam, David joined them at Parkfield Preparatory School, a long and tedious train journey far away to the south at Haywards Heath in Sussex. With his brothers already established on the rolls as 'Major' and 'Minor', David was 'Wanklyn Minimus' — an appellation that underlined his lowly status in the school hierarchy. The senior Wanklyns protected him from the inevitable early brush with the bullies, but he was too far removed from their sphere for them to have much to do with him. A few years can make a lot of difference; in adult life they were to see little of each other, though David was probably closest to his eldest brother Jack.

The harsh realities of the first few months of life at Parkfield produced the common reaction in a youngster already unsettled by his family's peripatetic existence. At home for the holidays, he shared a room with Jack: 'I was supposed to see that he didn't wet his bed; one night I didn't wake up and he did it again — so mum gave me a beating instead of him.'[6]

This seems harsh, yet Marjorie, so much younger than her husband, was naturally better attuned to the boys. Their letters to her are written in an affectionate shorthand, as might be employed with an understanding elder sister. William, though kindly and much loved, figured more remotely in his children's perceptions.

At Parkfield, home must have seemed far away. Jack describes the perils of the long haul back at the end of term: 'We left to catch the night train and were told to wait under the clock at Victoria, where Dad's secretary was to pick us up and take us across to Euston — Dad was back with Partridge Jones as a working director by this time. Anyway, he never turned up and we waited for what seemed like hours. Peter and I had sixpence between us and David had nothing, so in the end we got a taxi and told the cabby our problem — that we only had a short time to make our connection.

'When we got to Euston we were met by a crowd of porters who ran to us on seeing our red school caps and we were hustled to meet the station master, resplendent in his frocked coat and topper. He had held up the express train for ten minutes as Dad had asked him to take care of us — he was a friend of his — and he paid for our tickets, First Class. At the first stop, at Tring, we went off to see the engine and chat with the driver and stokers. They knew all about us — Dad knew a lot of people on the railways . . .'[*][7]

---

* William Wanklyn drove a railway engine during the General Strike of 1926 — a 'patriotic' action typical of his class at the time.

Back at school David soon found his niche. Before his voice broke he was a good singer. His mother, in addition to her sporting accomplishments, was exceptionally musical having studied piano at Weimar and David could pluck the heartstrings with *Under the Deodars* and other sentimental Victorian ballads. More readily appreciated by his schoolfellows was an athletic trick he was still able to present as a Wardroom show stopper twenty years later:

'He was practically double jointed and could wrap his legs around his neck, supporting himself on his hands and bottom — it used to nearly make me sick,' remembers sister Joan.[8]

With his hopes still centred on the Navy, he applied himself diligently to meeting the required standards, but sometime before he was due to go before the Selection Board a perceptive master at Parkfield noticed a congenital disorder that would have dished his chances from the outset, had it been discovered; he was colour-blind.

'It would obviously have failed him,' Joan observes, 'but the master patiently coached him to differentiate between what he thought he saw and what he was seeing in reality and he managed to get through the medical.'[9]

Surgeon Captain Frank Golden, Fleet Medical Officer at this time of writing, agrees that he could have learned to recognise colours by the degree of light intensity they reflected — 'but it would have been virtually impossible for him to get by our tests today.'[10]

Colour blindness, which persists throughout life, is fairly common — about one in fifty suffer from it to an appreciable degree and it is more prevalent in men than in women. David's problem, an inability to distinguish red from green, is its most usual form. *Black's Medical Dictionary* notes laconically that 'the importance in testing for colour blindness anyone who is to be a signalman or an engine driver is evident.' It is hardly less so in one who is bent on a maritime career, where quick recognition of a variety of signals can lead to life-or-death decisions. The almost uncanny visual judgment David Wanklyn would exhibit at a later date is all the more remarkable.

At any rate, he passed the written examination required for entry into the Royal Naval College at Dartmouth and Marjorie took him to the Admiralty Selection Board in London. They stayed at a small hotel off Wigmore Street and spent the evening at the cinema to take his mind off the worst hurdle — the viva voce test.

There is no such animal as the 'naval type'. Certain characteristics may be observed as marking the man of the sea and in the Senior Service an apparent conformity to traditional patterns of behaviour is noted by outsiders. But they are, like French verbs, more widely divergent than the rules would seem to permit. Submarine command — a particularly specialised field, one might assume — has always offered membership to a surprising range of personalities; a psychologist, trying to correlate success to sensibility here, must inevitably subside into bafflement. Although in those days it was said the Admiralty chose its raw material 'to type', trying to discern in the young candidates a fixed set of qualities that might mature into competent leadership potential, some latitude was allowed. David's marked shyness, which he never quite overcame, did not mask a sensible, if not intellectually brilliant, approach. Nor did it preclude a growing, quiet popularity, even now tinged with respect. He was not particularly keen on team games and tended to be a loner — hardly the standard passport to social eminence in any school environment. Yet in his last few months at Parkfield he was elected prefect.

David entered Dartmouth in the St Vincent Term of 1925.

Chapter 4
'Very much his own person'

He once told his wife they sent him into the Navy with five shillings in his pocket . . .

Jack Wanklyn remembers that they used to call him 'The Admiral' when he first went to Dartmouth.[1] It is the sort of unoriginal sobriquet any non-naval family might apply to one of its number beginning a career at sea and signifies nothing beyond the fleeting status of a novelty, for there were, at first, no intimations of any particular promise. At home on leave he never gave himself airs; in any case, his mother's healthy pragmatism would soon have nipped any such tendency firmly in the bud. There were already signs that the Wanklyn coffers, once well-lined, were wearing thin, so there was no room for complacency. The post-war slump hit them hard, as it did so many upper middle class families conditioned to the easy prosperity enjoyed by their strata in the Edwardian era before the events of 1914-18 turned their world upside down. William had returned from India materially, if not physically, 'quite well off'. Unfortunately — and against the advice of his contacts in the stock market — he invested all his money in the steel company that had given him his chance in South Wales. His deep sense of loyalty clouded his judgment and he failed to see the writing on the wall.

Home meanwhile allowed appearances to mask the underlying unease. In 1923 the family moved to Peterscourt at Benington near Knebworth in Hertfordshire — an old rectory with a small home farm that gave Marjorie further scope for her talents in husbandry. When on leave David went hunting with the Puckeridge Hounds with his mother. While the Wanklyns could still afford a stable he became expert in the saddle and horses 'went kindly for him'. At one time Marjorie owned a part-bred Arab stallion, 'Grey Boy'. 'He wasn't meant to be a stallion,' says Joan, 'but he had been inefficiently gelded as a foal. He was what is known as a 'rig' and used to enliven tedious moments in the hunting field by giving a macho squeal, which set any mares in the vicinity dancing. Apart from mother, David was the only one for whom he went well.'[2] Peter, however, recalls that he preferred cycling, shooting and tennis. At Dartmouth he developed interests more suited to the introspective side of his nature — philately and bird watching. By the time Joan began her own 'much more amateurish' stamp collection in the early 1930s — in which David gave his little sister much help and encouragement — his catalogue was so large that he decided to specialise in United Kingdom and British Empire issues.*

Ornithology went hand-in-hand with photography and he compiled albums of well-observed studies of the birds of the Dart estuary. They are the clear result of careful planning and attention to detail and it is a curious paradox that his success in these quiet and homely pursuits was due to qualities that were of equal value in his career as a submarine commander — more effective, it might be argued, than any skill in the robust 'character building' team games favoured by the Dartmouth curriculum. He never excelled in organised sports and his natural diffidence in this area was hardly likely to impress his personality upon his fellow cadets. Commander Dick Raikes was one of his contemporaries:

'He was a couple of terms senior to me, which of course means that at the time he was only a recognisable name. My distinct impression of him is that he was very ordinary — rather uninteresting. While I was rather over-keen on games, I seem to remember that he didn't shine at all in this respect.'[3]

Even after the passage of seven or eight years, when both had joined the Submarine Service, Raikes was still struck by a strangely solitary character that seemed to rely solely on its own inner resources — and this in the most 'clubbable' of Service environments.

'By then he was very much his own person, to use a modern expression, and I don't think he really had any *friends*. I don't mean that he had enemies — merely that he was such a loner that he didn't encourage friendships. Looking back at this period I can't seem to see him ever laughing, which the rest of us did a great deal.'

But there was, even in the convivial atmosphere of the Mess from which he was often so noticeably detached, something about him that inspired serious interest. He was not a nonentity to be allowed to fade into the background.

'I realise that this may be hindsight, but I do think we recognised that he was a very strong character in his quiet way. He was very conscientious and we all saw that he was single-minded in his determination to master his subject.'[4]

There was, in fact, always a danger that he might stretch himself too far — and after the first few months at Dartmouth he was close to burning himself out. Glandular fever was the outward result of an adolescent frenzy of undisciplined study and he had to relearn the art of relaxation through weeks of enforced idleness in the sanitarium.

He loved sailing and when his parents came down to visit he would meet them at Kingswear and, scorning the use of the ferry, take them across the Dart himself. In his senior terms he whipped in to the

---

* After his death his widow was forced to sell it to help make ends meet.

Britannia Beagles with some skill, but the truth is he had little money for entertainments outside the college. Five shillings did not go very far, even in 1925, and he later told his wife he could not even afford the price of a hat.

'When I asked him why he hadn't asked his parents for more cash, he simply shrugged and said he wasn't quite sure. He couldn't even "go ashore" when he arrived because he hadn't got a hat and the college authorities insisted the young officers wore one then. Eventually someone from the Lower Deck was very good to him and lent him the money to buy one.'[5]

About this time his brother Jack, to whom of his siblings he was closest, was packed off to make his fortune in the Argentine, where the Wanklyns still had connections. Jack and Peter had followed their father to Marlborough where Jack set his sights on a cavalry regiment. He excelled at boxing and running and was a fine cricketer. Joan Wanklyn: 'He actually had a trial at Lords — I think for the Public Schools' Eleven — which he just missed, and then he failed the Army exam and came home to Peterscourt very depressed. He went for a long walk with mother, pushing me in a pram and was made my godfather — not much compensation for his disappointment — and the upshot was that he was sent out as a "jackaroo" on a cattle ranch, working for Liebigs, the "Oxo" people — it was just like the Wild West!'[6] With their fondness for nicknames, the Wanklyns inevitably tagged Jack 'Oxo'. Eventually he managed several large estancias and at the time of writing still has his home in Argentina.

David found a more immediate goal in the then current Dartmouth system of two watches. The cadets were divided 'port' and 'starboard' and rivalry between the two camps was intense. This competition gave an edge to his endeavour and he began at last to enjoy the company of a small circle of friends. Prominent among these during his early years in the Service were Tom Worthington and Anthony Collett, whose families both lived in Goucestershire — to which county the Wanklyns repaired in 1929, about the time, on 1 May, that David was gazetted Midshipman after passing out top of the list in five subjects. It was a highly creditable result. Sydney Hart, prefacing a racy history of *Submarine Upholder* in 1960 with a short biographical sketch, put it down to 'constant, unflagging application. It may not be a record, but for a boy who never claimed to possess sheer brilliance it was certainly nothing to be ashamed of,' he wrote in a curiously downbeat aside to an otherwise eulogistic account.[7]

In spite of this academic success, however hardly attained, Wanklyn did not excite attention. He had something over a year in the battleship HMS *Marlborough*, his first sea-going appointment. 'The Brough', as she was known to her intimates, showed the flag at an endless parade of foreign ports — although her young Midshipman's albums are concerned less with the ceremonial of those last heady days of Empire when the Royal Navy was its principal ambassador at large than with scenes of quotidian shipboard life. His was still the eye of the photographer, watchful of the minutiae of life. A year later, when he was appointed to the first class battle cruiser *Renown*, Vice Admiral Sir Peter Gretton was a fellow Midshipman:

'I am afraid that my recollections are rather sparse. I remember a rather quiet young officer with a pleasant personality. He was very keen on his profession and I remember he was a good handler of the picket boat — other than that I have no firm views and it would be easy but dishonest to invent any.'[8]

Acting Sub Lieutenant Wanklyn, as he became at the end of his time in *Renown* in September 1931, began his long courses of instruction to qualify for his second ring as a full Lieutenant. He was soon deep in study at Whale Island, Portsmouth — the gunnery school, HMS *Excellent* — and Greenwich, where he learned more of the art of navigation. It was during this period of concentrated academic effort, the make-or-break time at the beginning of any young officer's rise up the ladder, that his father died, quite suddenly, of pneumonia. The Wanklyns found themselves, in the context of their class, for a time practically penniless.

His mother was left with £98. The investment her husband had made in the company which launched his career had virtually disappeared in the stock market crash that heralded the Depression. William, in his innate generosity, had run himself further short helping out a relative with the result that he was overdrawn at the bank. The bank foreclosed and almost the entire family assets were swallowed up. Marjorie and her daughter moved to another house in the Cheltenham area, Little Manor, Charlton Kings — really nothing more than a small converted farmhouse — where they found an understanding landlord who offered a reduced rent.

Peter Wanklyn: 'Mother had her marriage settlement . . . and also about 40,000 shares in Partridge Jones and John Paton which the bank did not sell (although they were lodged as security for a £10,000 loan to Dad) because Jack guaranteed the loan and interest. He called me — I was working in India at the time — about Dad's death and told me of the temporary money shortage. I managed to scrape up £80 which I sent to Mum and which she insisted on returning to me when I married.' Eventually the bank overdraft was paid off and the securities were bought to provide Marjorie with an income. Far removed from the scene of his family's difficulties as he was, Peter can easily be forgiven for regarding them as representing a "temporary shortage".'

Yet as Joan recalls: 'Things were very difficult indeed for a number of years. Mother had to sell furniture, silver and personal possessions to make ends meet and with great courage and unquenchable joie de vivre kept the home going for my brothers and myself. David, always frugal, managed to give her some money from his pay to help her through that difficult first year of widowhood. That's almost incredible — in those days it was the norm for junior officers to be subsidised by their families, not the other way around.'[9]

David, in common with his brothers and sister, had been devoted to his father. He had been a somewhat remote figure but they all recognised the kindliness that lay behind the facade of the Victorian paterfamilias. David was very much his father's son and the blow was bound to come hard. For a while the news was kept from him. He was sitting his Lieutenant's examinations then and Marjorie worried that it might distract him. She asked his CO's co-operation and he wisely acceded to her request. Afterwards he was granted three months' leave — those were more spacious days than our own — and returned home to console his family in their grief.

As an engineering executive William had never been content with desk work. He had loved the practical side of the business and was never averse to donning overalls and getting his hands dirty — a trait that endeared him to the rank and file of his profession. He left behind a sizeable workshop and here David saw an opportunity to divert his sister.

'He taught me a bit about tools and model making and once he and his brothers got my father's miniature steam railway to work. There was an engine with a tender and a single carriage large enough for children to sit in. We also tinkered with various steam boilers and steam-powered engines. They were all sold during the bad years . . .'[10]

Beyond his domestic preoccupations David was privately committed to a new direction in his career. When Jack made a dutiful return from South America he confided his hopes to him.

'We slept in the same room when I came home to Little Manor and spent a long time talking about our lives. He was already thinking about specialising in the Submarine Service — this was the future for the Navy as he saw it.'

At the end of Jack's visit, David and his friend Tom Worthington drove in a sports Bentley to meet him at Paddington Station.

'We got in behind a fire engine and raced all across London to get to the Docks in time for drinks and dinner on board the *Walney Grange* before she left for the Argentine. That was the last I ever saw of him.'[11]

Chapter 5
'A mode of warfare which those who command the sea do not want'

David's decision to transfer to the submarine arm of the Service was not wholly intellectual — he wanted a challenge which his present circumstances had failed to provide. Some flavour of the year he spent in the gunroom of *Renown* with a score of other fledgling officers is provided in the sharply observed memoirs of his later friend and mentor Rear Admiral George 'Shrimp' Simpson. He wrote that gunroom life in the big capital ships had become a futile anachronism left over from the days of sail — though the petty tyrannies and often outright sadism of bullying Sub-Lieutenants were likewise by now largely a thing of the past, they were really the product of boredom. And the boredom remained.

'The duties of the wardroom officers in capital ships at sea were sinecures compared with those of their contemporaries in destroyers, submarines, small craft and flying. Whilst in harbour these duties were child's play, which is why they were often carried out by midshipmen . . .'[1]

David came to HMS Dolphin in May, 1933 — just over a month after Hitler made himself master of Germany. In his later quest for a wider empire it is fortunate that the Austrian Corporal's understanding of sea power was as weak as that of Napoleon — likewise a usurper whose career was limited by that fatal blind spot history has shown to afflict so many military commanders whose vision did not extend beyond the horizons of a campaign on land.

In 1917 Britain had almost been brought to her knees, not by the skill of the Kaiser's generals on the Western Front, but by the depredations of the U-boat fleet in the North Atlantic. Grand Admiral Karl Dönitz, who was briefly to succeed Hitler as Fuhrer in 1945, would fail to impress upon him that this lesson was no less valid in 1940 — and thus, perhaps, could World War II have been lost for Britain when she stood alone. Dönitz had asked for 300 U-boats. On 3 September 1939 he had 46 — and of these only 22 were suited to operations in North Atlantic. And yet Winston Churchill would one day declare that the submarine menace had been 'the only thing' that really scared him.

But in 1933, when that single, all-important warning from World

War I should have been fresh in the minds of the Admiralty, a sense of reality was only just beginning to seep through.

The Royal Navy had had its own share of success in submarine operations between the years 1914 and 1918. Most of these had been conducted away from the strategically vital transatlantic lifeline however, in the 'side-show' areas of the North Sea, the Adriatic and the Dardanelles. And the British Government, while recognising the uncomfortable truth that her large and expensive surface fleet was vulnerable to a small and relatively much cheaper underwater armada, fell back in spirit to the dictum of Earl St Vincent, First Lord of the Admiralty of over a century before, who considered it foolish in 1804 'to encourage a mode of warfare which those who command the sea do not want, and which, if successful, will deprive them of it.'[2]

In the context of his time, St Vincent's view was understandable. A year after he made his observation — prompted by Prime Minister Pitt's interest in the American Robert Fulton's prototype submersible *Nautilus* — Nelson secured British naval supremacy for the duration of the late Georgian, Victorian and Edwardian eras with his victory at Trafalgar, an encounter in which superior seamanship and gunnery had the upper hand, with no new-fangled 'secret weapons' to complicate what was really a foregone conclusion.

The attitude of St Vincent's successors 120 years later is less easy to defend. Once the reality of the threat had been proven, instead of turning their minds to submarine research and development — and today the submarine is itself the most potent of anti-submarine weapons — they pressed for its abolition in the international naval community. Naturally enough, few other countries, most of which were unable to bear the expense of a large surface fleet, were eager to identify a cost-effective method of countering the challenge posed by those that could. So there was little support for the idea.

After the Armistice many submarines were scrapped. Two types of patrol submarine remained in service with the Royal Navy: the short-range H Class and the larger L-type boats. Some of both survived to see action again — Wanklyn himself was to command *H31* and *H32* in the early months of the next war — and there was hardly any new building until the mid-1920s. Much time was wasted on experiments with huge, unwieldy submarine cruisers and monitors. The 3000-ton *X1* mounted four 5.2 inch guns in twin turrets and the *M1* actually carried a monster 12 inch gun taken from an obsolete battleship. Variants of the M Class — they were actually diesel conversions of the steam-powered K boats* (see footnote opposite) — were the seaplane carrier *M2* and the minelayer *M3*. Both *M1* and *M2* were lost in accidents, *M2* with all hands off Portland in January 1932 while Wanklyn was serving in HMS *Renown*. These experimental boats mostly had unhappy histories. They carried out a number of successful trials in the roles for which they were designed — but these were essentially alien to the proper business of submarines, which have always prospered better solo, under more or less free-ranging briefs, or in loosely confederated 'wolf packs'.

More conventional types were constructed from the mid-1920s on. The O, P and R classes were conceived in the light of the expansionist policies of Japan and their consequent threat to British possessions in the Far East and were developed with extended endurance as a prime requirement. Still more specialised models were introduced from 1932, the five minelayers of the Porpoise Class and yet another return to the Fleet submarine concept inaugurated by the ill-starred K-boats. *Thames*, *Clyde* and *Severn* at least benefitted from conventional diesel-electric propulsion and were very comfortable by the standards of the day, but they were not particularly successful. Dating from the same period and continuing in build with variations in three groups until the very end of World War II were the short-range S Class boats which eventually totalled sixty-two units commissioned. They were to operate with renown in all theatres during 1939-45.

This, then, was the state of the Submarine Service when Lieutenant David Wanklyn arrived at Gosport in the Spring of 1933. Three months of intensive training followed, mostly classroom work with occasional trips in an elderly training submarine, after which he passed the necessary examinations with credit. In September he received his first submarine appointment, to HMS *Oberon*. With the exception of two experimental Fleet boats of 1915-16, *Nautilus* and *Swordfish*, *Oberon* and her eight successors in this leading post-war design, initially designated 'O' Class and built between 1926-29, were the first to bear a name. A rather ungainly craft, weighing in at 1311 tons with what for the time was the large complement of fifty-five, *Oberon* presented a considerable target when surfaced, having a high freeboard and a massive conning tower mounting a four-inch gun. But she had an impressive range — 8500 nautical miles at ten knots.

Oberon's birth at Chatham on September 24, 1926 had been spctacular. Delays had caused the launch grease to ooze out beneath her keel and she slid down to the channel on almost bare wood,

---

* Six of the 18 infamous K Class submarines, built in the latter part of World War I, came to grief in tragic circumstances and none saw action. They were designed to operate with the battle fleet and were powered by two steam-geared turbines generating 10,000 hp to give the necessary high surface speed of 24 knots — a rate not exceeded by Royal Navy submarines until the arrival of the nuclear powered HMS *Dreadnought* in 1963. Among the K boats' most bizarre features were two funnels which retracted on diving. Around 339ft long with an unmanageable length-to-beam ratio of 12:8:1, they had a safe diving depth of only 200 feet — and thus their bows could quickly reach crush depth if the angle of dive was too steep. Irresistible is the story, quoted by Don Everitt in *The K Boats* that has one C.O. telephoning his First Lieutenant in the fore-ends: 'I say Number One, my end is diving — what the hell is your end doing?'

according to one of the shipwrights, 'with reports like rifle fire and louder, with flames and smoke coming from the ways.'[3] She was based in Malta as part of the 1st Submarine Flotilla, Mediterranean Fleet, where she was visited in 1932 by the Prince of Wales, later Edward VIII and Duke of Windsor. There is a famous photograph of him clinging to her conning tower rail with his cousin 'Dickie' Mountbatten. Wanklyn sailed in her Spring and Winter cruises of 1934 for exercises in the Atlantic, visiting Gibraltar and returning via Bormes Road near St Tropez and Leghorn in Northern Italy; and then to Bone in Algeria in company with the submarines *Thames*, *Regent*, *Regulus* and *Rover* and the destroyer *Douglas*. These were not altogether pleasure cruises but the lack of any serious intent behind submarine planning in this period is indicated in Simpson's memories of the Staff College at Greenwich that year: '. . . one hour was devoted to submarines and not one minute to the 1917 U-boat crisis or to subsequent anti-submarine measures to prevent its recurrence.'[4]

In October David transferred to *L56*, a slightly smaller, middle-aged vessel built by Fairfields in 1919. This class, of which 34 were completed for the Royal Navy and two for the Yugoslav Government, developed out of the famous E class of World War I and had many variations in build. *L55* had a curious and tragic history which reflected some interest in her immediate successor. On 4 June 1919, during the Russian Civil War, she was forced into a minefield off Kronstadt in the Baltic where she was sunk by the destroyers *Gavril* and *Azard*. The Soviets raised her in 1928, refused permission for a British warship to enter their territorial waters, but eventually agreed to allow in the steamer *Truro* to pick up the bodies of her forty officers and men. When *Truro* departed, the Russians observed the niceties. Warships of the Baltic Red Fleet lowered their flags and provided a guard of honour. Later the *Truro* was met by the destroyer HMS *Champion*, which took off her sad cargo of coffins for the remainder of the voyage back to England. Three years later, when *L55* was re-commissioned into the Soviet Navy — under her original pennant number — the *Illustrated London News* published three pages of photographs of her sister *L56*.[5]

Wanklyn spent a year in her before his appointment as First Lieutenant to *H50*, one of the last of a class of over forty built around the end of World War I and now given over to training — although they would return to active service in home waters for the next war. Very small with a surface displacement of only forty-four tons, they had a crew of twenty-two, which would make them quite the lightest manned submarine craft — apart from the midgets — to operate between 1939-45. Even so, *H50* was 'eminently suitable for breaking in a First Lieutenant whose all-embracing duties ranged from store supervision, discipline, father confessor to the ratings, to controlling the ship's diving trim'.[6] Wanklyn would later be reminded of her delicate ways — she could dive to only 100ft in safety — when he had command of *H31* and *H32* in the first half of 1940.

The living was relatively easier in the brand new S Class submarines *Sealion* and *Shark*, in which Wanklyn served for much of 1937 and 1938, a period of intense diplomatic activity which culminated in the Munich Crisis. *Shark* was destined to play a role in maintaining the uneasy limbo between peace and war as the lines were drawn up for the coming power struggles in the Mediterranean and it was in *Shark* that Wanklyn returned once again to Malta — to a chance meeting that would bring him all his brief store of personal happiness.

Pat Norman, one of *Shark's* officers who was to become a close friend, recalls that it was 'a delicious time' in Malta then.[7] In the last years before the war the little archipelago enjoyed a certain affluence — in marked contrast to most Mediterranean communities which were still suffering the effects of the Depression. The population of a little over a quarter of a million, basically of Semitic origin, while hardy and somewhat frugal in character, was easy-going and well-disposed towards the British in general and the Royal Navy in particular. Towards the latter, years after the United Kingdom severed its formal ties with the place, they retain to this day a deep affection that transcends any change in political attitudes. The ordeal they were shortly to suffer as the host of a power surrounded by enemies would prove that the ties that had bound them to the British Crown since the end of the Napoleonic Wars were strong indeed. It had been, in fact, a contract actively encouraged by all levels of Maltese society and the presence of the Mediterranean Fleet had long been the mainstay of Malta's economy. Leaving these considerations aside, the Navy liked the Maltese and the Maltese liked the Navy. There had been a good deal of intermarriage and the union had been blessed with many children.

Shark's workload was slight. She spent only a couple of days a week at sea, so there was ample opportunity for recreation. Picnics were a favourite diversion. 'That's where the love potion worked,' says Pat Norman — and he saw it work for David Wanklyn, sometime in the summer of 1937, with a speed that astonished and delighted him.

'He was such a naive chap that way, that we were all surprised when he hit it off with Betty so quickly. I'm absolutely certain he'd had no girlfriends before her — I could cross my heart on that one . . .'[8]

Joan was likewise sure that this was 'the first girl he'd ever been interested in. It's not so surprising, after all, in one so dedicated to his career and quiet pursuits. Early on, when he was helping mother out financially, life must have been pretty boring for him on leave . . .'[9]

Elspeth Kinloch — always known as Betty — hailed from David's spiritual home and her antecedents, unlike his own, were pedigree Scots. Just under a year his junior, she was the second of the four children of James Kinloch (himself the second son of Sir John Kinloch) at Broughty Ferry, now part of Dundee. The family were based at Meigle in Perthshire. An illustrious forebear was one George Kinloch, a renegade politician of the early 19th century who, according to a commemorative plate in her possession, 'was forced to flee his country and proclaimed an outlaw for having advocated the cause of the people and the necessity of reform' and was, on 22 December 1832, 'proclaimed the chosen representative of the town of Dundee in the reform House of Commons'.

Betty was possessed of a gentle, unaffected charm that was seen by some as the clone of Wanklyn's own. Yet, despite a fairly sheltered upbringing and a school career blighted by illness, there was, too, a liveliness about her, expressed in sudden bursts of uninhibited behaviour and unexpected candour — still apparent today in her seventies — that took him aback. It was quickly to exert a valuable influence — she 'brought him out of himself', people said.

While still in her teens, at Queen Margaret's School, Scarborough, she suffered bouts in quick succession of measles, pneumonia and mastoiditis that kept her away from her classes for a full year. The latter infection, a serious complication of inflammation of the middle ear, has more recently been effectively treated with sulphanomides and penicillin. This treatment was not available then and it left Betty stone deaf in one ear. She moved to St Steven's School, Folkestone, where acute appendicitis caused her to miss her final examinations. After a period of convalescence she worked for a while breeding Cairn Terriers at Coupar Angus, close to her family home. And then, in 1937, she came to Malta.

'We had a friend who had an old aunt — a famous lady who lived in Malta called Miss Knight — who was rather ill. They didn't like her being alone so I went out as a companion. Shortly after I arrived she died and I took a job with some Army people, looking after their small boy, and then I met David.'[10]

The same friend who gave her the introduction to Miss Knight knew a submariner stationed at Malta, Pat Ryan, and it was Ryan and his wife who brought about the meeting that was to change her life for good — and bring Wanklyn a little way out of his self-containment towards a new confidence. Hitherto he had been shy of social contact, especially with his superiors. Soon the influence of Betty Kinloch would be a catalyst in cementing the most important professional friendship of his life; at the beginning, however, his lack of familiarity with the opposite sex was painfully apparent. They were brought together at one of those picnics on the beach:

'We'd been playing around with the Ryans, with a ball or something and I — I don't know, I think I just threw myself across him to get something that was being held out of my reach. And I think he was a bit surprised, you know — I don't think he really thought a girl could behave like that. But it was a perfectly normal thing to do, I thought . . .'[11]

For David Wanklyn it was anyhow a pleasant shock. Betty gaily insists that he was 'bowled over from the start'.[12] For her part, there was the complication back in Scotland of a suitor of some five years' standing and, sensibly deciding to remove herself for a while from the heady romance of the Mediterranean days and nights, she returned to the UK. Fate intervened to send *Shark* back for a short refit. When David arrived about the same time, she went straight to her mother's home and there they were formally engaged.

Chapter 6
'Franco's lot were the worst'

For almost the entire period of Wanklyn's tour of duty in *Shark* the Spanish Civil War was the major foreign policy problem for the European Powers. When he joined the boat in October 1936, four months after hostilities began, the Insurgent Navy was in control of the Mediterranean coasts near Gibraltar and the northern coast of Spain and its destroyers were intercepting Soviet freighters as they approached Valencia.[1]

Britain had adopted a policy of non-intervention. This was the era of Appeasement and the politicians were interested primarily in containing the struggle, keeping it apart from the wider implications of the Continental power game — and above all in pursuing a workable agreement with Hitler, which became, after May 1937 when Baldwin was succeeded as Prime Minister by Neville Chamberlain, a preoccupation which dictated almost every aspect of the Spanish issue.[2] The Admiralty had other interests. First Sea Lord and Chief of the Naval Staff Admiral Sir Ernle Chatfield was determined to rebuild the Royal Navy, sadly run down in terms of both ships and men since the Armistice. He saw in the Spanish Civil War an opportunity to justify a policy of expansion. In fact, while ships of the Royal Navy were busy throughout the war in evacuating refugees and patrolling the coasts, the Government was criticised for its unwillingness to let them have their head in carrying out their traditional role as a protector of the country's merchant fleet. This was widely believed to indicate a pro-Nationalist bias — which Chatfield largely shared together with Sir Samuel Hoare, the First Lord of the Admiralty, who came out strongly in support of Franco. Indeed, while confusion reigned in the Foreign Office's attitude to the opposing factions and in the Government's view of the economic questions, the naval policy was quite overtly anti-Republican and made a positive contribution to Franco's final victory.[3]

At the outset, neither the Republican nor the Nationalist navies (the latter then practically non-existent) posed much of a threat to British interests. But when Hitler and Mussolini stepped up their backing for Franco the situation changed dramatically. In November 1936 Italy sent submarines and warships to intercept Russian supply ships and Foreign Secretary Anthony Eden worried about the extent of their involvement. By the following August the sea campaign mounted by the Nationalists — whose right to blockade the British tacitly recognised — was intensified. Eden's opposite number in

Italy, Count Ciano, sent four more submarines to operate under the rebel command, with instructions to raise a Spanish flag if they had to surface.[4] (Italy, incidentally boasted the world's largest submarine fleet at this time — eighty-three units to France's seventy-six and Britain's fifty-seven.)[5] In the last three weeks of that month there were no less than twenty-six attacks on shipping. Of seven casualties flying the British flag, five were known to have fallen victim to Italian, officially 'unknown' submarines and when on 31 August the destroyer HMS *Havock* was attacked, British public opinion was outraged.[6] It was obvious that such a wide-ranging scale of operations — stretching beyond the South East coast of Spain to the African coast, the central Mediterranean and as far to the east as the Dardanelles — could hardly be the work even of the combined numbers of Republican and Nationalist submarines alone. International peace was threatened and even the appeasers in Chamberlain's cabinet could no longer afford to stand back. Mussolini had gone too far — the Duce's 'Mare Nostrum' was fast becoming a reality.

A conference was hastily convened at Nyon, a small town on Lake Geneva in Switzerland, to explore the problem of these acts of 'piracy' — always a label the British found irresistible when attached to submarine operations conducted by outsiders. Under the threat of recriminations from the Soviet Union, Germany and Italy declined to attend and suggested the matter be discussed by the international Non-Intervention Committee. But the Chamberlain administration was for once insistent. Britain and France were joined at Nyon on 10 September by Albania, Yugoslavia, Greece, Turkey, Egypt, Bulgaria and Romania and in four days — to the fury of Mussolini — they agreed a system of patrols. The burden fell on the principals — Britain and France, who had issued the invitation — to watch over the Mediterranean by dividing it into six zones covering the main shipping routes. Any unidentified submarine would be sunk on sight.[7]

The Tyrhennian Sea was later reserved for the Italians — a decision which amused Ciano, who observed cynically that the Italians were now 'policemen of the Mediterranean' while the Russians, whose ships they were sinking, were left out of the scheme.[8] Ten days later he agreed to supply Franco with two more submarines while Mussolini assured Hitler that, notwithstanding the Nyon protocols, he could continue his attacks.

Italy's parallel adventure in Abyssinia had meanwhile brought about the removal of the bulk of the Royal Navy's Mediterranean Fleet to Alexandria and the only units left in Malta were a few destroyers and submarines. In the last months of 1937 *Shark*, together with *Snapper* and *Sealion*, repaired to Gibraltar — to help the local destroyer flotilla with anti-submarine exercises, the crew was told — and was duly emblazoned with the Nyon recognition mark, a red, white and blue tricolour.

Commander James Sladen, who later had a distinguished wartime career in HMS *Trident*, was in command. Other notables in the wardroom included Lieutenant Pat Griffiths — who was shot in the back when the Royal Navy took over the monster French submarine cruiser *Surcouf* at Plymouth in 1940 — and a Lieutenant Hopkins, who had lost a finger and 'enjoyed the revolting trick of shoving the stump up his nose'.[9] Wanklyn relieved him as First Lieutenant. And there was a 23-year-old newcomer who was to become one of Wanklyn's few close friends.

Pat Norman was a robustly cheerful young officer with an attractively self-deprecating style — and it is noteworthy that almost all the select band with whom Wanklyn opened up to a degree of intimacy were of similar colour. He came from a notable Army family — his father, grandfather and great-grandfather all commanded a battalion of the Royal Welch Fusiliers — and they might have looked upon him with horror as an irredeemable black sheep when his choice fell on the Senior Service. Yet to his everlasting credit his father, Brigadier Compton Cardew Norman, CMG, CB, DSO, one-time Inspector General of the King's African Rifles, was disposed to allow a degree of latitude in his son's options.

'When I was about eleven he took me for a long walk on the marshes at Sheerness where he was stationed at the time. There we were, living in an Army quarter just outside the gates of the Dockyard and I'd already been out in a submarine and explored every nook and cranny of the place. He said: "Well, it will have to be either the Army or the Navy" — and when I said the Navy he was as good as his word and put me in for Dartmouth. The Regiment and the Generals and so on were outraged . . .'[10]

Norman was fourth hand in *Shark* when Wanklyn returned as Number One. The two hit it off immediately, though Wanklyn's quiet ways still set him apart from the general stamp of wardroom society.

'He wasn't a rip-roarer — not the rather devil-may-care type which was so often the sort you encountered in submarines in those days. The sailors took a while to get used to him. He was a very strict disciplinarian — what he said went — and he never set out to be popular with anybody. But for all that, he was utterly straight with the Ship's Company; in dealing with defaulters and so on he was eminently fair and they all came to love him for it.'[11]

Wanklyn's touch in his dealings with his men was beginning to excite favourable comment and there would come a time when disciplinary problems of any kind were a rarity under his eye. Troublesome cases were often deliberately transferred to his command — and were quickly and magically settled. And this was due not to any marked measure of severity in his judgments, but rather to an innate kindliness and a vision that constantly flickered aside the narrow corridor of Service regulations. Personally austere in his habits, he was sympathetic towards the common human frailties and Norman never forgot the lesson.

'I learned a lot from him when I got on in the Navy and looked back to remind myself of the way he would have done things. His dealings were not all "according to the book" by any means — if he thought it would be better for the man he might not punish him at all.'[12]

By his mid-twenties Wanklyn had grown to an imposing six feet two: very spare and gaunt, he seemed taller still. His nose, broken in a riding accident, was prominent and slightly crooked, hooked above a strong, square jaw. In contrast, the ears were small, pinched at the tips beside straight, heavy brows that fell close over wide-spaced dark eyes that gave his otherwise craggily severe features a curious, dreamy sensitivity — and coloured a quiet, sardonic smile. In profile he appeared hawkishly intent; face-on, oddly vulnerable.

The life he shared with the 38 crew in *Shark* — by now fitted with a three-inch gun and painted in the deep blue livery adopted for operations in the Mediterranean, as opposed to an original very light shade of grey — was distinctly uncomfortable. Working out of Gibraltar between the Rock and the Balearic Islands and out to Cape Trafalgar and Cadiz, the men were forced to live on board the whole time. There were no bathing facilities. 'Eventually Sladen sent a signal saying we were getting absolutely filthy and we were then allowed to live ashore in lodgings — but we still put in a lot of sea time, so we stayed filthy all the same.'[13]

Wanklyn had one vice at least that did not help conditions on board: 'He stank us out every morning with that beastly briar of his. It was never out of his mouth and, waking up in a tiny submarine wardroom, it didn't imrove the atmosphere at any time, either in harbour or at sea if we weren't dived. The moment he woke, before his eyes opened, he would grope around for his pipe. It was Service tobacco he used, too — really acrid stuff.'[14]

You learn tolerance of your fellow man in a submarine, so this too was allowed, or at least suffered, by non-smokers, it may be imagined, with a markedly lesser degree of equanimity. The pipe soon became a trademark. Coxswain William 'Cuts' Curtis remembers it as a more or less permanent fixture, even when the boat was dived and smoking forbidden.

'He used to sit between the two hydroplanes when I was on aft, sucking his empty pipe. I asked him one day "Do you get any satisfaction from that?" and he said "Well, it allows me to think." It was part of the calmness about him. He never seemed to panic about anything. I never saw him tear through the boat like some of them did when something went wrong somewhere — never saw him rushing, never heard him swear. You never heard him tick anyone off — he'd tell somebody something and his manner of telling it was sufficient. He never raised his voice or lost his temper. "The gentle giant" some people called him. We never had any trouble-makers in *Shark* . . .'

Curtis, having come to her in June after two years in the Fleet submarine *Thames*, found *Shark* particularly cramped. It was, he told his mates, 'like moving from the *Queen Mary* to a tramp steamer'. But when they managed a few days ashore in Gibraltar the crew found the life there was pleasant enough. They were considered honorary members of the Sergeants' and WO's Mess in the barracks and most of them found their entertainment inside camp. 'We didn't go to the bars much, though one or two of the places in Main Street were pretty good — Ivy Benson's all-girl band used to play in one of them.'

Curtis always had a nagging feeling they were 'fiddling while Rome burned' for the signs of the Spanish tragedy were 'right there at your elbow'.

'We met quite a few refugees who had fled from Franco. They knew what the score would be if they returned and they were staying put. Some of them were still there when I returned to Gib during the war.'[15]

Pat Norman was also struck by the weird situation of a peacetime community surrounded by war — civil war, the worst kind.

'There was fighting at one time just across the frontier. It was an extraordinary set-up because the dockyard workmen still came over the border. They were mostly Spaniards, working in the Gibraltar Docks, and it was closed to everybody except them.'[16]

Through it all the refugee ships — including on more than one occasion the submarine depot ship *Cyclops* — plied their dismal trade. By July 1937 the British had evacuated nearly 28,000 of all nationalities: French, Italian and German as well as the indigenous population. 'This was the Navy's chief and happiest work' according to Chatfield.[17]

It must be said that to the majority of Britons at this time the whole deeply sorry business was little more than a vaguely troubling embarrassment. Even at the diplomatic level, while it offered opportunity to the Dictators, it was 'an irritant to the Democracies'.[18] There were those who cared passionately about the issues on either side and who volunteered for service and fought and died in their cause. Orwell and Hemingway and other distinguished literary commentators have left the impression that such depth of partisan feeling was more widely shared; the truth was that to the average newspaper reader at home the conduct of both of the protagonists was equally repellant — an appalling catalogue of massacre, torture and rape that seemed to belong more to the Thirty Years War of the

17th century than to the domestic troubles of modern Europe. And yet the Holocaust was but a short step into the future.

From *Shark*, alongside in Gibraltar Bay, Wanklyn heard the sound of the bombs and saw the smoke rising to the north of Algeciras as the German and Italian pilots put in practice for the wider conflict to come. Closer still, he was sickened by the sight and sound of the daily executions of prisoners by Franco's firing squads. His sister noted his revulsion: 'I once asked him who were the worst offenders, the insurgents or the Government forces. He said both committed atrocities, but marginally he thought Franco's lot were the worst.'[19]

Shark never became personally involved in any action — though Curtis remembers one incident early in 1938 that put her role in the Nyon patrols sharply into perspective. It happened shortly after their customarily clandestine morning departure.

'We had to slip at 4 a.m., which wasn't too clever after a good run ashore. It was left to me to take her out, though the captain would watch the speed. I'd have to miss one buoy that wasn't lit at all and then steer direct for the light on the end of the detached mole and wait until the light on the end of the South Mole was abeam, and then turn hard to port to get out of the harbour. It was quite a tricky business. And then we started to get hydrophone effects where there shouldn't have been any and our escorting destroyers told us to stay on the surface while they moved away from us a bit.'

The orders remained the same — all unidentified submarines were to be sunk on sight.

'Suddenly a German U-boat surfaced about a mile away. It was known they were operating around the area and if they sank any ships we'd be blamed for it. Nothing passed between us — no exchange of courtesies, not a word. We just sat there, silently looking at each other and after a while we carried on . . .'[20]

Eden had been confident that the cover provided by the Nyon agreement would prove successful — so confident indeed that he told reporters he would 'eat his hat' if there were any further attacks.[21] For three months his optimism appeared to be justified — and then, on 31 January, the SS *Endymion* was sunk. Other sinkings followed and the patrols were intensified. But Chatfield still declared his unwillingness to take action against the Nationalists. Franco had the sympathy of the Royal Navy, he believed — not surprisingly in view of the fact that at the beginning of the war the Republicans had shot or imprisoned many of their own higher ranking naval officers who were suspected of favouring the rebellion — and he advised that the Nationalists had obviously been unable to countenance the increase in traffic of essential coal supplies to Barcelona.

Meanwhile Chamberlain anxiously pursued a naval agreement with Italy. This was eventually signed on 16 April but by then it was becoming obvious that the Nationalists were going to win the war. In the next two and a half months twenty-two British ships were bombed — eleven of them sunk or disabled — by Franco and his supporters. The politics of appeasement only invited contempt. As a later commentator observed: 'The Nationalists could barely conceal their scorn for a government which obviously desired their victory but which simultaneously demanded compensation for the damage done to British ships carrying cargoes for the Republic.'[22]

And so, in the final analysis, the Nyon patrols were a failure — though they were later seen to mark 'the first and last real attempt to take swift and aggressive action against illegal and bullying tactics of either Italy or Germany until World War II.'[23]

Shark and her crew returned to Malta for an idyll in the sun while the clouds rolled in over Europe. To their delight, one ray of Spring sunshine had been reserved as Wanklyn's very own.

Chapter 7
'Very close to him, in his problems'

David and Betty were married at Holy Trinity Church, Sliema, on 5 May 1938. Pat Norman was best man. After the service they passed under the traditional arch of swords provided by David's fellow officers — all dressed in the frock coats and cocked hats of the Royal Navy's ante bellum full dress uniform.

The crew of *Shark* towed the couple away in their car to be ferried over the water in a dghaisa — the Maltese version of the Venetian gondola — to a reception in the old submarine depot ship *Resource*. Stella Danvers, the wife of one of the towing party, was struck by the 'ordinariness' of the pair:

'In those days the Lower Deck didn't mix with the officers and their wives — but Wanklyn never showed any 'side' whatsoever. He actually did get on better with us than he did with the officers — it was his naturalness that made him so popular. Later on I would go down to Sliema when the boat came in and he and Elspeth would always come and speak to us . . . He was obviously very happy at his wedding, she was what he wanted and she seemed so right for him. And she looked radiantly happy, in her beautiful white gown with her honey-coloured hair. She struck me as rather shy until you got to know her. I think she wondered what she was getting into . . .'[1]

To others Wanklyn appeared ill at ease in his formal rig, but at least most of the guests were known to him. Betty was confronted by a sea of strange faces. On the voyage out for the ceremony she had been befriended by Mrs, later Lady, Campbell, whose husband was an officer serving in destroyers. Her two small sons acted as train bearers.

'But apart from them I hardly knew any of the guests. Afterwards, when we went to someone's house or to a party or something, people would say "Oh yes, I met you at your wedding" and I'd say 'Did you? How nice." I couldn't cope with all that mass of people at once. As time went on I got to know some of his friends, but practically all of them were lost in the war . . .'[2]

She hardly had time to get to know her husband really well either. In the four years of their marriage, owing to the normal exigencies of Service life and the much longer separations of the war to come, three months was the sum of the longest period they had together at one stretch. In her seventies she looked back on a honeymoon fate would allow never to end.

'Naval officers never really like to talk about their work at home — and Naval wives, I think, are never supposed to know anything of the Navy. I really did not. We bathed, picnicked, walked, talked and made love according to time and place and there wasn't much talk of the future — except that we both hoped for a house in Scotland one day . . .'[3]

They took ship in the *Knight of Malta* to the beautiful Sicilian resort of Taormina. Their fortnight's holiday was blessed with glorious weather but David was tempted to mix business with pleasure, bearing in mind the likelihood of some future confrontation with Mussolini's Italy.

'When we were in the train he spent the whole time looking out of the window, trying to see if he could spot anything he ought to report back. I don't know what he thought that might be — he wouldn't tell me!'[4]

He was, of course, intent on sorting away landmarks that would be of use to a submarine officer operating off a potentially hostile coast. Later he relaxed at a sandy bay with a distant, sometimes dazzlingly clear view of Mount Etna and turned his full attention to his wife. They treasured an incident following one long laze in the sun that caused them to miss the bus back to town.

'We started walking up a very steep hill — but then the bus came along after all. As we were at the half-way stage they just gave David one ticket and one for his baggage. He always used to carry that ticket around with him, I was his baggage, you see . . .'[5]

Back in Malta they took a flat in Charidud Sliema. The place was bombed in the war — David would write home 'The flat's flattened'. And then, in June, *Shark* was sent off to Yugoslavia.

'All the Fleet went and it was just a lot of wives in Malta,' Betty recalled ruefully. She felt they had 'just gone off to enjoy themselves'.[6] It was a pardonable conclusion for any young bride to arrive at — but Pat Norman, in retrospect, felt it was uncomfortably close to the truth. A dangerous laxity was prevalent in submarine training in those days.

'There were certain COs at that time in Malta whose nerve had gone — carrying out a mock attack with a glass of gin at their elbows. I used to be absolutely horrified and I'm no prude, but, God almighty, there were one or two. I don't suppose any submariner ever went to sea totally calm inwardly. Nowadays it's different — you're driving a great big ship, really, and everything's under control. But when you think of the old H Class submarines, for example, they were First World War boats and it was all run on bicycle chains. I was never really happy until we were actually down — and then not until we were back up again . . .'

The need for an urgent reappraisal was soon underlined by the Munich Crisis — in the middle of which, in September, the Wanklyns came home to spend a few weeks' leave at Betty's family home in Scotland. The Fleet was mobilising for war and David's next appointment was to be as First Lieutenant to the minelayer HMS *Porpoise*, then attached to the Second Submarine Flotilla at Devonport. His CO, Commander 'Shrimp' Simpson, recorded his impressions of his war orders as issued by the Admiralty. They certainly left a lot to be desired.

Porpoise was to lay her mines across the approaches to the River Ems — which seemed reasonable enough until he discovered that the positions selected lay in only 50ft of water, while *Porpoise* required at least 70ft to cover her and allow room for manoeuvre. He reported his findings to his superior, Captain Jock Bethell, whose commonsense verdict was acidly to the point:

'Good. Now my orders to you are that you should lay these mines to the north and west of the positions given, *provided* visibility allows you to fix where you have laid them, *provided* there is adequate depth of water during approach and lay, and *provided* . . . you return here safely. I am not going to lose one-third of our total submarine minelaying force during the first week of war due to stupid orders stupidly labelled. The next lot of orders will be issued by Flag Officer Submarines, so we won't have any repetition of this suicidal stuff . . .'[8]

In the event, Chamberlain returned from Munich on 1 October, waving his infamous piece of paper and declaring 'peace in our time' to a relieved public that was only too happy to share his delusions. For a while the crisis was over. The submarine force stood down.

It was at this point that Simpson and Wanklyn came together for the first time. George Walter Gillow Simpson was the son of a Guildford cleric, born on 6 June 1901 — just a few months before the Royal Navy launched its first submarine, *Holland 1*. He was an experienced submariner, having joined the Service in 1921 and he noted his 'good fortune' in having the 27-year-old Lieutenant as his Number One.[9] They quickly cemented a close friendship, despite the disparity in age and rank. What they shared in common was a dedicated, serious-minded attitude to their calling. And both possessed that vital pre-requisite of command — the ability to inspire confidence in others. Simpson too, even in a Service traditionally given to understatement, was modest to a fault. One of the young officers who knew him during his finest hour as Captain of the 10th Flotilla at Malta described him as 'ever an engaging and friendly personality, full of fun, with a twinkle in his eye.'[10] Not much more than a hint of this comes out of his determinedly professional autobiography *Periscope View*, in which his own career progression is kept firmly subordinate to his theme of a personal view of the naval policies and the politics that built up to the Mediterranean campaign he would conduct with, in the end, rather poorly rewarded distinction. He likewise treats any tendency to vainglory in the published reminiscences of his brother officers with withering contempt. Simpson pulled no punches in his critiques of the military and political establishment, but after the war, when asked his opinion of a popular memoir by one of his young commanders which, though controversial, tended towards self-aggrandisement, his verdict was crushingly succinct. 'Shrimp', drawing his thickset figure to its full height — not much over five feet — threw his craggy head back and pursed his lips three or four times in his characteristic way before delivering judgment: 'I had no idea I had such a distinguished officer under my command . . .'[11]

But he recognised the solid worth of his new First Lieutenant straightaway.

Early in the New Year, after a fortnight's intermediate docking at Devonport, *Porpoise* sailed for Gibraltar with the two other minelayers of the Second Flotilla, *Cachalot* and *Narwhal*, to take part in the combined Home Fleet and Mediterranean Fleet exercises. The war in Spain was nearly over, but while hostilities continued the diving areas were still a long way from the Rock, which necessitated a lot of day-running with the attendant chore of charging batteries at night in order to be ready for the next day's activities.

Lieutenant George Gay was newly joined as Engineer Officer. It was his first submarine appointment and he was immediately impressed by the First Lieutenant's quiet professionalism in the midst of this maelstrom of activity.

'He just "knew" and as a result he always seemed relaxed. He pressed on with the job, wrote things down, crossed them off as he did them and looked at the list to see what was next. If you wanted to know the answer to anything, the chap to ask was Wanklyn — no matter whether it was some highly technical point about the submarine, a point of law, the next item on the boat's programme, how best to set about buying duty free wine in Gibraltar, or the prospects of getting any fishing. If he didn't know the answers, he generally knew where to find them. He always seemed to have time for all this, without hurry or fuss . . .

'It was this professionalism, I think, combined with his natural kindness and the fact that he always had time to listen, which made for his easy rapport with the Ratings at all levels. They had the greatest respect for him and his ability — and genuinely liked him as a man, too . . .'[12]

Simpson, as Senior Submarine Officer at Gibraltar, noted among those assembled the presence of 'a radical, determined younger set' who were to score high marks in war.[13] The invigilators' verdict on their performance in these exercises provides as inaccurate a forecast of actual achievement as one could expect to find in the school reports of boys branded as failures who are later to succeed as men. This sort of oversight has become a cliche — but the lack of vision the examiners exhibited on this occasion was almost total.

Military exercises seldom produce results that mirror the actuality. There are far too many imponderables, of which chance is an inestimable factor, and each of the various factions involved is naturally predisposed to give a sympathetic account of its own contribution. Here the submariners themselves judged that out of a theoretical 200 torpedoes fired the number of actual hits scored was 44 — not a bad return, they argued.

'I knew that this was quite true and a very reasonable estimate,' Simpson averred, adding: 'I also felt in my bones that it would have serious repercussions . . .'[14]

He never spoke a truer word. The exercise 'wash-up', convened in a coal shed on Gibraltar Mole, was packed with a thousand officers. After they heard the unfortunate young Commander chosen to deliver his opinion of the submarine effort, no questions were allowed. Then the Commander-in-Chief Home Fleet, Admiral Sir Charles Forbes, rose to his feet.

'I wish to disabuse the mind of the young submarine officer who has just finished his statement,' he observed with some asperity. 'The sea power that will win the next war will obtain three per cent of hits with the gun — and his opponent will have scored two and a half per cent hits with the gun.'[15]

Sitting beside Forbes was Admiral Sir Dudley Pound, the Commander-in-Chief Mediterranean. Perhaps wisely, he made no comment. Perhaps wisely — probably not. Two and a half years later, when the Battle of the Atlantic was at its height and the threat posed by Dönitz's scanty U-boat fleet was self-evident, he took Churchill and Beaverbrook to America in the battleship *Duke of York*. He decided to cast off his destroyer escort and run through the U-boat stream alone, arguing, as Churchill recounted in *The Grand Alliance* that 'we were more likely to ram a U-boat than to be torpedoed by one ourselves.'

Wanklyn's thoughts are not recorded. Doubtless he shared Simpson's frustration. But he was careful, nonetheless, not to impart any sense of the unease he might have felt to the crew, for whom his concern — at least for the minutiae affecting their daily welfare — was helping to forge a common bond of trust and respect. *Porpoise* sailed for home at the end of March. Two days before her departure the cook came to see Wanklyn and told him he was shortly to be married and that nothing had been arranged for the reading of the Banns. A submarine's cook is an important man — his skill is one of the most important factors in maintaining morale, as Wanklyn well knew. George Gay witnessed how he rose to the occasion.

'There was little time to spare and it was necessary, if the cook's girlfriend was not to be disappointed, for the Banns to be read for the first time the next Sunday, when *Porpoise* would be at sea. A study of King's Regulations confirmed to Wanklyn that under these circumstances the Captain could read them — and right away, with the doubtful assistance of the Wardroom, he wrote them out in the language of the Prayer Book.

'And so, on a Sunday evening somewhere in the Bay of Biscay, the hands were piped to prayers in the Control Room. Simpson came down from the bridge and read from Wanklyn's piece of paper, on which were typed the familiar lines ending "and if any of ye know just cause or impediment why these two persons should not be joined together in Holy Matrimony, ye are to declare it."

'The silence which followed was broken by a loud stage whisper — "Can she cook?" '[16]

After Easter leave, *Porpoise* sailed from Devonport to Portland to prepare for her summer cruise. Two months were largely given over to day running, to provide anti-submarine training for units of the Home Fleet. Simpson was later to confess that in this period Wanklyn spent as his First Lieutenant he felt 'very close to him in his problems'.[17] He does not explain what these problems might have been but Wanklyn, despite the easy rapport he had established with his men, was still not altogether sure how he stood with one man at least whose confidence in him never failed, despite at one later stage a heavy weight of evidence that it might have been misplaced.

His wife recalls a revealing incident that gives a rare insight into the self-doubt that lay behind the facade of quiet containment that so impressed most of his contemporaries. One day in early May Wanklyn came in to see Simpson and 'Shrimp' rather brusquely cut him off. He was devastated.

'He came home terribly hurt. He said "I thought Shrimp quite liked me — and he didn't want me at all . . ." '[18]

That evening Simpson sent one of his staff round to Betty with a present — a rolling pin and the following address:

> To Mrs M. D. Wanklyn, upon the occasion of the first anniversary of her Wedding, this Memorial is respectfully dedicated by the Wardroom of HMS *Porpoise*.

> *The Unspoken Appeal*

> A year ago! Ah, woe is me!
> I wed this fiery tempered squire.
> What can I do? What is to be?
> How can I rule his reckless ire?

Now Mrs Wanklyn, calm your fears,
We must co-ordinate a plan
To save us from all frequent tears,
To calm the brute and feed the man.

Protected as we are, on board,
By all the Articles of War,
Plus safety that K.R.s. afford,
We sympathise with life ashore.

So through this life, in hours of strife,
In summer, autumn, winter, spring,
Just flatten him; devoted wife!
And please accept this rolling pin.[19]

Thus Betty was given the solution to the apparent snub her husband had suffered — 'I think Shrimp was busy composing it when David came in and he didn't want him to see!'[20] She has kept both the rolling pin and the address to this day. They were clearly delivered with an affectionate irony that cannot have been lost on anyone who knew the principals involved — not even Wanklyn's worst enemy would have labelled him a 'fiery tempered brute'. In a rare moment of effusion Simpson himself, when he came to set down a series of pen portraits of the officers under his command in the Tenth Flotilla, declared that Wanklyn's modesty 'made him loved and respected by all'.[21]

The two months at Portland were pretty much routine, George Gay recalls, with plenty of time for recreation:

'From time to time on a weekend afternoon we would take a boat away fishing — David just adored any sort of fishing. He had infinite patience and insisted on the greatest attention to detail. We had a lot of fun — and a few fish for supper, too.'[22]

On the evening of the first day of June they had just finished enjoying the harvest of one of these excursions when news arrived of an event still remembered today as the Submarine Service's single most traumatic experience — perhaps because it happened in peacetime, on the eve of war. George Gay remembers it clearly — just as later generations can recall exactly where they were and what they were doing when they heard of the assassination of Kennedy.

'We had just returned from sea and sent the watch ashore, and in the Wardroom we were just finishing supper . . . when a pale-faced Lt Commander Anthony Miers*, Staff Officer Submarines to the Commander-in-Chief Home Fleet, burst in. He told us *Thetis* was

---

* Later Rear Admiral Sir Anthony Miers, VC, wartime commander of HMS *Torbay*, Flag Officer submarines and President of the Submarine Old Comrades' Association.

down in Liverpool Bay and that we and *Cachalot* were to go up there with all speed.'

'There was no time to get the watch ashore back so the deficiencies in *Cachalot's* and our crews were made up from some S-boat crews who were on board at the time and we set off as soon as possible. Throughout this episode a great deal of the organising — much of it inevitably off the cuff — fell to Wanklyn. There was no fuss, everything was done efficiently, and we might have been going to sea on a routine exercise. Time for a word with the "new boys" and to get them settled in. And I don't remember him appearing to hurry . . .

'In the event *Cachalot*, who had docked in the Easter leave period, was able to make better speed than we were and when we were somewhere off the Cornish coast we were ordered to return to Portland and leave *Cachalot* to go on alone. By the time we got back, we knew the worst about *Thetis* — and a very sad time it was.'[23]

It would be difficult to conceive of any circumstance that might have dealt a heavier blow to morale at this time. *Thetis* was a brand new boat incorporating 'everything that Britain had learned about submarines and submarining over a quarter of a century of peace and war'.[24] She failed to surface during routine trials out of Birkenhead and was found with 18 feet of her stern pointing out of the water like an accusing finger. It was a very public tragedy. Of 101 people on board — 14 naval officers, 48 ratings and 39 assorted civilians — only four managed to escape. A flooded torpedo tube was the cause of the disaster. When the tubes were being checked — two were actually supposed to be flooded to weight her down for her test dive — one was flooded that should not have been. And when the door to this tube was tested it flew open and the sea rushed in to pull her to the bottom. A fail-safe device, known ever after as the 'Thetis Clip', was later introduced and remains in use to this day. At the time, nothing could be done for the men entombed in *Thetis*, whereas the escape facilities incorporated in modern submarines would have been easily equal to the task in the shallow waters of Liverpool Bay.

Commander Richard Compton Hall describes *Thetis's* dilemma: 'Two officers, a Leading Stoker and a Cammell Laird employee did manage to escape by using Davis apparatus, and when the news came through that the submarine had been found and that the remaining ninety-seven on board were safe, there were joyful scenes at the company's offices.' But it was a cruel and premature respite to the agony of waiting.

'The original hope that oxy-acetylene equipment might be used to burn a hole in the stern to release the men came to nothing. The Admiralty said that strong tides allowed only an hour or two for such work, and it would be impossible to complete it in time. There was also the added hazard that any pronounced movement of the boat would have doomed the men immediately.

'As it was, *Thetis's* stern failed to reappear at low tide on 2 June, despite a variety of attempts by salvage teams and divers to keep it afloat. On the afternoon of 3 June, Cammell Laird officially announced that all further hope of recovering the men had been abandoned . . .'[25]

Thetis was raised a few months afterward, repaired and commissioned under a new name, HMS *Thunderbolt*. She later distinguished herself by sinking a U-boat and several supply ships as well as carrying out a number of special missions. But she was a ghost ship to the end. It is said no amount of scrubbing or repainting ever hid the high water mark that ran along her bulkheads — the legacy of that first, fatal dive.[26] Off Sicily on 13 March 1943, after claiming a large steamer sailing in convoy, she was hunted down by an Italian escort. The duel lasted 28 hours, and then the final pattern of depth charges found their target.

For a moment, before she plunged to her grave 3000ft below, her stern rose again — as it had in sight of home nearly four years before.

Chapter 8
'Our chances weren't going to be very good'

In July, with the memory of *Thetis* still hanging like a pall over the Submarine Service, Wanklyn returned to HMS *Dolphin* at Gosport as First Lieutenant of a group of boats in reserve. Betty was in her eighth month of pregnancy and took a furnished house at Havant to be near her husband. He was to be far away when her time came.

War with Germany was by now a racing certainty. Among the young jockeys assembled at the starting post there was a feeling that the going would be tough. Wanklyn was joined by Lieutenants Hugh Mackenzie and Edward 'Tommo' Tompkinson. These two were also headed for distinction — Tompkinson's war record would almost match Wanklyn's own — but at this time they would have viewed such a prospect with laughing incredulity.

'Rufus' Mackenzie remembers long discussions late into the night, in which they attempted to bolster up a fragile aura of self-assurance none of them felt at heart.

'We wondered what the hell we would bloody well do if war broke out — we hadn't joined submarines to fight a war and our chances weren't going to be very good — "Oh hell, it's going to be the end of the world for us" and all that. Actually, I think when war did come we were confident, possibly over-confident. But we very quickly learned that our training really hadn't fitted us for fighting a 1939 war.

'When I look back now, although we were quite good at firing torpedoes and the technical side of how to conduct a patrol tactically, we had no training there — and it was almost criminal that right up to the outbreak of war in any Fleet exercises, submarines were told to surface at sunset for safety reasons, and withdraw with navigation lights switched on until dawn.

'That was appalling — the enemy doesn't withdraw from the war at sundown. We were only just realising the dangers of this practice at the time. The Mediterranean submarine squadron had persuaded the C-in-C Med to alter the rules and allow his submarines to dive at night but, generally speaking, the old rule applied. So our tactics were not so well-developed as were the Germans'. And yet we'd been training as submariners for six or seven years beforehand, most of us. About once every commission, every two years, you might, if you were lucky, do three or four days' simulated war patrol when you would be able to dive at night. It wasn't enough . . .'[1]

With Tompkinson Wanklyn was to enjoy both an easy-going rivalry and the most celebrated of his few friendships. They were quite unalike. 'Tommo', though only an inch taller than 'Wanks' (as he was by now universally known) was much the more powerful in both physique and the outward show of personality — a burly, breezy extrovert. Before the war he was for two years the Navy golf champion. He had a good eye for ball games — a quality, some have said, that marked out the expert submariner, but one that Wanklyn never shared. But Pat Norman felt there was a deeply serious vein running beneath his apparent lightheartedness.

'He was very cautious — I don't mean timid in any way, but everything had to be absolutely right or he wasn't bloody well going to sea, you know . . . Wanklyn and he made an interesting contrast, because the more obviously likeable chap — the "nice guy" — was Tommo really. But the truly dedicated one was Wanklyn.'[2]

Simpson would mark the difference between them when the pair came under his authority in the Tenth Flotilla.

'Like Wanklyn, his ability, presence and intelligence made him a born leader, but unlike Wanklyn . . . Tompkinson did not accept all my ideas as either good or reasonable ones. When some deep-rooted conviction on his part was in danger of being disregarded by me, he would come and see me and state his case from which he could not move. This quality of his was of value to me, partly because I knew his mature criticism was always checking over my problems . . .'[3]

Wanklyn still held back, even among his contemporaries in rank and age. Always generous with opinion — and advice once his experience and success made it highly prized — he was not disposed to offer it unasked, which is, after all, an attractive trait. For the most part, he kept his own counsel.

Hugh Mackenzie: 'He was a loner, he was reserved, he was serious-minded. The rest of us, well — we were pretty young and we tended to let our hair down a lot. I think he could relax, though — possibly more within himself, in his own interests. He read a lot. I can picture him, sitting reading instead of standing at the bar — and then after a while he'd come and join us.'

Wanklyn was noticeably reluctant to join in the boisterous horseplay that characterised submarine Wardroom life at this period — it still does, though the wider spread of social background obtaining in the modern Service has tended to make it less prevalent. The organised violence of 'Mess games' often appears to outsiders to be little removed from the hooliganism of today's soccer fans. To the conservative middle-classes — and the even more innately conservative working classes — the spectacle of supposedly well-bred, grown men in formal attire 'letting off steam' produces a reaction of disgust that is probably in itself based in insecurity — a sense of awe at the supreme self-confidence born and bred in the public school system that can so blithely shrug off all cricitism by those who 'do not belong'. Yet the pressures that fall upon those who lead usually require a safety valve. Wanklyn, by and large, lacked the means — or the inclination — to let it blow. Mackenzie, not untypically, was one who did: 'One tended, if one was to last the course, to treat things pretty lightly.'[5] And Dick Raikes, observing Wanklyn at an earlier stage of his career, thought 'he would have been an even greater man if I could have discerned any "sense of the ridiculous" in him.'[6]

From all the evidence, it seems the Lower Deck — with whom, as Raikes agreed, he enjoyed an easy familiarity he did not extend to contemporaries of his own class — did not think less of him for it. There is no paradox in the fact that witnesses to his character from this quarter almost without exception refer to him as 'a great gentleman'. If he had the common touch, it was not tinged with the slightest condescension.

Oberon, *Oxley* and *Otway* were the three training submarines of 'A' group at HMS *Dolphin* to which he was assigned as First Lieutenant under Lt Commander Henry Cumberbatch. To begin with there was only one crew available to take whatever boat was in the best running order to sea for exercises. Mobilisation saw them divided into three, one-third forming the nucleus of the ship's company of each of the boats. The rest were all reservists, ex-submariners who had been in civilian life for anything up to ten years.

'They were a right shower,' according to Leading Stoker Fred Matthews, a regular assigned to *Otway* with Wanklyn and Cumberbatch — the latter was replaced in command within a few days by Commander 'Granny' Conway.

'To us active service blokes they were largely Scousers, Geordies and Brummies, pissed as puddings in harbour, but good as gold at sea. This was what David Wanklyn had to cope with — Conway was an efficient skipper and a great character, but he left a lot to his Number One. It was a motely crew and a "dodgy" boat . . .'[7]

Matthews' lasting impression of Wanklyn — he met him for the first time this July of 1939 and last spoke to him on the casing of *Upholder* in early March, 1942, shortly before his death — was of 'a very caring and considerate person. He could overlook human frailties when the efficient running of the boat was not in question.'[8]

Matthews had a personal problem of his own, to dispose of which Wanklyn bent the rules to reveal details of *Otway's* forward programme. 'The girl I was going with at the time was pregnant and he tipped me off we'd be home in February. "I'll have to be home to get married by then," I said. "You leave it to me," he said.

'He was such a tall, lanky bloke — always banging his head as he walked through the boat. He had nicknames for us all, I was "Fred the Bear".'[9]

Otway left Gosport for the Mediterranean on the 24th of August to relieve one of the newer 'S' boats for service in home waters. Five days later she stopped off at Gibraltar to take on water and fuel and left at once for Malta. On 31 August, while she was still at sea, Wanklyn's son Ian was born. It would be five weeks before he had the news.

Chapter 9
'Little chance of shooting up a Hun'

As the leonine hulk of Gibraltar loomed in the early dawn of 29 August, Conway handed over to Wanklyn: 'You can take her in, Number One.'

Otway was scheduled to make the briefest of calls at the gateway to the Mediterranean — a few hours to take on fuel and water and then on to Malta. There was a hold-up ahead as a large P & O liner made her own ponderous entry into harbour. Should he make a signal to her, Wanklyn queried his skipper laconically — 'If you don't hurry up, you'll have a big submarine up your arse?'[1]

Fred Matthews, at his station on the auxiliary panel, chuckled as the story was relayed through the boat. Good old Wanks . . . The Jimmy's occasional dry bursts of coarse humour were all the more effective for being so totally out of character — and he knew exactly when a crack like that was needed to lighten the mood. They were all apprehensive. The lights of the Rock, soon to be extinguished under the depressing regime of the blackout, gave only a flickering illusion of security. And the usual buffeting through the Bay of Biscay had done nothing to lift their spirits.

At 8.30 a.m. *Otway* pulled away from Gibraltar and pressed on, arriving at Malta in the early afternoon of 2 September. She tied up alongside *Porpoise* (which had arrived the day before) in Lazaretto Creek. The submarine base on Manoel Island — a small peninsula, 'fifty acres of rock' just west of Valletta — was the home of the 1st Submarine Flotilla under Captain Philip Ruck-Keene. Its offices were in the ancient Lazaretto itself, a massive two-storey building once used to quarantine incomers against the risk of importing bubonic plague. Facing directly south onto a waterfront 40 feet deep, 500 feet long and 100 feet in breadth, it was solidly built of limestone blocks and protected on the northern side by a sheer rock face. The rooms were big and airy, providing excellent barracks, and the easily quarried but resilient sandstone beneath was soon to be extensively tunnelled out for bomb shelters.

In loaning the place to the Navy, the Government of Malta had insisted that the names carved on the walls by various illustrious visitors condemned to idleness there by the quondam quarantine regulations be preserved. As it turned out, these graffiti survived the worst attentions of the Axis bombers — among them a couplet by

Byron, who at the close of his sojourn there in 1811 scratched irritably:

Adieu thou damndest quarantine
That gave me fever and the spleen.

These facilities — not, after all, custom built for the requirements
that were now to present themselves — were as near-perfect as
circumstances allowed. But while those circumstances were certainly
not unforeseen nothing had been done to anticipate them. The need
for submarine pens cut deep into the rock under Valletta had often
been discussed but not, to the great detriment of the Submarine
Service, acted upon. When the fall of France secured for Germany
the availability of bases on the Atlantic coast, the Nazi war machine
would move with ruthless efficiency, making use of slave labour to
construct almost impregnable concrete-lined bolt holes for U-boats
returning from patrols against the Allied convoys. A similar refuge in
Malta would have been invaluable for our own submarines which
were to work in turn to savage reinforcements of men and material
being sent over the Mediterranean to Rommel in North Africa.
Instead, they made do with a hospital that betimes enclosed the
island's lepers — an irony that was not wasted on those whom many
still affected to despise as the piratical pariahs of the Senior Service.

At the beginning, even these doubtful amenities were not afforded
Otway and her crew, for by this time the submarines were denied the
advantage of a depot ship. It was felt that the valuable new
acquisition of the *Maidstone* 'must not remain at Malta with Italy's
pro-Nazi affiliations, and her fleet and air force which make Malta's
future problematical' and she was removed to Alexandria, where
Admiral Sir Andrew Cunningham, Commander-in-Chief of the Allied
Mediterranean Fleet, was to have his headquarters. Hugh Mackenzie,
arriving in Malta in *Osiris*, remembered that the ratings were
boarded out in lodgings while the officers took the lease of a house in
Sliema Creek.

'We didn't have many runs ashore but we were very content — we
had a very happy little Mess. Wanklyn was there with us and I got to
know him very well then. He was always game for anything — but he
never let go the end. He was quite austere — one might say almost
religious. A deep-thinking man.'[2]

He had a good deal to think about. Leaving his wife at an advanced
stage of pregnancy worried him greatly — particularly in view of her
troubled medical history.

On the morning of 3 September all hands in *Otway* were employed
in painting ship. At 11 a.m. a note in the log recorded: 'Britain
declared war on Germany' and a little later 'Crew recalled from shore
leave'.[3] The following day they were at sea for exercises. The pattern
of these outings continued through the month — shakedown trials,

the firing of dummy torpedoes and practice attacks with destroyers and other submarines. *Otway* and *Osiris* were there to relieve the more modern S-boats for service in home waters. Though there would be for some time to come no 'shooting war' in these waters — Italy did not come in until the following June — their purpose, as Fred Matthews put it, 'was to show the flag and frighten the Eyeties'.[4]

At the end of the month *Otway* sailed for Alexandria. Several darkened ships were sighted and challenged on the way but the passage was completed without incident. She berthed alongside *Maidstone* on 2 October and spent another month engaged in desultory exercising.

The period of the 'phoney war' produced its own pressures. Fred Matthews: 'Once late at night at Alex, someone came aboard "Franz Liszt". I was having a smoke on the casing, talking to the sentry. We had managed to get him over the gangway when Wanklyn came up. Together we got him down below and into the heads, where he made one hell of a mess, mostly over himself, because of his action in blowing the thing.' (The usual conveniences in submarines at this period required the operation of a complicated sequence of valves which had to be observed in strict order to discharge sewage outside the pressure hull if one was to avoid the unpleasant — and occasionally fatal — result of an error known as 'getting your own back'.) 'The Jimmy and I managed to strip him down and get him into his bunk and then we both had a quiet drink in the Wardroom — the rest of the officers were ashore and most of the crew had their heads down, so no-one was the wiser . . .'[5]

The cable that brought Wanklyn the news of the birth of his son was soon followed by letters from home. At the end of November he wrote his mother — at this time temporarily removed from London to Cheltenham: 'I am so delighted at receiving a son — isn't it great?' he enthused. He found a likeness in the baby's first photographs to early portraits of both his sister and brother Jack and expressed the hope that the war would not affect him 'in any permanent way'. While his family were preparing for winter he reminded them that he was still 'in tropical rig — just white shorts and open shirt in blazing weather down east.' He speculated about the possibility of his sister Joan joining the WRNS: 'With shorthand typing she'll be jolly useful. At one time there was talk of each boat here having a secretary to take the piles of paper off our hands, but that fizzled out with our dispersal. What fun if Joan were attached to us!' (She was just 15 at this time, too young for the Wrens, but interrupted her art studies to join the Women's Voluntary Service and later worked in the Home Office.)

There was, he concluded, 'just a hope of being home for Christmas as the Command Courses are starting up again in January and I ought to be relieved in time for the first one.'[6] So he was — but not, alas, in time for the holiday, which he spent enduring one of those interminably uncomfortable journeys by ship and rail across Europe which were the lot of so many Servicemen at this period of the war, before the fall of France. Betty's feelings as she awaited his arrival at her family home at Meigle may be imagined. When he was finally able to join her he described the trip in graphic detail to his mother:

'I left Malta a week ago, Saturday 23rd, and arrived at Marseilles on Christmas Day. What a Christmas! Nothing but luggage and French station hotels and steamers and smoky trains. Before we left at 9.50 p.m. we had half a Christmas dinner in the Army HQ Mess. There are no sleepers, so we had to sit up all night in a full but very cold carriage. Lots of snow and frosted trees south of Paris. Fortunately a breakfast car was put on at Dijon so we were all full of hot coffee by the time we stepped out at Paris. I had only summer underclothes and a light Burberry, so I noticed the frost. We had to spend most of Boxing Day in Paris getting bathed, shaved and even manicured before taking a taxi ride around the Arc de Triomphe and the Eiffel Tower etc.

'At Cherbourg we arrived at midnight and spent a beastly night on a lousy mattress with two horse blankets in a room with a broken window and no black-out shutters. Anyway, I crossed next day in an old Isle of Man steamer which was not allowed any booze and arrived at Blockhouse to report and eat an enormous dinner at 8.30 p.m. Even a hard naval bed was heaven that night. So I caught the train north on Thursday, taking a First sleeper as I had a free return ticket.'[7]

Wanklyn started his Command Course on January 8 and Betty travelled down to Portsmouth to be with him for its duration. Roger Keyes, appointed Inspecting Captain of Submarines just before World War I, had early identified the qualities necessary for submarine command: 'The military value of a submarine lies in the skill of her captain and in his powers of leadership. If you can add the hunter's instinct to a first-class, steady nerve, you will probably have a first-class submarine captain. But skill in attack is not enough. Unless the captain has the absolute confidence of his crew . . . you will not have a first class submarine.' Soon after the Armistice, with the lessons of the war still fresh in mind, it was felt that those qualities should be examined more closely. Beyond the basic and obvious resources of coolness, patience and rapid decision making, the need to master the art of attack by the use of a periscope and to acquire an eye for range were recognised. For many candidates these were natural attributes — but they could also be learned. The Commanding Officers' Qualifying Course which evolved from these studies was known colloquially, as it is today, as the 'Perisher'. The name reflects its make-or-break character. At the end of all the long years of experience in every branch of the submarine officer's profession, if you fail your Perisher you are out of the Submarine Service and back into General Service.

At Fort Blockhouse, Gosport, in an underground mock-up of a submarine control room, Wanklyn stared through a periscope at a representational seascape painted on a canvas screen, across which model targets moved according to the direction of the Attack Teacher. It was, owing to the urgency of the situation prevailing, something of a crash course. Four British submarines had already been lost — *Oxley* within a few days of the outbreak of war. Disturbingly for Wanklyn and his fellow Perishers, *Seahorse*, *Starfish* and *Undine* had all gone to the bottom of the Heligoland Bight in the second week of January, just as the young hopefuls entered the first intake of 1940.

Mackenzie, a relatively young candidate in late 1941 — by which time many of the older men were lost — observed that the news from submarines on patrol in the North Sea spread around fairly quickly. 'Fortunately we had nine months or so of the "phoney war" period to get ourselves trained up. A little broadsheet was hurriedly got together by the Staff, based on World War I principles — about half a dozen pages of foolscap, telling us how to patrol at night. You weren't to go across the line of the moon, you had to go up and down, not backwards and forwards across it. Things like that we were told about — but not until after war had broken out and, after all, we had been training as submariners for six or seven years by then . . .'[8]

In the middle of his course Wanklyn was given a temporary appointment to one of the old H boats left over from a class of over 40 built around the end of World War I.

'I have been away for the past week with my first command,' he wrote to his mother excitedly on 2 February. 'I took over *H31* at Portland and had one day at sea before bringing her round for refit — sorry, mustn't say where she is.' (It was Sheerness, he revealed in another letter a fortnight later.) In the depths of the severe winter of 1939/40 conditions were bad, the weather had been 'beastly' and it had been 'a nasty trip with fog or thick snow most of the way and a gale the rest of the time.'[9] He was glad to know his mother had managed to complete moving house before being snowed in — after five months in Cheltenham, she and Joan had decided to move back permanently to London.

On his return, baby Ian arrived with Betty's mother at the Wanklyns' digs in Southsea — but Wanklyn himself, on completion of his Perisher, was given *H32* and he was quickly off to join her at Portland.

'Now I have got my command permanently I am very pleased with life,' he wrote. 'She is only a small submarine, but none the less thrilling for all that. We are fairly busy, but at the moment have little chance of shooting up a Hun. That will come later in the year.'[10]

The H-boats were far from comfortable, even by the minimal standards of the day. *H32* was the first submarine to be fitted with the underwater detection device known as Asdic. This was done at Portsmouth in 1922, when she was the last vessel to occupy No 2 Dock before Nelson's flagship HMS *Victory* claimed it as her permanent home. Two experienced submariners who visited her at Larnaka when she was undergoing trials with this equipment were reportedly 'frankly horrified' at the conditions in which her people were expected to live. In the Suez Canal, it was noted, the temperature in her engine room stood at 127°F. Like the rest of her class, she suffered excessively from condensation, even in cooler climes — with the result that clothing, along with everything else, was permanently damp. But they were hardy enough — *H32* had an operational life of 26 years, being finally scrapped in 1944 — and handy, steering very well, particularly when submerged. Yet, being only 170 feet overall, they pitched badly and in rough weather the screws often came out of the water.

Jack Philip-Nichols has provided a grittily evocative memoir of *H32* in her heyday in the early Thirties. Writing in *Ship's Monthly* magazine in 1979, he recalled a two-year stint in 'this lovely little submarine'. It was an endearment only a submariner dyed in the wool of his distinctive roll-necked, definitely off-white sweater, redolent of that potpourri of 'diesel smoke, shale oil, Bluebell polish, cooking, battery gas, salt water, drying paint and the queer smell of vapourised methylated spirit from the arc-type wireless set'[11] could appreciate. (In curious contrast, today's nuclear submariner, used to breathing the scrubbed and tasteless air generated by electrolysis from desalinated water, is actually nauseated by his first gulp of so-called fresh air when the hatch is opened at th end of a long patrol.)

Life in a modern 'nuke' may not be as picturesque, but it has to be a whole lot healthier. An occupational hazard of service in *H32* was constipation. '. . . everyone had an interest in the workings of everyone else's bowels. As you made your way for'd after a visit to the after WC or "heads", the engine room staff asked by signs (too noisy for speech) how you got on. A lift of the eyebrows, a raised thumb if you had been successful, produced a smile on the face of the enquirer . . .'[12]

Most of the crew lived in the motor-room, amid a jumble that included two mess tables, four switchboards, an electric boiler and cooking range and an oxygen manifold for the Davis escape apparatus. Philip-Nichols swore that 'nobody felt crowded' — yet 'Leading Stoker, Leading Seamen, Leading Signalman, two Telegraphists, two Stokers, two Asdic ratings and two Leading Torpedoemen plus the Officers' Steward all lived in the space of a normal room in a suburban house.

'Up forward, the two officers huddled behind a green curtain at their small table, with the ERAs, a Stoker PO, Torpedo Gunner's Mate and Submarine Coxswain the other side of the curtain. Polite remarks were passed from the Wardroom to Chiefs and POs and were answered . . .'[13]

This then was the little realm into which Lieutenant David Wanklyn was piped with due ceremony on 5 February 1940 — for the first time absolute monarch of all he surveyed.

The weather showed no sign of improving. 'It is beastly cold here even on land and at sea, on my tiny, open conning tower, it is bitter,' he complained. Aunt Rosa, his father's elder sister who lived nearby at Sherborne in Dorset, had thoughtfully sent him a cheque to pay for a foul weather outfit (it was the cause of some discontent in the Service that the German U-boat men were much better provided for in this respect). 'It was a surprise and most welcome, as I had been shying off the expense of anything but woollies', he told his mother.

Even so, though he would not receive his promotion to Lieutenant Commander for another year, he was pleased to note that his pay 'at the moment gives me quite a pleasant surprise, as it includes Lieutenant's pay at the highest rate, submarine pay, command money, marriage and child's allowances and lodging and provision allowances as I have no accommodation in the depot ship. I nearly forgot travelling expenses at ninepence a day; though I am nearly always so early that I take a workman's Fourth Return. 6 a.m. is damned early in the morning and I am always ready for bed after supper.'[14] All this hardly amounted to a fortune but it enabled the Wanklyns to engage a young nanny to move in with them in the small house they took in Rodwell, Weymouth for the three months of cheerful domesticity that would be practically the most they would ever enjoy.

'It had a garden and he was very happy planting out vegetables,' Betty recalls. But the pressures of his new responsibility were ever intervening. 'I remember him feeling very ill once and taking a thermometer in to him and he said "Take that bloody thing away — I've got to go to sea." It was the only time he ever got cross with me . . .'[15]

The question of the strain experienced by submariners conducting war patrols was at this time worrying Winston Churchill who, returning to his old job as First Lord of the Admiralty before the collapse of Chamberlain elevated him to the Premiership, was busily canvassing young officers for bright ideas — and confronting their seniors with their conclusions, presented as his own.

'It was naughty of him,' Admiral Sir Max Horton, appointed Flag Officer Submarines in early January, confided to Shrimp Simpson. 'Churchill sent for me at midnight. He said he thought I should have two crews for every submarine. (Churchill had heard, not quite correctly, that this was the German practice.) 'Just imagine it! Suddenly to produce another sixty submarine crews! The dissolution of efficiency!'[16]

The inevitable destruction of continuity and *esprit de corps* that such a measure would have effected — even if it had been realistically practicable — was appreciated at once by Horton. Simpson wrote: 'This question of crews changing submarines was to become a live issue in Malta and to prove Horton right.'[17]

For the rest of the winter and the early part of spring Wanklyn was kept busy with exercises out of Portland. Then it was the turn of *H32* to go into refit. At the end of April he took her back to Sheerness where *H31* was restored to him. There was time for another week of trials and dummy attacks and three days on patrol in the Channel — but the vegetable plot at Weymouth would be harvested by other hands. On 3 June Wanklyn embarked for the little port of Blyth on the Northumberland coast, whose strategic value in opposing the threat of enemy excursions out of the Skagerrak, directly 400 miles to the east across the North Sea, had — as it was in World War I — brought it into service as a submarine base. The Battle of Britain would not be declared officially open for another five weeks, but these waters had seen many of the preliminary skirmishes. Somewhere between Great Yarmouth and Cromer, a single note in the log of an unseasonably fog-bound but otherwise uneventful passage recorded the discovery of one of the casualties: 'June 5 0940: Passed human body in flying kit.'

Over the next two months Wanklyn and *H31* would roam the North Sea for the space of several patrols. By now 14 British submarines had been lost in or near home waters, including *Shark*, off Norway, on 6 July. Her loss caused Wanklyn much personal grief, for several of her company remained with her from his own period as First Lieutenant. He was not to know that most of them had survived an attack by German minesweepers near Stavanger. After being forced to the surface they had scuttled her while she was being put in tow. They then endured a long forced march to a POW camp in Germany. (En-route Percival Danvers, wrote a letter to his wife Stella — she who had watched the Wanklyns' wedding two years before — offering all the cash he carried, some £10, to a Norwegian civilian to ensure it reached its destination. The man was as good as his word and the letter subsequently brought the Admiralty the first news of their fate.)

German air attacks on British convoys in the Channel began four days later. In all, 40 Allied merchant ships totalling 75,698 tons would be sunk during this month, as well as the destroyers *Brazen*, *Codrington*, *Delight* and *Wren*. *H31's* first significant share of the action came on 18 July while she was on patrol off the Dutch coast.

The boat had sailed from Blyth on the 14th and for the first three days of her passage encountered light winds, but on the morning of the 18th it blew strong from the south west and caused a moderate swell. As she moved on eastward it was difficult to maintain periscope depth in the shallow waters of the North Sea — but now at last Wanklyn got his opportunity to 'shoot up a Hun'.

'0633. Sighted three trawlers bearing Red 135° to 160°.'

They lay in line ahead about a mile apart north west of Terschelling Island. Wanklyn assumed they were sweeping for submarines in an area where activity had earlier been reported by the submarine HMS *Sturgeon* — they were not minesweepers as far as he could tell and were flying no signals.

It took him an hour to line up on the port wing vessel — since he was by then some distance to the east of her he felt he would not thereby give his position away. 'Previous reports from this zone show that it is not necessarily likely that other enemy forces will appear after the passing of this sort of patrol,' he noted. '. . . the state of the sea, which was rapidly rising, gave a good prospect of escaping the surviving trawlers.'[18]

He took her bridge as his point of aim and at 0737 fired at 900 yards, having selected a track angle of 125° to bring all the ships nearly in line and offer the chance of hitting at least one of them. The torpedo's run was clearly heard through the hydrophones, as were the target's movements fully half an hour beforehand, her own Asdic transmissions having failed to hold contact. A little over two minutes later a series of heavy explosions reverberated through the submarine — followed almost at once by the crash of a couple of depth charges away to port, which Wanklyn assumed must have been dropped indiscriminately. When the counter attack developed properly he noted that the enemy appeared to be using the 'directing ship' method — 'On one side an Asdic would be heard, then HE (hydrophone effect) would start on the other side as the second ship came in to attack.'

He found that contact was lost as soon as *H31* pointed towards the Asdic and was 'almost certain' that only two vessels were engaged in hunting him. He was right — the submarine chaser *UJ126* had gone to the bottom. The hunter was blooded.

A total of eight depth charges were counted in the next thirty minutes, the closest falling 250 yards or more distant, but it was not until a further hour and a half had passed that the enemy finally gave it up and retired to the eastward.

'The behaviour of the crew was most satisfactory,' Wanklyn recorded.[19]

This was the only patrol encountered before *H31* arrived back in port — and they were no doubt relieved to have completed yet another journey in which the chances of a safe return were becoming increasingly problematic. Submarine losses were not publicised and Betty, who stayed with her mother in Scotland while her husband was at sea, joining him at Blyth at fortnightly intervals, was for long blissfully unaware of their extent.

'I don't know that I realised quite how bad it was until afterwards. I met a Captain's wife and she had to do all the going and telling people the sad news . . . It was a difficult time, rushing home to pick up the baby and then back down for our meetings at Blyth.'

The Wanklyns had rented a couple of rooms in the house of a miner at Seaton Sluice. Dick Raikes, who took them over a few months later, remembers their hosts — 'a truly wonderful family. The old man was dying of a miner's respiratory disease and one son was nearly blind from his underground work. The younger son was still down the pits. My wife and I both clearly remember how *all* of them thought Wanks was a "great gentleman". This was perhaps the impression that he left with the working classes and, of course, the Lower Deck. He was genuinely fond of these people and I honestly think he was more "natural" with them than with his contemporaries in his own class.'[21]

Perhaps their worlds were not so far apart. There is an obvious bond between those who work beneath ground and sea. Today the Submarine Old Comrades' Association is particularly strong in the mining districts of the North and 'exchange visits' continue to fascinate both communities with the common experiences they endure in their — to others — unnatural way of life.

The Wanklyns' digs were provided with an air raid shelter, to which Betty repaired on one occasion wearing her first pair of slacks. The sight of women in trousers still had the capacity to shock in 1940, though their adoption by the Land Army girls was making them acceptable via the newsreels, but Betty's unconscious ability to surprise her husband dated from their first meeting and she was amused by his reaction: 'He was actually horrified — but he didn't mind in the end, because he found everyone else was wearing them.'[22]

In any case, he had a surprise for her, too. In August he was moving across to the north west coast of England, to Barrow-in-Furness where a new submarine, HMS *Upholder*, was building. A new command — and a whole lot of new faces. Most of them would be his constant companions for nearly two years.

Chapter 10
'An almost intuitive perception'

'I was his biggest headache . . .'

At 19, Ordinary Seaman George Curnall was already marked down as a troublemaker. The only son of a respectable East London family — his father was a printer in Hackney and his mother an accomplished pianist and music teacher — he dismayed his parents by bouncing from one job to another after leaving school at 14: 'I just felt I was being pushed into something I didn't want to do.' After two years, to his mother's further chagrin and to the delight of his father — who had served in World War I and earned a string of medals for his prowess at football along with his campaign ribbons — he decided to join the Navy. At once, while under training at Sheerness, he fell foul of the Master at Arms and was three times flogged with the birch 'for overstaying leave and going adrift'. Towards the end of 1937 he embarked on a troopship at Southampton to join HMS *Birmingham* at Hong Kong. He loved every minute of it, but the good times on the China station nearly came to an abrupt end when he fell down a forty foot cliff and fractured his skull. 'I hovered on the brink for three weeks and cables were sent to my parents — but I pulled through.' Arriving back in England early in 1940, he became engaged to his childhood sweetheart, took the torpedo course at HMS *Vernon* and, having already volunteered for submarines, went on to learn the ropes at HMS *Dolphin*. He came to *Upholder* still fighting a losing battle against an ingrained resentment of authority — 'lively and adventurous with a big chip on my shoulder.'[1] For a while he was the youngest member of the crew. Ruddy complexioned, short and stocky, his eyes staring belligerently from beneath black brows that contrasted startlingly with a shock of blond hair, he was a tough nut to crack. Perhaps only Wanklyn could have managed it — and that would be due to a mutual respect that Curnall, for his part, was to grant few other men in the whole of his life. In the end, even Wanklyn's patient application could not keep him out of trouble — but that failure, ironically enough, was to be his salvation.

But to Michael St John, also newly arrived at Barrow as *Upholder's* First Lieutenant, he was just one of a type who met the need of the hour. 'Those were the sort of chaps you wanted with you in a war, they were only branded as scamps because they were bursting out of their skins with energy. More often than not they turned out to be the most valuable members of the crew — and Wanklyn knew how to bring out the best in them. Most submarine officers were very good with the Lower Deck, but Wanklyn was certainly amongst those who found it easiest and most natural and he commanded their respect without having to stamp on them in any way. He was always particularly understanding with welfare cases.'

St John had just turned 24. Like George Curnall, he had spent two years in Hong Kong, where he had been 'third hand' in the Fourth Flotilla. There followed a spell as Number One in *L26*, patrolling the North Sea on the flank of the Dunkirk evacuation. At Barrow he found himself in distinguished company standing by the production line of U Class submarines. Vickers Armstrong Ltd, under the direction of Charles Craven — himself an ex-submariner from World War I — made sure the likes of Wanklyn and Tompkinson had everything they wanted.

'We were beautifully looked after, given the most tremendous perks. Everything was of the best, you only had to raise your little finger and they bent over backwards to get whatever you wanted in connection with building the boat. We had lunch every day with the directors and their senior staff which was very useful because you could talk shop with them, and being very busy men it was difficult to got hold of them at any other time.'[2]

Vickers were employed at full stretch. The lead submarine builders for the Royal Navy from the beginning of the century — as they are to the present day — they were to construct all but two of the highly successful U's, either at Barrow or at their subsidiary yards at Newcastle-upon-Tyne. *Upholder* was the tenth of the class that began with *Undine* in 1937. Each of them, from the fourth of the series, *Umpire*, onwards, had their names changed to a pendant number, but these later reverted — on Churchill's orders — to their original appellations (*Upholder's* number, 99, was coincidentally that of the U-boat commanded by Germany's leading ace, Otto Kretschmer.) Initially designed for training, they were very small but handy boats of single hull construction with internal fuel and ballast compartments.

This might be a convenient point at which to examine *Upholder's* specifications in some detail. Along with the rest of her type, she met the requirement the Navy had perceived for a short-range patrol submarine for operations in northern waters and the Mediterranean that would be economical, especially in manpower, for training anti-submarine forces. The earliest designs, *Unity*, *Undine* and *Ursula*, were fitted with four internal torpedo tubes and two external tubes within a characteristic high bow. These caused problems. It was found that the boats were hard to manage at shallow depths — after firing a full salvo of six torpedoes it was practically impossible to avoid breaking surface. Early in 1940 it was decided to leave out the external tubes but the decision came too late for *Upholder* and the rest of the six boats in line as it would have led to unacceptable delays in construction. Later a flush bow was introduced.[3]

Upholder was a slimline submarine — a 'lethal, venomous shark of a ship' (*sic*) Sydney Hart called her.[4] A bit of over 60 yards long with a maximum beam of only 16 feet, her single hull construction with internal frames and rivetted sections allowed a safe diving depth of 200 feet — nothing like the latitude enjoyed by larger submarines of the period and hardly sufficient to obscure her outline from the air in the clear blue waters of the Mediterranean.

In diving the submarine, six internal main ballast tanks were employed. These had hydraulically operated vents at the top, those at the extremities having free-flood holes at the base while the four between were fitted with hand-operated Kingston valves. In emergencies, to allow quick diving, an extra tank known as 'Q' tank came into play. This, fitted with both a hydraulic vent and a Kingston valve, lay beneath the forward end of the accommodation section. Direct, high-pressure air blew this and the main ballast tanks at both ends. Once dived, the depth was controlled by two sets of hydroplanes. The forward set was above the waterline when surfaced and in rough weather could be folded flat against the casing to prevent damage. To submerge, the ballast tanks were filled, the hydroplanes inclined and the speed raised to at least seven knots. As the boat went down, Q tank was blown empty and she levelled off at the depth ordered. Periscope depth was 27 feet.

The trim was adjusted by pumping water in and out of a number of compensating tanks positioned throughout the submarine until the required depth could be regulated at slow speed with the least use of the hydroplanes. The vents on the main ballast tanks remained shut. In order to surface, the forward and after tanks were blown and the hydroplanes inclined in the reverse direction. After the conning tower hatch opened, a low pressure blower emptied all the remaining tanks — though in fine weather they were kept lightly flooded to accelerate a 'crash' dive. In most submarines these tanks were set along the sides; *Upholder's* ran all the way around the bottom, which made for good stability in diving without the usual tendency to list.[5]

Even so, guiding the boat through the constantly changing conditions she would encounter below (varying levels of salinity and temperature are among the factors which combine to affect a submarine's trim) required constant vigilance and a certain instinct, which St John soon noted Wanklyn possessed to an almost uncanny degree.

Betty, newly installed in digs in nearby Ulverston — 'two rooms and the use of the owner's bathroom, it was all very primitive but it was the same for everyone in those days' — missed *Upholder's* commissioning owing to a sharp attack of 'flu that left her particularly low after she ignored doctor's instructions: 'They gave you a tablet called "M & B" which they said turned you blue if you ate eggs with it. I forgot and ate some eggs — I didn't turn blue but it made me feel desperately ill . . .'[6]

Once again worried by his wife's poor health, Wanklyn took *Upholder* off for her torpedo trials at Loch Long. St John, knowing of his preoccupation, marvelled at the way he masked his unease. 'From the moment I met him — and I'm not talking from hindsight — I realised that of all the people I had served under in submarines up until then he created the most tremendous atmosphere of confidence that wore off on anyone who was anywhere near him. You would suddenly realise that this chap, a flash before anyone else, would always know what was the right thing to do. He had almost intuitive perception, he just never did anything wrong. Without any fuss or bother or showing off about it, he was just always in the right place at the right time — or if he saw somebody who was about to make a mistake, he would quietly take some sort of tactful action to stop it.'

An instance of this at Loch Long directly concerned St John — who to this day cannot recall it without feeling a shiver running up his spine.

'Diving was often very tricky in the Loch. There was a lot of fresh water coming down at certain times of the year, so you had density trouble when you fell into a sort of funnel of fresh water out of salt. So keeping a trim at very slow speed on a torpedo range was always a bit of a monkey. That was my job, of course, as First Lieutenant, and I do remember on one occasion it was particularly bad. We'd got so far and managed a certain amount of the work and then, on the final run — and it's a thing as a commanding officer you're told never to do, to interfere with your Jimmy — he did just that . . .

'He was at the periscope, watching the bearings and waiting to let his test torpedo down the range, when he suddenly said "Blow one and two tanks" to lighten the load. I don't know how he could tell, whether he'd seen something through the periscope that reflected the difference, but we went straight into a pocket of fresh water at the very moment when he wanted to fire and if it had been left to me we would have 'plongéd au catastrophe', as the French say.

'As it was, he spotted what might have been going to happen and he gave the order to blow which was a very drastic matter, but it kept us up and he fired the torpedo. If he hadn't, we would have missed that one and had to start all over again.

'I can't explain it — it was a very minor but interesting "for instance", I suppose. He just said "Sorry, Number One but I thought I saw that coming." I don't know how he knew. It's a mystery, naval historians have always said, how Nelson always knew where the other people were. They call it an intuitive perception — ESP, if you like. It wasn't really that with Wanklyn but he was so well-informed that his instincts always proved to be right.'

St John observed him to be of 'a philosophical turn of mind. He liked a bit of theosophy and enjoyed an argument — though he never forced anything down anyone's throat. He didn't go in for small talk, though, and he wasn't a social animal at all. He didn't shine at parties.'

It was in the open air, in the wild and beautiful uplands of Argyllshire and the Lake District, that he saw him in his element. 'He was a countryman at heart. I thought of him as a Scot — erroneously, as I now understand — because most of my experience of him was in Scotland and he took to the hills so well. Whenever it was possible he was out shooting and fishing and people were very generous to us. The Kennedy family in Ulverston were the owners of valuable iron ore mines up in Furness and they had a lot of land. Wanklyn and I would go out partridge shooting with them. He would often move off from us — he was a bit of a loner that way and I suppose that's why people said he was a sort of enclosed, private person. It's not true — he just didn't appreciate going to drinks parties very much.'[7]

Towards the end of his time at Barrow, when *Upholder's* trials were complete, Wanklyn had ample leisure for his favourite pursuits and made the most of what were to be his last opportunities to enjoy them.

'Life up here is nice and quiet and very pleasant,' he wrote his mother on 9 October. 'I have had three days' shooting and another tomorrow and any amount of fishing.' He went on to regale her with an account of a protracted battle with a salmon. 'I had one on three days' running . . . but was broken after being snagged every time. Of course I had to go in every time in a forlorn attempt to clear it, but I didn't mind going in to gaff him the fourth time . . .'[8]

Betty shared his love of angling — he caught the salmon with her own trout rod — but their fishing expeditions en famille could be trying. 'It wasn't very suitable for the baby. I remember sitting in a field trying to keep him entertained. There was nothing for him to look at and he was at the age when he would rather have seen the traffic going past. But David and I saw so little of each other that it was really like being on honeymoon each time. I don't think we ever got to the stage of "give and take".

Yet her husband was long unused to domesticity and his occasionally quixotic behaviour in the home at once amused and exasperated her.

'There was one time when I was putting Ian to bed and David said he would gut the fish and get them ready for supper. After I'd given the baby his bottle I came down — and there was David with the fish cut open and all the insides arranged in a neat row along the draining board. He said "Look, darling — it's eaten this and that and so and so." It didn't really help to get the supper ready — but that's the sort of thing he would do.'[9]

His sister was astonished at the skill with which he performed these dissections: 'His fingers were like two bunches of bananas.'[10] But they belonged to the hands of a natural surgeon — as he would soon demonstrate when it fell to him to apply treatment to a badly injured sailor (see page 73). Meanwhile Wanklyn saw no incongruity in the use of the fore-ends of his submarine as a game room in which to display his trophies from the field. The crew, who must ordinarily have been counted the least fastidious of hosts, objected strongly to their presence, however. St John remembers an unrecorded mutiny over the matter of a hare.

'One beautiful day in Loch Long that autumn he had his twelve-bore on board and he said: "Let's go ashore, Number One, and see if we can bag some game. You take the submarine back to the pier and get the Folboat out and I'll go ashore with some sailors and join you again at the other end." So we erected the Folboat — it was a collapsible thing used in cloak and dagger operations and its assembly in itself was a major evolution seldom undertaken by any sensible submariner — and ferried him and half a dozen Jolly Jacks in relays to the shore on the north east bank of the loch. I took the submarine back and put her alongside and waited. They spread out and walked the moor up the head of the loch and the sailors all came back absolutely exhausted after a stiff hike in their bellbottoms and gaiters — with Wanklyn in triumph with the biggest brown hare I'd ever seen, which was the sole item in the bag.

'Marvellous,'' he said. "We'll hang this, Number One, and jug it." ' I said 'I can't jug a hare' but he said 'I can do it.' And so this bloody thing was strung up on the bulkhead door which separated the fore-ends from the seamen's mess and there it stayed, with a cup under its nose to ripen — which it did rather faster than expected, thanks to the warm, damp atmosphere. After a week I went to turn the hands to at 0800 and the Coxswain, who should have come to tell me they were ready, fallen in and told off at the casing, came instead with a very straight face and said: "Very sorry, sir, we have a mutiny on our hands. The sailors absolutely refuse to do any work at all until that bloody animal's been ditched, because they can't stand the smell any longer."

So I said 'Tell the hands at once that they'd better fall in or there'll be trouble — but you can also tell them that I will pass their sentiments on to the CO and let them know what he has to say.' And so the mutiny was averted and the hands turned to — everybody pissing themselves with laughter. I went to Wanks and said "Look, we had a mutiny this morning, sir . . ." Well, they were right, the smell was really getting beyond belief.'

It appears that the hare was indeed by now so gamey that Able Seaman Young, the submarine's gunlayer and cook, was ordered to remove it to the after casing for gutting and cleaning. *Upholder* was tied up alongside the depot ship *Forth* and the operation took place immediately below Captain Submarines' cabin porthole — into which a good deal of the aroma duly travelled, to its occupant's immediate and explosive rage. 'Anyway,' St John concludes the tale, 'Wanklyn jugged the hare and the sailors were given a share as a reward for putting up with it for so long — and very good it was, too.'[11]

The idyllic autumn days in the country that Wanklyn loved best came to an abrupt end when he received a signal ordering him to proceed to Gosport. He had started the full black beard that most people were ever after to associate with him and it came as something of a shock to his mother and sister, whom he arranged to meet for a farewell lunch at the Trocadero in London's West End. The famous restaurant was still doing a roaring trade, despite the attentions of the Luftwaffe.

'Mother and I sat waiting for him as the crowds of officers came downstairs to leave their coats and caps. In the dim lighting imposed by the blackout we failed to recognise the lean, bearded Naval officer until he turned to the cloakroom hatch — and then mother recognised the back of his head!'[12]

They were not to know, though the thought lay naturally in their minds, that this would be their last meeting. A more certain parting was soon made clear to Wanklyn at Fort Blockhouse, where he found that St John, whom he had come to value highly, was to be taken off to do his own Perisher.

'I hadn't expected it to come as early as that,' St John admitted, 'but I counted it a great privilege to have had even a short acquaintance with Wanklyn because even in that brief period he impressed me as a very exceptional person with that uncanny ability of his to foresee problems and furthermore to take the right action to deal with them.'[13]

St John left a small — and possibly unique — legacy. Wanklyn had objected to *Upholder's* official crest — 'an insipid dish served up by the powers that be' that took the form of a representational classical deity, arms broken off in the style of the Venus de Milo, incorporated in a Greek column — describing it as "an armless Greek tart with her legs in a gash bin." 'He ordered me to do better and I hit on the idea of using the Atlas Insurance Company's logo — a full-frontal depiction of Atlas supporting the world.'

It was a happy thought, St John's robust pragmatism had been visited by true inspiration which Wanklyn at once appreciated. 'Wanks had it carved and put in the boat. He was adamant that he would have nothing to do with the Admiralty's effort and thereafter *Upholder* had my Atlas and no other crest.'*[14]

Wanklyn was understandably irritated by the removal of his right hand man. 'He was a bit put out: "Why the hell go and give me a First

---

* But the 'armless Greek tart' remained on the Admiralty register. She returned to haunt the new HMS *Upholder* — and was again summarily exorcised by Wanklyn's successor. St John's Atlas was 50 years old when it finally won official approval.

Lieutenant and then take him away from me just as I'm going to sea?" I heard him complain. But he was very lucky because he got Tubby Crawford in my place . . .'[15]

Michael Lindsay Coulton Crawford's nickname probably owed less to his girth, which then as now hardly merited this title, than to a pleasantly rubicund countenance that still splits wide in a wall-to-wall grin that is instantly infectious. When war broke out he had been serving in *Sealion* with the redoubtable Ben Bryant, a much older submarine skipper by the standards of the day who later won great renown in the Mediterranean in command of *Safari* and survived the war to become Flag Officer Submarines. *Sealion* had returned early from Malta with the S boats Wanklyn helped to relieve in *Otway* and had operated in the North Sea out of Harwich. She had an exciting time of it. Crawford left her 'after she had her periscope swiped off in the Skagerrak' and went to Scapa Flow to spend three months in his first job as 'Jimmy' to *L23* before his posting to *Upholder*. It was his first experience of the type and he was given just two days to get to know her before she set off for Malta.

'We went out for a day's exercises and then back into harbour. It was purely done for my benefit. Exit the last First Lieutenant and that was it — I had the boat.'

He found her 'very lively underwater in rough weather', noting that with her very shallow periscope depth she was 'very difficult to control when heading into a head sea at that level.' It was his first experience of Wanklyn, too, apart from a brief sighting in *Otway* at Malta the year before. He discovered him to be 'calm, quiet and straightforward. He accepted me as any CO does — sorry to see the last chap go. It was one of those things we all have to suffer — you get a good team going and then you have to lose part of it.'[16]

His first lastingly vivid impression of Wanklyn — who parted from his wife and son for the last time on December 9 — derived from an incident a few days later while on passage through the Bay of Biscay, during which *Upholder* had a taste of the severe weather for which those waters are notorious:

'During a particularly heavy roll Chief Engine Room Artificer William Baker — at 44 by far the oldest rating on board — lost his balance and grabbed at the jamb of the bulkhead door. At the same time the door broke free of its retaining catch and smashed on his hand, practically taking off the tops of three or four fingers. It was a problem Wanklyn dealt with remarkably well. With infinite patience and a very delicate touch, having given the man morphine to ease the excruciating pain, he sorted out the mangled fingers and splinted them up. During the next three or four days he painstakingly changed the dressings and when we got to Gibraltar Baker was taken off to the military hospital. As far as I can tell, he got the full use of his hand back apart from the malformation of one of the fingers. It was entirely due to Wanklyn's skill and patience, the doctors said. In the circumstances, he would have been entirely justified in amputating — and I bet he could have made a good job of that, too.'

Wanklyn's success in this matter had a magical effect on the crew. 'They were all very impressed. Wanklyn had actually turned a nasty accident into a morale booster. Coming just before we went into the area of operations it gave them confidence to know how well he could cope with that sort of emergency. After all, you only got a pretty perfunctory First Aid course as a submarine officer — it was all down to the individual. In my own Perisher, when we did a quick refresher, one of my fellow budding COs turned green and had to leave the room when he was just being *told* about the sort of thing he might be called upon to do . . .'[17]

Upholder passed the New Year at Gibraltar in storing and carrying out a few minor repairs. CERA Fred Frame was taken on in Baker's place. It was an important position he held; the U Class carried no engineer officer so an experienced Chief Artificer was essential. The boat left the Rock for Malta on 3 January. Wanklyn was ordered to patrol off the west coast of Sicily before reporting to base. A convoy was going through the Sicilian Straits and he was told to intercept any Italian surface forces that might threaten its safe passage. None were seen — though they heard the sound of a number of explosions which were assumed to come from bombing attacks on the ships.[18]

Italy had entered the war seven months before and in that time the Allies' situation in the Mediterranean had deteriorated. On land, in North Africa, the battle raged to and fro along the coast. In the skies above the Central Mediterranean the Luftwaffe and the Regia Aeronautica had the advantage. And while the Allied supply lines stretched 12,000 miles around the Cape of Good Hope, the enemy's route to Africa was only a few hundred miles long — comfortably 1000 miles distant from the Allied Fleet bases at Alexandria and Gibraltar. The year that had just begun was going to be critical in this theatre of the war. Perhaps the most vital requirement was the limitation of the flow of reinforcements and material from Italy. Already the role of Malta was threatened by continuous air raids and the shortage of spares and ammunition for the small number of fighter aircraft based there — and the surface forces could not operate adequately without air cover.[19]

Submarine operations out of Malta had met with very little success during these months and nine boats, together with forty-one officers and 407 ratings, had been lost. They were too big and too old for the work they had been called upon to do — mostly O, P and R classes recalled from the Far East. Some had been claimed by intensive mine laying by the Italians and they were further hampered by a restricted 'sink at sight' area imposed on them. And though mines were initially blamed for the submarine losses, six had fallen to Italian destroyers and torpedo boats. On the other side of the balance sheet lay only nine Italian merchant ships, one U-boat and a torpedo boat sunk, totalling a scant 37,000 tons. In fairness, this figure has to be seen in the context of the limited stocks of torpedoes available to the Malta submarines. In general terms, they were told 'not to fire on northbound merchant vessels and never to fire a salvo of more than three unless attacking a major war vessel.'[20]

To Shrimp Simpson, who had been appointed Commander Submarines Malta and arrived there in the destroyer *Janus* on 8 January, the protracted agony Malta was to endure over the next 20 months was the unnecessary result of 'a stupid policy'.

He realised that Malta 'if *defended* from air attack, could support a vast surface force of cruisers and destroyers which would have caused the Axis to abandon the North African campaign virtually at British dictation.' The island's resilient limestone afforded superb natural air raid protection — although 16,000 tons of bombs were to fall there, destroying 35,000 buildings, the number of civilian casualties claimed by the bombardment would be comparatively light at just over 1500. Yet the orders to Malta-based aircraft were to attack — 'not to defend the island and its unique qualifications as a sally port for slaughtering the enemy fully committed in North Africa by fast surface gunships supported by submarines.'[21]

And so, with no aircraft suitable for defence, the lack of air cover left a few of the Royal Navy's smallest — next to the H boats — and slowest submarines as practically the sole naval force operating from the island.

On 14 January, *Upholder* was among the first of these to arrive.

Chapter 11
The Illustrious *blitz*

Upholder checked in just four days after the second great siege of Malta began in earnest. It came within an ace of closing her career before it even got started.

On 10 January the first dive bombing attack was directed against the aerodrome five miles away from Lazaretto — where the submariners had 'a grandstand view'.[1] Just after noon, fifty miles to the west, the carrier HMS *Illustrious* was struck by six heavy bombs delivered in a concerted attack by 30 screaming Junkers 87 Stukas that has been described as 'one of the great flying achievements of the war'.[2] It was certainly the first practical demonstration of the vulnerability of surface units to the threat from the air and the skill and precision of the German Air Force was admired even by those on the receiving end. 'Admiral Cunningham', wrote Ernle Bradford, the author of the definitive surveys of both of the great historic investments of Malta, was himself 'so engrossed that he hardly seemed to notice when a thousand pound bomb hurtled over his own bridge and, missing the foredeck, struck the fluke of the battleship's (*sic*) starboard bow anchor'.[3]

That *Illustrious* survived at all was due only to the frantic efforts of a flight of her own Fulmar fighters, which managed to get away as the attack began — actually flying through the spray raised by the first bombs that luckily fell short. Circling out of control with her steering gear out of action and with huge fires ranging below, she suffered further attacks mid-afternoon and after sunset. These were bravely broken up by the slow-climbing Fulmars — no real match for the Messerschmidts that accompanied the later strikes — which had gone to Malta to refuel, re-arm and return to the fray.

Steering solely by her main engines — amazingly still intact — the great ship limped into Grand Harbour at 10 p.m. and tied up in French Creek, reeking of 'burning cordite, of aviation fuel and oil and blood and tired sweat'.[4]

Upholder, visited by the usual defects that plague any new vessel and lying under repairs prior to her first war patrol, was in the next berth when *Illustrious* came under fire again six days later.

Until now the air assault on Malta had been conducted by the Italian air force, the Regia Aeronautica, whose pilots were less inclined to come in low, where the better chance of accuracy was balanced by the risk of an equal opportunity afforded to fire from the ground and counter-attack by the island's meagre fighter force.

Consequently these ineffectual raids had become something of a spectator sport for the local populace, who gathered on the rooftops to watch the show 'as if it was all some spectacular opera.'[5] This time the authorities knew it would be quite different: General Geissler's crack Fliegerkorps X merited a barrage of fire so dense that the chances of anyone out in the open being struck down by the resulting fall of shrapnel were much the same as those affecting its intended recipients — and the Maltese were warned to take cover.

At 2 p.m. wave after wave of Messerschmidt, Fiat and Macchi fighters swarmed in before a dark cloud of over 70 bombers. Only four Hurricanes, three Fulmars and two of the island's soon-to-be-legendary Gloster Gladiator biplines were available to counter the largest concentration of enemy aircraft it had seen to date. From the ground, every single gun in Malta seemed to be joining in the barrage, including some of the heavy guns in the forts which had been useless against the earlier high-level attacks. The din was indescribable, with every ship in the harbour — including *Illustrious* herself — adding to the clamour as they opened fire with their own armament.

Upholder, her nearest neighbour, brought her Lewis guns into play. From the bridge 20-year-old Second Coxswain Gordon Selby witnessed the drama. He had joined the Navy as a Seaman Boy in 1935, volunteered for submarines during the Munich Crisis and had seen war patrols in *Oberon* in the Channel during the Dunkirk evacuation and in *H44* out of Harwich before joining *Upholder* at Barrow, but nothing had prepared him for this taste of modern warfare in all its fury. *Illustrious* sometimes disappeared from his view entirely behind mountains of water thrown up by bombs falling into the creek.

'I saw the — miraculously single — direct hit she suffered on her quarterdeck . . . As duty Killick I was on the bridge and Crawford was there with me during all the bombing. We were literally just 50 feet astern of her.'[6]

The whole bombardment lasted about ten minutes, according to Simpson who admitted 'he could not bear to see the "inevitable" catastophe of *Illustrious* either blowing up or sinking alongside the wall' and took shelter. When he emerged he noticed that a cloud of dust had risen 1000 ft into the air around French Creek and privately concluded that this alone must have saved the ship.

'Just seventeen months later smoke cannisters lit around the harbour proved most effective in frustrating bomb attack, but nobody had the vision to learn the lesson from this vivid demonstration.'[7]

Crawford noted that *Upholder*'s guns produced 'little effect, even though the enemy aircraft dived very low. Some submarines in the dockyard suffered minor damage, but *Upholder* was unscathed . . .'[8]

She was luckier than she knew. Lying at the opposite end of the creek was the merchantman *Essex*. Thirty-eight men were lost, dead and wounded, when her engine room was struck but fortunately the compartment's bulkheads contained the blast. Her hold was crammed with 4000 tons of ammunition and torpedoes. If this lethal cargo had been ignited *Illustrious* and *Upholder* would have gone up with her.[9]

Three days later, on Sunday 19 January, came the last raid on the carrier, raising 'terrific clouds of dust, flying masonry and iron'.[10] This time *Illustrious* suffered underwater damage from bombs that exploded close by her on the bottom but she took no direct hits. Nineteen of the raiders were shot down — about a quarter of the attacking force, a rate of loss the Luftwaffe could hardly sustain. Even so, a further attack was prepared but at sunset on the 23rd *Illustrious* sailed at high speed for Alexandria, where she safely arrived two days later. In *Red Duster, White Ensign* Ian Cameron was to observe that 'no warship of any Navy ever lived through such bombardment'.[11] That she survived the *Illustrious* blitz as it came to be known was, Simpson felt, a 'miracle';[12] that *Upholder* passed through the ordeal intact was little short of miraculous, too.

Chapter 12
By guess and by God

As night fell on 24 January *Upholder* slipped out of harbour to begin her first patrol. The way led along the swept channel that was hopefully clear of mines. She made her first dive to check her trim and was able to surface again in just eight minutes — careful preparation alongside had meant that few adjustments were required. The boat headed on at a steady 12 knots for the rich hunting grounds to the west of Tripoli.

A little over 24 hours later the Asdic rating made contact. He had picked up the hydrophone effect from moving propellors, bearing 090 degrees . . .

Up on the bridge, Wanklyn could see nothing. All was shrouded in darkness. He ordered diving stations and tension mounted below as the men fell to their allotted places. *Upholder* continued on the surface. At 1.30 a.m. the Asdic operator announced that his contact was moving to the left — and as Wanklyn altered course he saw the faint shadows of a merchantman with a single destroyer in escort. He decided to undertake a surface attack — the more difficult of his options.[1]

Upholder carried a full load of eight torpedoes, four of them ready loaded in their tubes. These were the standard 21 inch Mk 8 variety introduced in the early 1930s that were to remain in service for half a century. Straight-running at 45 knots, they had no homing devices and so were intended to be fired in 'hosepipe' salvoes, one after another along the same course. Thus the submarine itself must be aimed ahead of the enemy's track to allow for the delay in reaching their target.

To some extent the method was 'hit or miss', even when applied by an expert. Two torpedoes fired, for example, would hardly account for any margin of error. When dived, the captain's necessarily hasty glance through the attack periscope would have to produce most of the information on which he must base his calculations. He had to make an accurate relative bearing before checking his observation with the gyro compass; compute the inclination by angle-on-the-bow (which together with the true bearing would produce the target course); and then measure the range with a tiny rangefinder built into the periscope against some part of the target's known or guessed height — the funnel or masthead, say. By this means an idea of the target's speed could be arrived at. There were other useful pointers such as the propellor revolution count obtained from the Asdic operator together with anything known of an identified target's capabilities and it was also worthwhile measuring the distance of the second bow wave from the bow to give a good indication of speed.

All this intelligence was processed by a simple calculating machine known as the ISWAS — later replaced by the slightly more advanced 'fruit machine' — to give the lead angle on which to point the submarine. Mackenzie maintained that 'any CO in those days could not rely on the fruit machine entirely. He had to work it out in his head by mental arithmetic as well — the fruit machine was a pretty Heath Robinson affair . . .'[2]

Richard Compton-Hall has observed that a capable captain would customarily produce a target solution accurate to within 'a couple of knots for speed and ten or twenty degrees for course. He then endeavoured to fire so that the torpedoes ran at more or less right angles to the enemy's course from an ideal range of about 1000 yards. At that range the fish took only forty seconds to cross the enemy's track or, hopefully, impact on the target. This gave little opportunity for the ship under attack to take evasive action if the torpedo wakes were sighted, while the chances of him altering course in the normal way, on a standard zig-zag pattern, were minimised.'[3]

It was not an easy business — especially when bearing in mind the escorting destroyers which had to be dodged on the way. Curiously, a night attack on the surface was often even more difficult. Wanklyn, judging his first attack from the bridge, could not make use of the periscope's rangefinder, so it was truly a case of 'by guess and by God' — 'although some old hands said it was always 10 degrees whatever and more often than not they were right!'[4]

Just after 1.30 a.m. Wanklyn, at a range of 2500 yards from the merchantman, fired two torpedoes at eight second intervals. He at once altered course to avoid the destroyer, and as he did so spotted two more ships following in very open order. As the minutes ticked by without the crump of an explosion, it was clear that his first shots had missed — he had allowed for a target speed of 15 knots whereas experience had already shown that convoys seldom exceeded eight or nine. With this in mind he fired two more torpedoes at the next two ships. This time the range was about 3000 yards — again, far from ideal and again both missed. Captain Sydney Raw, the Captain of the First Submarine Flotilla at Malta, later noted that an error in director angle of only one degree would have caused both to miss ahead and at one-and-a-half degrees to miss astern — which represented a speed error of only one knot. So it was an easily pardonable miscalculation and he considered that Wanklyn's decision to remain on the surface and carry out a second attack when a counter-attack as a result of the first might have been expected was 'most creditable'.[5]

Wanklyn, having finally given the order to dive and waiting intently for the sound of an explosion which never came, could hardly be expected to share this charitable view of his efforts. He had expended half his precious stock of torpedoes with no result. That the submarine was spared the recognition of a counter-attack or a sudden change of course by the transports that would indicate that the track of his torpedoes had been spotted was not much consolation either — he might suppose he had been well wide of the mark. But he betrayed no emotion, we are told, beyond a thoughtful stroking of his beard.[6]

After an hour had gone by he ordered 'Surface — blow main ballast'. He had to keep his batteries charged — a submarine skipper's constant pre-occupation — and now he was more conscious than ever of the need to conserve his depleted arsenal for worthwhile targets. While surfaced the following night he caught sight of three more merchant ships — but broke off his attack when he noticed they were sailing light, unloaded.

Close inshore, early in the morning, what seemed at first to offer a worthwhile target was eventually discerned to be a house set on the tip of a promontory — in the gloom the whitewashed eminence had been taken for the bridge of a ship!

As the day slowly lightened however, two large ships appeared: an 8000 ton merchant vessel escorted by an armed merchant cruiser. Wanklyn was determined to make no mistake this time and closed to 900 yards. Shortly before 4.30 a.m. he fired two torpedoes, again at 12-second intervals — and a minute later Upholder echoed with a solid thump. One torpedo had struck home, the other having missed through gyro failure. As an exultant cheer rang through the boat, Wanklyn gave the order to dive.[7]

He waited over two hours before raising the periscope to check the result and found the ship — later identified as the German transport Duisberg — lying bows down, slowly sinking, it seemed, with the water lapping almost to the bridge. Thus satisifed, he moved off to the western end of his patrol area. Here, during the afternoon of 30 January, Upholder heard the sounds of a convoy approaching from the west — two large supply ships escorted by a pair of destroyers. Wanklyn elected to attack the second of the transports, estimated at 5000 tons. This time he fired two torpedoes at the extreme range of 4000 yards at 20-second intervals. He had guessed the enemy's speed at eight knots by checking the revolutions of the screening destroyer — and Raw later felt his tactics in not attempting to close the range at speed when he lay so near the escort ship were entirely correct.[8]

Once again the rumble of a distant explosion echoed through the submarine. But as Upholder dived to 80 feet the first shock of retribution was visited upon her. Wanklyn knew his torpedo tracks had been spotted — he had seen a destroyer racing full tilt towards him at the moment of firing. Now his crew were to experience the horror of depth charging for the first time. The detonations crept nearer and nearer, each one a huge tremor hammering the hull and

Wanklyn began the deadly game of cat and mouse. As the destroyer stopped, he stopped too, and when he heard the sound of movement above he moved in turn on a new course, diving deeper, full speed ahead. In the interval, the deck plating shuddered, light bulbs tinkled into splinters . . .

The tactics of evasion were interpreted differently under other hands. Survival was their only justification. Hugh Mackenzie preferred to hold to a straight course: 'It's not absolute luck, avoiding being depth-charged — you've got to grit your teeth and keep your head down. I always went dead slow. It's always a temptation to speed up and get away from the scene as quickly as possible, but you make a noise by doing that and that puts the enemy on to you. Sticking to one direction only, not twisting and turning — that was my recipe. That was when you were being hunted by hydrophones, I would change my tactics if I thought the chap could make contact with Asdic. As he came in to attack you, as you thought he was going overhead, you would speed up and try to get away under all the kerfuffle that the depth charges would make, when he wouldn't be able to distinguish them from the flow of water you gave out at high speed. Then you'd have to slow down again and stick to going slow and steady. That worked for me, anyhow.'[9]

On this occasion Upholder's ordeal lasted only 15 minutes but in that time 25 depth charges crashed around her and the crew were uncomfortably aware that only a half-inch thickness of steel separated them from extinction. Wanklyn got away with it, though. One hundred and fifty feet below, as he registered the Asdic operator's quiet report: 'Bearing drawing slowly right — getting fainter,' he was able to creep away.[10]

Upholder's first 'hammering' actually had a beneficial effect on morale — it reassured the crew that the captain could get them out of trouble. Luck or skill? Well, these were early days. Mackenzie 'sat at the feet of the master' at a later date when Wanklyn's celebrity was established and knew how his matchless calm under fire inspired confidence.

'This varied with the individual, but I can just see him — he would never be unnerved or show he was rattled in any way. He was a tremendously strong character that way, I think.'[11]

As Upholder set course for Malta, where she arrived on the first day of February in time for yet another air raid, the watchkeeper entered in his log 'probably a 5000-tonner'. They all felt some cause for satisfaction but Simpson weighed the results of Wanklyn's first patrol in his mind. Was it sufficient return for eight valuable torpedoes? And, as it turned out, the Duisberg had not gone to the bottom after all. Badly damaged, she was towed to Tripoli for repairs, which nevertheless kept her out of action for four full months.

Chapter 13
'Obviously a very disappointed man'

Though Raw considered *Upholder's* first patrol to have been 'extremely well carried out' and reflected 'great credit on the determination and resource of the Commanding Officer', noting that Wanklyn's tactics on the surface at night illustrated 'the advantages of the small, quick-turning submarine over the large, cumbersome type'[1] that had met with so little success in this theatre, Simpson's concern deepened over the next three months as Wanklyn conducted three patrols that met with no success at all.

Yet they were not without incident and some moments of high drama which produced several examples of Wanklyn's singular qualities of judgment and leadership.

Morale continued to be high as *Upholder* embarked again on 12 February, in spite of the already alarming shortage of food ashore — and of beer, which was by this time just a memory. The crew were forced to resort to the noxious local brew known as 'ambeet', popularly styled 'boiled oil' or 'Stuka juice', the latter a more accurate appellation, in the opinion of Sydney Hart. It hit a man, he said, 'with all the stunning impact of a bomb'.[2]

Not a few of them were still nursing hangovers when *Upholder* left at 11 a.m. for an afternoon of exercises with the destroyer *Havock* before heading once more for the western approach route to Tripoli. Early in the evening, just 25 miles to the south of Malta, Wanklyn was called to the bridge. A shadow steering north towards the island could just be made out against the darkening sky. It was too low in the water to be a transport — just possibly it might be a German E-boat.

Wanklyn called for diving stations but continued towards the target on the surface. Searchlights suddenly blazed over Malta, signalling the start of another air raid — and against the eerie cone of luminous white the unmistakable silhouette of a submarine was suddenly clear. A U-boat, perhaps, and the richest prize of all in the eyes of the Admiralty. Such a target merited a full salvo.

But was it a U-boat? Wanklyn could be forgiven for assuming so, for the situation report indicated no British submarines in the area and U-boats were known to scavenge these waters for stragglers making for the haven of Malta. Perhaps the second sense Michael St John has described was working against the appalling danger he faced by delaying too long — for it could be that *Upholder* was herself being lined up for attack. Even so, the unthinkable consequences of an error of identification had to be counted.

Wanklyn closed to 2000 yards and ordered the signalman to make a challenge. The flash of the trigger lamp would give his own position away, but though it was still hard to be certain it now seemed to him that the image in his night glasses might be that of a T-Class submarine. Three times the identifying letters for the day shone over the water. It was dead calm and though visibility was poor *Upholder* herself must have been a clear target by now.

No reply.

A quarter of an hour went by. Wanklyn altered course and challenged again. The click of the lamp sounded like machine-gun fire in the stillness of the night. Why was the skipper exposing them like this, the crew wondered as they sweated it out inside the darkened hull? He had only to challenge once to justify completing his attack — and at this range he could hardly miss. Nearly fifty years later Tubby Crawford still shakes his head in wonder. 'He was a very cautious, thinking chap who weighed up all the risks. He had very good vision — mine was pretty good but he could really pick out detail better than I could — and he just said: "No, that's a T-Class — leave it alone." So *Truant* got away with it . . .'[3]

At a similar distance, Sydney Hart was even more appreciative — and with good reason. 'I was on that submarine that night. I was on watch in the engine room at the time *Upholder* was stalking her. I have never since failed to be extremely thankful and grateful for Wanklyn's keen eyesight . . . The chances of a submarine escaping unscathed from such an attack as he mounted that night would have been infinitesimal.'[4]

Simpson, once he had the full facts at his disposal, observed that a fatal accident had only been avoided by Wanklyn's 'good judgment'.[5] It turned out that *Truant's* wireless transmitter had broken down in the course of a long and arduous patrol. She had taken part in a surface gun battle, fired 15 torpedoes — one of which had struck a mine close by — and lost the sixteenth from its tube in a depth charge attack. In the circumstances, Simpson felt her captain's decision to return to Malta a day early was quite in order — 'but since Malta's swept channel was being approached 24 hours early without being able to inform anybody, it was more than ever imperative to keep a particularly keen look-out.'[6]

The moon was favourable to *Upholder*, he noted, and the searchlights had probably distracted attention from the immediate horizon. Even so, he concluded grimly: 'The challenge lamp is certainly dim, but to fail to see four challenges from about one mile is inexcusable.'[7]

As it happened, *Upholder's* own W/T transmitter was also out of action and Wanklyn was unable to report the (at the time still unidentified) submarine's course and position until early the following morning.

Over the next five days, while patrolling off the Tunisian coast south east of the Gulf of Gabes, *Upholder* logged a number of sightings but most of the likely targets were so close inshore that the risk of missing and detonating a torpedo along the rocky coastline (which would give warning of a submarine to one and all) was unacceptable.

In the late evening of 19 February they encountered a heavily escorted eastbound convoy — three merchant ships with three destroyers. This was worth a chance and Wanklyn closed to 1500 yards of the leading ship, 2000 yards ahead of the starboard wing destroyer from which he could expect a heavy counter-attack. Two torpedoes were fired and both missed. Wanklyn had allowed a speed of ten knots, which he surmised must have been too slow.

Mercifully they remained undetected. Night attacks like these were to be preferred — during the daylight hours, in the often glassy calm and clarity of the Mediterranean, the forward casing could be clearly discerned through the periscope at 25 feet. Wanklyn realised how easily the submarine could be spotted from the air. If the periscope broke surface for even a few seconds it would leave the distinctive mark of its wake behind. The boat's blue livery helped reduce visual detection, but he must have prayed for the slightest breeze to help cloud the outline of their passage. On this patrol barely a ripple disturbed the clarity of the mirror above — and aircraft were seen almost every time the periscope was raised. It appeared these were large bombers and troop carriers on their way to Castle Benito, so perhaps they posed no real threat, but the information on their movements Wanklyn relayed back to Simpson was useful.

On the homeward passage to Malta he set his course along the enemy convoy route and arrived there on 23 February, disappointed by what he termed an 'uneventful' patrol.[8]

For all his lack of success in this and two subsequent forays in March, Wanklyn's reports were meticulous in detail. His notes on communications and defects and remarks on equipment in general were followed up — and the innate, quiet good humour with which they were imbued made for easy reading. On this occasion he had embarked five Army men from a special Commando detachment — a Lieutenant with a Sergeant and three others — to give them experience of submarine conditions. Wanklyn enjoyed their company, sharing none of the Service's traditional mistrust of 'outsiders', and employed them variously at the helm, in cyphering and as additional look-outs.

'They were most useful, relieving messmen and Asdic watchkeepers of all duties except their special ones,' he wrote. Games of Ludo

('Uckers' as the Navy call it) were a popular means of relieving the long periods of tedium that separated the perils of life on patrol. The undemanding pastime had its devotees in the Wardroom, too — if only for the arguments it produced: 'One most important duty for the (Army) officer was to make a fourth for Uckers — usually a noticeable defect in a "U" Class submarine complement,' Wanklyn observed.[9]

During this month *Upholder's* run of bad luck continued. On the afternoon of the 5th a small northbound convoy sighted off Tripoli was allowed to pass unmolested — the ships were heavily escorted but they were all unladen and none of them exceeded 4000 tons. Three days later a small escorted southbound group was attacked. Two torpedoes were fired at the only reasonable target, a well-stocked schooner. Simpson generously allowed that the attack was well pressed home to 900 yards — but no hits were scored: 'It is possible that if the first torpedo which was set to eight feet missed ahead, the second set to 12 feet passed under, though the vessel appeared to be at maximum draft.'[10]

By this time he appears to be struggling to make allowances for his protegé: '. . . the target was unfortunately too small to make certain of a kill,' he rather lamely concluded his remarks — though he was at pains to praise another comprehensive report on aircraft movements that indicated substantial reinforcements to the Italian base in Tripolitania.[11]

Wanklyn had also detailed 'an unpleasant but fortunately innocuous accident' which occurred while changing the submarine's recognition flares. 'One was set off in the Control Room, causing a glow like an electric fire and giving off enormous volumes of smoke. The whole submarine was quickly filled to capacity with a dense fog which fortunately was not excessively choking.'[12]

It was easy, in hindsight, to play down an event which men at sea fear beyond all else. Fire in a surface ship is harrowing enough; in a submarine it grips with a terror that not even the grim ordeal of a prolonged depth charging can equal. To describe *Upholder's* experience here as 'innocuous' stretches the Navy's traditional preference for understatement too far. Wanklyn calmly noted that 'the contents of two foamite extinguishers were played on the flare without making it falter for one moment.'[13] Later, when visibility improved and it was found that no damage had been done, the cause was investigated. It seemed the flare's safety pin had been stiff and came out with a sudden jerk which pulled the striker far enough back to set the thing off. Wanklyn recommended that flares be kept at 'safe' until they reached the bridge and that a longer lanyard be supplied to the safety pin and Simpson made an immediate signal to this effect.

Later in March *Upholder* was despatched to carry out a survey along the eastern coast of Sicily. Wanklyn's orders were explicit — he was not to carry out any attacks near the survey position unless the target was particularly worthwhile. When he began his task early in the morning of the 21st he sighted three schooners very close inshore. He let them pass — they were indeed of 'doubtful value' for torpedo fire and *Upholder* was not really suited to gun action as there was no gun hatch and the only access was via the conning tower.

He returned home, reporting that towns and railway trains on the coast were 'carelessly and ineffectually blacked out'.[14] On the 22nd he had seen a hospital ship, which Simpson thought might have been trying to recover airmen ditched in the Malta channel. This had been a black day for the RAF. Seven Hurricanes chasing a few bombers away from the island were thought to have been attacked by a number of German fighters and only two returned. Daylight raids were by now almost routine. The Luftwaffe were determined to establish air supremacy and wear down the small defending force — for which the Messerschmidts were more than a match.

The following day the hospital ship was seen again. The first proper Allied convoy of the year, four merchantmen escorted by the battle fleet and the new carrier *Formidable* from Alexandria, had reached Grand Harbour unobserved. But reconnaissance flights from Sicily soon spotted the arrival of the newcomers and two transports were sunk alongside before they could even be unloaded. A month before Admiral Cunningham had warned First Sea Lord Dudley Pound: 'The most drastic and early measures are needed to restore the situation at Malta, which alarms me seriously. Enemy air forces operate over the island as they please.'[15]

Three days after *Upholder's* return the Italian Navy, 'relinquishing its sensible policy of avoiding action and remaining a fleet in being', struck at the British convoys making their way between Egypt and Greece — and was routed off Cape Matapan. The Mediterranean Fleet had reasserted itself, confirming both the value of its air arm and the Italian High Command's reluctance to face the Royal Navy in a major action at sea. Malta was probably spared actual invasion by this event but, as Ernle Bradford has observed, 'after this one success it would be the Luftwaffe which would dominate the inland sea.'[16]*

The raids continued, making life almost impossibly difficult for the submarine base personnel. They did them one good turn, however. A lucky hit destroyed the Naval Store Office's records and the Flotilla Engineer Officer, Commander Sam MacGregor, to whom paperwork was the one drag on a matchless talent for improvisation, could not have been better pleased. 'As a cloud of paper forms and

---

* No submarines took part in the Battle of Matapan, although *Rover* and *Triumph* patrolled off Suda Bay and south of Milo in case the Italian Fleet intended to break into the Aegean.

flimsies floated away on an easterly breeze . . . Sam was heard to remark with satisfaction: "I reckon that must have loosened things up a bit".[17] Thereafter 'submarines helped themselves to whatever stores they needed without formality.'[18]

Rough seas and a persistent swell dogged *Upholder's* efforts throughout her next patrol on the convoy routes between the Kuriat Isles and the Kerkenah Bank between 3-14 April. Periscope depth was 'uncomfortable but just tenable,' Wanklyn wrote.[19] Bad weather notwithstanding, he still had three good opportunities against merchant ships travelling without surface or air escort — but expended his full load of torpedoes without result — 'which can only be considered extremely disappointing,' Raw noted irritably.[20]

Still more damning were his comments on the first of these abortive attacks, carried out around noon on the 10th at the extreme range of 6400 yards. After an hour-long approach the target altered course much further to the north than Wanklyn had expected. Raw's directive to Simpson that torpedoes were not to be fired at ranges over 2500 yards except at valuable targets had allowed some latitude: 'In the present instance, however, even if the attack were correctly carried out, I consider that this discretion was misused,' he wrote.[21]

Later the same afternoon *Upholder* had closed at full speed on two merchant vessels seen approaching from the north. Wanklyn fired three torpedoes at the larger of the two which appeared to harry him through the first two hours of the following morning.

After this the day wore on uneventfully and then, in bright moonlight, he chased a 4500 ton, fully-laden merchantman. His last three torpedoes were aimed individually at 2000 yards. Once again, all of them missed — one, Wanklyn said, had a gyro failure and the other broke surface. By the time the 'wanderer' had sunk and he was able to break surface, he was too late for a gun action.

Simpson was still inclined to be sympathetic: 'It was at first considered unfortunate that *Upholder* should have carried out this attack on relatively unimportant targets in view of the information to him about a troop convoy leaving Palermo, but it is considered that *Upholder* acted entirely correctly not to let any target pass unattacked, in view of the fact that his information also told him that Swordfish and four destroyers were standing by to attack the troop convoy.'[22]

Raw, however, was still not making any allowances: '. . . I do not consider that the failure of the third attack can be attributed with certainty to the gyro failure which occurred. Such a conclusion pre-supposes that all the attack data was correct and that the torpedo which failed was the one which would have hit the target. While it is possible that this was the case, the evidence is not conclusive.'[23]

Wanklyn was only able to draw some credit from yet another abortive patrol when a signal came through from Simpson that four destroyers were waiting at Malta to operate on the convoy routes.

Submarines were to make reports on any distant sightings of a southbound convoy and Wanklyn replied that he would remain on station, even though his torpedo tubes were empty. At 2.45 p.m. on the 12th he spotted a group of five large merchant ships and three Navigatori Class destroyers with air escort approaching quickly from the north. That night he was ordered to break off and set a course for Pantellaria, the Italian island base midway between Sicily and the Tunisian coast. But on passage *Upholder* intercepted reports from Swordfish aircraft shadowing the convoy and saw parachute flares falling to the southward. This indicated that the convoy had altered course to the north and Wanklyn increased speed and ordered star shells to be fused, hoping to turn the ships back towards the destroyers. Two hours later he sighted the enemy vessels three miles west of Pantellaria and steering north. He fired his shells across their bows and hastily dived as their escorts raceds towards him. As he hoped, the convoy thought an attack by a surface force was imminent and turned on its tracks. (Four days later it was wiped out off Sfax by the strike force from Malta.)

Wanklyn then took a considerable risk by exposing his radio mast aerial in broad daylight to make his report in full view of four Italian aircraft circling above. Raw accorded him the rather backhanded compliment of observing that in this instance he 'had the fortune which favours the brave'.[24] Simpson loyally concluded that this last action of Wanklyn's had shown 'fine determination and correct appreciation'. The patrols had been well carried out, he maintained stoutly in his official communique, 'though a great disappointment to the Commanding Officer of the *Upholder*.'[25]

Privately he was less sanguine. Despite his continued high opinion of Wanklyn's capabilities, he was close to being forced into an agonising decision over one 'whose torpedo expenditure without result was actually making me wonder whether such a poor shot could be kept in command'.[26]

Crawford could tell his skipper was 'obviously a very disappointed man — but he never let it come out, he kept it very much to himself. Other boats were getting results, this was the worrying thing. Simpson — who still had a great respect for him — more or less said "One more patrol — and that's it".'[27]

Man and boy, Wanklyn had now spent over half his young life in the Navy and half of that again in the branch of the Service to which he had given his particular attention and loyalty. Now his career was in the balance. Found wanting in the only test that counted, he seemed destined to pass into obscurity.

Chapter 14
'Plain butchery'

'From Commander-in-Chief to Submarines Malta: Kesselring has established his HQ at the Miramar Hotel, Taormina. Eliminate him.'[1]

This was the dramatic signal that landed on Simpson's desk towards the end of April. Cunningham may be forgiven a touch of *Boy's Own Paper* military terseness — at least there could be no mistake as to his intention. Here was a chance for Wanklyn to vindicate himself. Taormina, it will be remembered, was the spot he had chosen for his honeymoon three years before. Duly summoned to help plan a 'cloak and dagger' operation, he pored over a detailed chart. 'There is the rock where we lay and sunbathed, and it has over 20 feet of water right up to it. I could take *Upholder* right in and put her bows against that rounded rock, which is ideal for landing from, and it is the nearest point to the hotel.'[2]

Wanklyn had never stayed at the Miramar, so he could give little more useful information. It lay about 200 yards from the rocky coast, cut into a hillside in the middle of an olive grove — a sizeable pile with maybe 200 bedrooms. It was assumed Kesselring would have the bridal suite. Including his entourage, staff and security troops, perhaps 200 others might be sharing these quarters with him.

They decided to fit *Upholder* with a large pudding fender around the bow to protect her from the rocks and embark a team of 23 commandos. In nine days' time, at 1 a.m. before the setting of the moon, it was intended that this force would creep ashore in their rubber-soled shoes and blow up the suite with 30 lb of plastic explosive. Four men armed with knives and hand grenades were to take care of the sentries while the rest of the party blazed away at any window that appeared occupied. It would all be over in about 40 minutes after landing, and then they would make their escape under cover of *Upholder's* Lewis guns.

Such was the plan. To Simpson, as he watched the team practise tossing dummy grenades through dummy window frames hung in a cutting behind the submarine base, it seemed chancy in the extreme — though worth the effort. He had no qualms over the morality of the venture; in the cold context of the military tally sheet it would be a fair return for the risk engaged by the attacking submarine.

But the the GOC Malta, General Sir William Dobbie, told him flatly that the plot was plain 'butchery'. Was it a naval or a military operation, he asked? And when Simpson answered that it was surely a typical example of a combined operation, he retorted that he very much hoped it was not. 'If your Commandos were training to bring Field Marshall Kesselring before me unharmed as a prisoner of war through a well-thought-out cutting-out operation I would approve, but if you intend to persist in this butchery I must insist that it be called a naval operation.'

Still smarting from this rebuke, Simpson walked down the sweeping marble staircase from the Governor's office past a row of suits of armour. To him they were at once the very embodiment of Dobbie's steely reproach and he felt a sudden surge of irritation at the Blimpish General.

'I walked over to the nearest, and tapping his cuirass I said: "The days of chivalry are over, chum. You might tell the boss." Then I felt rather ashamed that I should have sunk so low. I must attribute my fall to progress.'[3]

Yet it had been a grave insult for any Naval officer to have to bear from an Army man — especially from one whose generation had blithely countenanced the wholesale slaughter of the Somme, committing thousands of men in pointless frontal assaults against objectives that were bound to produce casualty rates out of all proportion to the value of their gain. Moreover Simpson of all people did not deserve it. Pat Norman, who came to know him well, recalled 'he took casualties so much to heart it was awful. He knew well he was going to send submarines on almost suicidal missions — and they really were suicidal sometimes — and he had to do it, had to send them out to the right position and take the punishment. It was a heavy load and he was a very human guy — loved his liquor, as so many captains of submarine flotillas did, and who can blame them?'[4]

In the event, the day before *Upholder* was due to sail, Cunningham signalled: 'Special operation with *Upholder* to be postponed until next suitable moon. Convoys loading at Naples likely to sail tonight and all submarines should be disposed to intercept.' Two weeks later a further signal advised: 'Kesselring has left Taormina'. 'So the outcome of this "butchery" was never tested,' Simpson noted wryly.[5]

Three more submarines were added to his command of five during April — *Union*, *Unbeaten* and *Urge*. The latter, with Tompkinson in the driving seat, had sunk the 10,500 ton Axis tanker *Franco Martelli* while on passage across the Bay of Biscay. Thus 'Tommo' opened a healthy account even before his arrival on station — and his was not the only early success. Dick Cayley in *Utmost* already had two ships to his credit and Simpson counted him his best CO at this time. Tubby Crawford felt his own skipper's recent failures keenly but was glad to notice that *Upholder's* crew remained in good heart.

'One might have thought that the morale of the ship's company would have suffered, particularly as other submarines from Malta were scoring hits,' he later wrote. 'The fact that this was not the case was entirely due to Wanklyn's personality and leadership. (They) still had every confidence in him and they went all out to give him the best support they could. It was a measure of the man that he was able to maintain that spirit under those conditions, particularly as he must have been undergoing considerable mental strain at the time. Being a perfectionist, he must have spent many worried hours pondering over the run of unsuccessful attacks. However, he remained outwardly calm, concentrating on the preparations for the next patrol, during which he was determined to break the run of bad luck.'6

The result would exceed his wildest expectations. In just ten days he would join the ranks of the submarine aces.

Chapter 15
The spell is broken

Upholder sailed on the evening of the 21st for Kerkenah, but 24 hours later was ordered to remain off the island of Lampedusa, midway between Malta and the eastern coast of Tunisia. Simpson had information 'from a secret source' that two enemy cruisers and two destroyers were leaving a port in Sicily to rendezvous with a convoy south of Kerkenah and escort it northwards before returning to their home port.[1] Nothing was seen, however, and it was later assumed the ships went north by an unexpected route.

So Wanklyn pressed on for the well-known area off the Tunisian coast and here, on the afternoon of the 25th, fortune favoured him at last. He closed at full speed on a large, fully laden merchant vessel, though Crawford remembered 'no sense of desperation',[2] Wanklyn himself recording that, owing to the heavy swell it was essential to keep moving at 'half both, grouped down'.[3] Even so, the range was closed to 700 yards before firing. The ship had no flag or markings, but an armed trawler had been seen a few minutes earlier so he had no hesitation in assessing her as an enemy.

Two torpedoes sped towards the target at 35 knots — and less than half a minute later *Upholder* was rocked by a heavy explosion. So close in was she that most of the lamp bulbs for'd were shattered by the concussion. Wanklyn had been forced to make a complete turn at the last minute. He had planned to fire a third torpedo but this was saved as the first struck home. He moved off to the north east, watched the target settling and then returned to deliver a *coup de grace*. None was needed — he saw that the after deck was well awash. The ship, which he identified as the *Bainsizza* of 7900 tons — later confirmed to be the rather smaller *Antonietta Laura*, packed with nitrates and bound for Italy — was going down slowly on an even keel. She sank six hours later.

And so the spell was broken but the relief Wanklyn must have felt was quickly replaced by a new anxiety, implicit in fresh orders that arrived that evening. He was to close Kerkenah Bank again and finish off a destroyer and a supply ship grounded there, but on an even keel and apparently little damaged, as the result of a successful skirmish by surface units ten days earlier. They might yet be salvaged and this Wanklyn must somehow prevent. But going into shallow waters where he could not dive in the event of enemy attack was 'a situation which no submariner relishes,' Tubby Crawford noted dourly.

In the early afternoon of the 26th *Upholder* surfaced and found the two ships in sight. Wanklyn decided to dive and leave his approach until twilight so he could get away under cover of darkness once the job was done. He hoped to torpedo both targets and set two fish to run on the surface — but as *Upholder* moved towards the destroyer she came aground herself, with just 29 feet of water showing on the guages. There might be other shallow spots in which torpedoes would be wasted and so he determined to go alongside the merchant vessel instead and set her on fire. She appeared to be deserted — but there could still be a gun crew left on board, mounting guard. As he blew his tanks and surfaced, inching his way across the treacherous bank, all his skill at seamanship was brought into play. Sydney Hart would observe: '. . . he had to be ready to put her full astern at the slightest touch. Five hundred and forty tons of ship moving only slowly ahead can drive herself well and truly into a sandbank.'[5]

At 10.30 p.m. he came close alongside to read the name *Arta* painted on the side of a 2500 tonner. In the moonlight he could see rows of trucks, cars and motorcycles covering the decks — vital transport earmarked for the Afrika Korps.

Lieutenant Christopher Read was chosen to lead the boarding party up her rusted side: 'I suppose being the most easily spared if things went wrong. Actually I was more scared of the chap who was meant to cover us. I think he was the cook, our regular gunner having been left ashore owing to illness. Anyway, there were no live Germans on board so, for intelligence purposes, we collected samples of those that were portable of the various items on board. It seems the *Arta* was carrying the HQ unit of a Panzer detachment.'[6]

In her holds he found munitions and evidence of accommodation provided for a human cargo of German troops who had evidently suffered heavy casualties. They gathered up quantities of arms, papers, flags, steel helmets — even a staff officer's picnic hamper.

'As the ship's captain had left, taking the keys of his safe with him, I had the welcome job of safe-breaking. A suitably placed charge (one of my hobbies when I could manage it) reduced the safe to its six component sides so I could rescue the contents. The explosion also set the tinder-dry woodwork on fire so we did not delay our removal.'[7] (Read's skill with explosives might seem unusual in one who would eventually enter the priesthood — but history is littered with bomb-happy clerics!)

They left the fire to spread — as the ship was flooded up to the 'tween decks in all compartments there would be no chance to examine the main cargo anyway. Able Seaman Lambert Saunders was attracted by a pair of boots that looked about his size — but dropped them smartly when he found a dead German's feet inside them . . .[8]

They cleared away and returned thankfully to deep water. The fire took hold well, spreading to the lorries on the deck. Soon the night was rent by a series of massive explosions and *Arta* became a huge bonfire, blazing high into the purple sky and illuminating the choppy sea for miles around. Wanklyn elected to leave the destroyer, which he knew lay in much shallower water, until the following day.

At first light they came to the surface and crept towards her but, not unexpectedly, they grounded in 15 feet of water while still 4000 yards clear. Wanklyn ordered: 'Blow main ballast'. It was no good, he concluded — it was simply not practicable to torpedo her and he doubted whether a closer approach could be made from any other direction. As *Upholder* bucked and thrashed, her reversed screws straining to clear her from the muddy shoal, she was helplessly exposed to attack from the air, but fortunately the skies were clear. They were lucky — the spectacular pyrotechnics of the night before must surely have been expected to draw the moths to the flame. And at the last moment, just as they finally pulled clear, the watchkeepers had a nasty jolt when all the buoys on the bank were unexpectedly lit.

Wanklyn moved on to a planned rendezvour with *Ursula* and *Upright*. HMS *Gloucester* and the 5th Destroyer Flotilla were at Malta, ready to take action against enemy convoys, and Simpson had planned to dispose his submarines to sink ships known to be embarking from Naples on 27 April and 1 May. They would set up a patrol line north of Kerkenah, shadowing them as they moved south through the night so they could be mopped up by the surface forces.

Upholder was given the westward position, the others being strung out at ten mile intervals on a line due east. At noon on the 28th Wanklyn contacted *Ursula* and checked his position with her at the same time on each of the two succeeding days. The first sight of their objective came at 8.15 a.m. on 1 May. A large merchant ship was moving west north west — too fast to be close to effective range. Wanklyn broke off. A little over six hours later he spotted a rich prize to the westward — five transports zig-zagging in company with four destroyers.

Wanklyn fired off a salvo at two of the largest ships, whose silhouettes were overlapping. The weather was rough, making depth keeping and periscope observations very tricky, but by now he had undoubtedly 'got his eye in'. As the men below held their breath the pin-drop silence was split by three heavy thumps. Two torpedoes had struck the 7386 ton German Fels liner *Leverkusen*, later seen sinking rapidly by the stern. A third had stopped the *Arcturus*, 2597 tons, dead in her tracks and she was already listing heavily by the bow.

Crawford noted that only a 'moderate counter-attack' followed as the remaining ships of the convoy streaked away.[9] By 7 p.m. Wanklyn was able to finish off the damaged ship with his last two torpedoes. His report gave the postscript to the drama in three terse lines:

'1940   Sighted stern of ship just showing above water; destroyer standing by.

1945   Ship plunged.

2100   Surfaced, and set course for Malta.'[10]

'Great fun entering harbour,' Christopher Read would recall. 'Wanklyn had all the upper deck personnel wearing German helmets — souvenirs from the *Arta* — with the German ensign beneath our Jolly Roger, and Captain Simpson was greeted with a guard of honour armed with the Panzer light automatics.'[11]

Simpson, whose dogged faith in his former First Lieutenant was now fully justified, was exultant. Three valuable ships totalling 19,000 tons had been sunk. 'I consider that this successful patrol is deserving of immediate recognition and recommendations for awards are being forwarded,' he wrote. Raw was pleased on this showing to make a reappraisal of Wanklyn, to whom he now accorded, 'the greatest credit'.[12]

Calcutta, 1911 — David Wanklyn with his brothers Jack (right) and Peter (left). *(Miss J. Wanklyn)*

William Lumb Wanklyn, aged 43, as a Major in the Royal Engineers After a year in the trenches in Northern France he was invalided home to lighter duties.
(Miss J. Wanklyn)

Popgun marksmen — David (right) with brothers Peter and Jack. *(Miss J. Wanklyn)*

Wanklyn's mother, the former Marjorie Josephine Rawson.
(Miss J. Wanklyn)

Lieutenant Alec Anderson, RN —
the cousin who fired Wanklyn's early
enthusiasm for the Royal Navy. He
died in the influenza epidemic of
1918. *(Miss J. Wanklyn)*

Countryman in the making —
Wanklyn 'Minimus' at Knockdolian,
Ayrshire, 1921. *(Miss J. Wanklyn)*

With his mother at Knockdolian,
Ayrshire, 1924. *(Miss J. Wanklyn)*

Wanklyn in his cadet uniform a few
days before entering Dartmouth in
1925. *(Miss J. Wanklyn)*

Wanklyn's camera records the battleship HMS *Marlborough* — his first sea-going ship — firing her port battery six inch guns.

Recovering torpedoes in *Shark* after practice firings *(Royal Navy Submarine Museum)*

Spanish Civil War, 1938 — Wanklyn on the bridge of *Shark* during the Nyon Patrols: "the first and last real attempt to take swift and aggressive action against illegal and bullying tactics of either Italy or Germany until World War II". *(Crown Copyright)*

The last of the *Shark* — in June 1940 she was brought to the surface near Stavanger, Norway after being disabled by enemy aircraft. Three of her crew were killed and 18 wounded — including her commander, Lt Cdr Peter Buckley. Survivors are seen here waiting to be picked up by a German trawler, having laid charges to scuttle her.
(Captured photograph released by the Admiralty in September 1945)

With *Shark* 'somewhere in the South of France' in 1937. Faultlessly turned out ashore, at sea Wanklyn wore 'the oldest jacket imaginable'.
(Mrs S. Danvers)

January 1938 — Lieutenant Wanklyn welcomes the Governor of Malta, General Sir William Dobbie, on board *Shark*. Dobbie would later condemn a plan for Wanklyn to land Commandoes to attack Field Marshal Kesselring at his headquarters in Sicily as 'butchery'. *(The Times of Malta)*

May 5, 1938 — David and Betty are married at Holy Trinity Church, Sliema, Malta.
(Mrs E. Wanklyn)

The minelayer *Porpoise* — Simpson in command with Wanklyn as First Lieutenant — shortly before her departure to Gibraltar for the combined Home Fleet and Mediterranean Fleet annual exercises of March, 1939. *(Royal Navy Submarine Museum)*

H31 — Wanklyn's first command — leaves Portsmouth Harbour. She was mined in the Bay of Biscay on Christmas Eve 1941. *(Royal Navy Submarine Museum)*

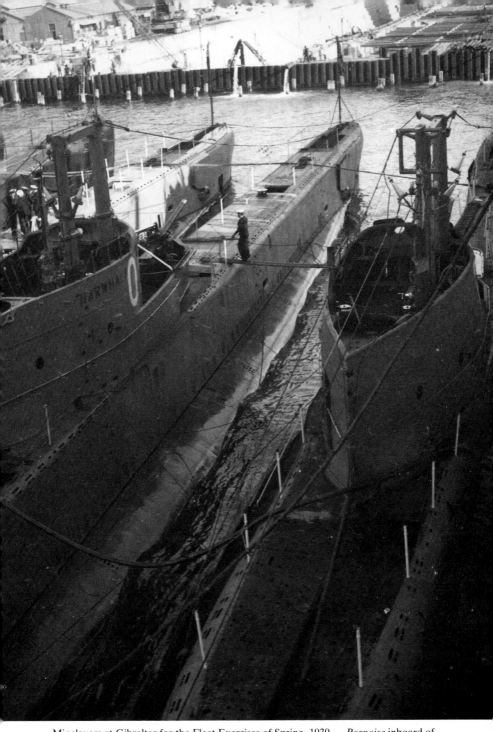

Minelayers at Gibraltar for the Fleet Exercises of Spring, 1939 — *Porpoise* inboard of *Narwhal* and *Cachalot*.

The first HMS *Upholder* is launched at Barrow-in-Furness on 8 July 1940. *(VSEL)*

Last days together — Wanklyn with his wife and son Ian in Cumbria in the autum of 1940. *(Mrs E. Wanklyn)*

Mrs Phoebe Thompson with her husband Hubert, Special Director of Vickers Armstrong Ltd, moments after launching HMS *Upholder* on 8 July 1940. She followed the submarine's fortunes closely and one of Wanklyn's last letters was addressed to her. Invited to the launch of the new *Upholder* in 1986, she died a few months earlier at the age of 89.

Target from the air — the submarine base on Manoel Island photographed from 10,000 feet. German and Italian bombers would eventually force the evacuation of the Tenth Flotilla from Malta. *(Royal Navy Submarine Museum)*

During her 16 months' service with the 10th Submarine Flotilla, HMS Upholder sank or damaged the following enemy ships:

Merchant) not marked		Sunk	28.1.41	**7** Conte Rosso (Troopship)	**Sunk**	24.5.41	**15** Submarine	**Sunk**	8.11.41
Merchant) on chart		Sunk	30.1.41	**8** Laura C (Merchant)	**Damaged**	3.7.41	**16** Destroyer	**Damaged**	9.11.41
1 Antoinetta Laura (Merchant)		Sunk	25.4.41	**9** Merchant	**Sunk**	24.7.41	**17** Destroyer	**Sunk**	9.11.41
2 Arta (Merchant)		Boarded and Fired	26.4.41	**10** Cruiser	**Probably sunk**	28.7.41	**18** Sirio (Merchant)	**Damaged**	4.1.42
3 Fels Liner		Sunk	1.5.41	**11** Merchant	**Sunk**	20.8.41	**19** Amiraglio St Bon (Submarine)	**Sunk**	5.1.42
4 Merchant		Sunk	1.5.41	**12** Tarvisio (Tanker)	**Damaged**	22.8.41	**20** Merchant	**Sunk**	27.2.42
5 Tanker		Damaged	20.5.41	**13** Oceania (Troopship)	**Sunk**	18.9.41	**21** Submarine	**Sunk**	18.3.42
6 Capitaine Damiani (Tanker)		Sunk	23.5.41	**14** Neptunia (Troopship)	**Sunk**	18.9.41	**22** Trawler	**Sunk by gun action**	19.3.42

UPHOLDER'S TALLY

Upholder's last reported position

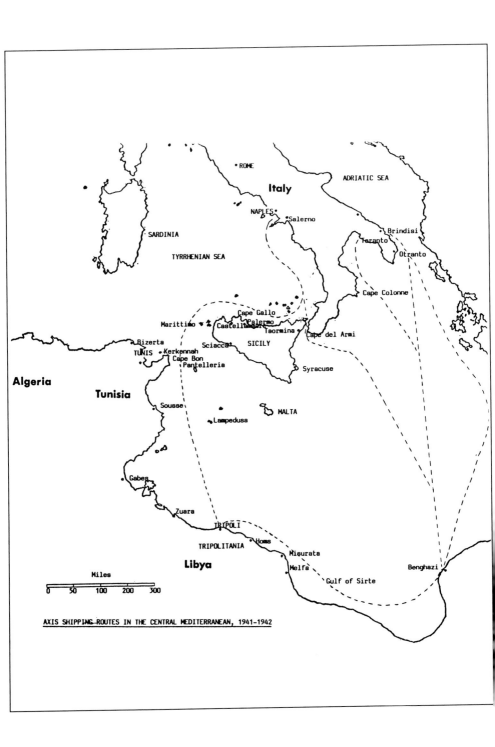

ROME

Italy

ADRIATIC SEA

NAPLES •Salerno

•Brindisi

Taranto

•Otranto

SARDINIA

TYRRHENIAN SEA

Cape Colonne

Cape Gallo

Marittimo •Palermo

Castellammare

•Taormina

Cape del Armi

•Bizerta

SICILY

TUNIS •Kerkennah

Sciacca

Cape Bon

•Pantelleria

Syracuse

Algeria

Tunisia

•Sousse

MALTA

•Lampedusa

•Gabes

•Zuara

TRIPOLI

•Homs

TRIPOLITANIA

•Misurata

Libya

•Melfa

Benghazi

Gulf of Sirte

Miles

0   50   100   200   300

AXIS SHIPPING ROUTES IN THE CENTRAL MEDITERRANEAN, 1941–1942

The cramped control room of *Upholder's* sister submarine *Utmost*. Lieut Cdr Dick Cayley at the periscope, Lieut Charles Oxborrow on the right. *(Royal Navy Submarine Museum)*

As enemy bombers approach, a harbour launch lays a smoke screen over the submarine base on Manoel Island. *P36* lies against the wall — where she sank in a raid on 1 April 1942. *(Imperial War Museum)*

Upholder outboard of *Urge* at Lazaretto — one of only two authenticated photographs of the Royal Navy's top scoring submarine of World War II. Note *Upholder's* characteristic high bow — later boats in the class such as *Urge* had a flush bow. *(Royal Navy Submarine Museum)*

Periscope view — a supply ship sunk by *Upholder* sometime in 1941. Photographs like these were rare, as submarine commanders were reluctant to expose the 'magic eye' longer than absolutely necessary to obtain data for an attack.

Wanklyn with members of the crew of *Upholder* at Lazaretto, sometime late in 1941. Left to right are: Lieutenant Francis Ruck-Keene, Acting Chief Engine Room Artificer Frederick Frame, Leading Seaman John Partleton, Acting Petty Officer Frederick Martin, Leading Seaman William Turner, Petty Officer Gordon Selby, Able Seaman Francis Lane, Wanklyn, Sub Lieutenant J. H. Norman, Able Seaman Thomas Brown, Telegraphist Patrick Newlands, Able Seaman James Smith, Stoker Ernest Self, Acting Leading Stoker Fred Topping, Engine Room Artificer Charles Burgoyne and Petty Officer John Swainston. Only Selby would survive from this group. *(Royal Navy Submarine Museum)*

Countryman at ease — Wanklyn tends the Malta submarine base pig sties. *(Miss J. Wanklyn)*

Upholder's officers congratulate their captain on the news of his VC. With Wanklyn (left to right) are Lieutenant Francis Ruck-Keene, Lieutenant James Drummond and Sub Lieutenant J. H. Norman, RNVR. The submarine in the background is P31 (*Uproar*). *(Royal Navy Submarine Museum)*

The Italian destroyer *Pegaso* at Piraeus on 24 August 1942 — three days after the loss of *Upholder* was officially announced. She was scuttled after the Armistice with Italy.
(Imperial War Museum)

Captain Robert 'Tug' Wilson DSO* of the Royal Artillery (centre), the dashing young 'special commando' who was the last man to see Wanklyn alive, seen here at Gibraltar on 18 April 1942 with Lt Cdr Teddy Woodward (left) of HMS *Unbeaten*. They were unaware that *Upholder* had been lost four days earlier. Shortly before Wilson transferred to *Unbeaten* for the first leg of his passage home.

"Full of fun, with a twinkle in his eye" — 'Shrimp' Simpson, Wanklyn's friend and mentor and later Captain of the Tenth Flotilla, clowning it up on the bridge of the submarine minelayer *Porpoise*.
(Royal Navy Submarine Museum)

A recent photograph of Capitano di Vascello the Barone Franceso Acton, commander of the Italian destroyer *Pegaso*.

Tubby Crawford, Wanklyn's longtime First Lieutenant (right) in the Lazaretto's sparsely furnished Operations Room at a later date when in command of *Unseen*, reading over the latest signals before going on patrol. With him is the CO of *United*, Lieutenant Thomas Barlow. *(Royal Navy Submarine Museum)*

Highest honours: Wanklyn's VC and three DSOs head his wartime medals, the top awards for gallantry awarded to a Royal Navy man in World War II. *(Royal Navy)*

'Pretty things and nice to hold' — Ian Wanklyn poses for the Press with his father's medals. *(Mrs E. Wanklyn)*

The new HMS *Upholder*, launched at Barrow-in-Furness on December 2 1986 by HRH The Duchess of Kent and commissioned on 9 June 1990. *(Royal Navy)*

Chapter 16
'The oldest jacket imaginable'

'I got in a week ago from a most successful patrol in which we sank three ships and burned another,' Wanklyn wrote home on 11 May. 'I have at last been recommended for a decoration — so here's hoping.'[1]

So many of his contemporaries have been at pains to stress Wanklyn's modesty and 'lack of side' that, taken together with the numerous attestations to a character that blended thoughtfulness for others with a reserve which discouraged intimacy, these qualities might seem to combine to produce an impression of almost monkish freedom from the common vices. One of the commonest of these is vanity and it comes as something of a relief to note that in the few private writings of his that survive Wanklyn was guilty of at least one of the faults that are part of the contradictory make-up of mankind.

It is a pardonable fault — Nelson and Mountbatten were sometimes guilty of the most overweening pride but it made no difference to the affection in which they were held by those who served under them. Wanklyn's public deprecation of his achievements was perhaps no more than his Service traditionally expected. He would eventually get a DSO for his work on this last patrol, the first of three he was to be awarded. The vexed question of honours and decorations in wartime has often been debated. Alistair Mars, who received a DSO and two DSCs for his work in command of *Unbroken* and *Thule*, wrote that it would be 'pretentious to maintain that captains, officers and men were not anxious to receive the decorations for which they had been recommended. Naturally they wanted them; for these were the outward signs of success in the arduous combat for which they had trained — and they wanted them before being killed! (Most of these honours could not be awarded posthumously.)'[2] He was irritated that while recommendations at home went through in a few weeks, in Malta the process could take many months. 'There were of course administrative reasons; but it was not nice to think that those in the forefront of the battle were at the rear of the honours queue.'[3]

Mars was a maverick whose forthright views often went against the grain — and were to lead him after the war to a much-publicised court martial. But he had a point which very few, perhaps, cared to discuss so openly. He declared his preference for seniority over ribbons on his chest, which, if it were honestly given, made a lot of sense, arguing that 'from the viewpoint of satisfactory performance of duty it mattered little whether a submarine commanding officer was a Lieutenant, a Lieutenant Commander, Commander or Post Captain.'[4] The amount of pay that went with the job, however, was quite another matter . . .

Pat Norman, on the other hand, speaks as one who fared moderately well under the system, who might have done better, could have done worse, and who, like most of his fellows, was glad to have survived the experience and expected nothing more. He looks back with a healthy cynicism that bears not a trace of rancour.

'The whole business of submarine decorations . . . well, I don't argue with Wanklyn's — they were well-deserved. But with the run-of-the-mill, rather like myself, you only had to chalk up a scoreboard and you got something. It really was a lottery.'[5]

Tubby Crawford points out that to sink an enemy submarine 'nearly always brought an automatic DSO, which in a way is odd. They were usually difficult targets but the one target where you got no sort of rebate or return. If you hit him he's gone and and that's it — they were not normally escorted, except when close inshore, so the attendant dangers of a counter-attack by depth charging seldom occurred.'[6]

Norman concludes: 'At the height of the Battle of the Atlantic to sink a U-boat was "wow" — but I think their Lordships saw reason after that. It was far more valuable to sink a troopship full of German soldiers.'[7]

For the present, Wanklyn had other preoccupations. Letters from home were long in arriving and caused a deal of anxiety for those left wondering how their families had fared under the bombing. In thanking his brother Peter for a letter he remarked: '. . . such a recent one, too. Only six weeks to come — that's pretty good these days.'[8] To his mother he wrote: 'You must be having a pretty thin time of it up in London, but perhaps you are hardened to it now and don't feel it too much. Here the raids are annoying at times, but are not really disturbing yet.'

He made a joke of the souvenirs he had acquired from the *Arta*, which included 'a very fine German tin hat, ensign and tommy gun. The first I wear during air raids. I'm sure they won't try to hit it.'[9]

The true situation was much worse, though Wanklyn was naturally pleased to make light of it to spare his family undue anxiety. Simpson wrote: '. . . daily life at Lazaretto throughout April 1941 and early May was one of apprehension. Our survival as a base was likely to come to an abrupt end at any moment.'[10] There had been 107 air raids in February and 105 in March. 'In April the bomb weight of raids increased dramatically whilst the method became more lethal. Attack both by day and night contained an increasing percentage of parachute mines.'[11]

When these exploded on land the effect was minimised by the solid masonry of most of the Maltese buildings, but their real purpose was to mine the entrances to Grand Harbour and Marsamxett, the gateway to the submarine base. *Upholder* and her sisters were able to creep in and out unscathed by hugging the Valletta side of the channel. There was no minesweeper at Malta capable of clearing these mines so it was down to the spare submarine officers to note the position of each one was it dropped and in this they were remarkably successful. So many had fallen across Grand Harbour, however, that the precaution was valueless.

A near-casualty of the bombing had been the submarine base pig sties. Simpson had establishing these out of canteen funds, partly to amuse his men who were sorely lacking in any form of diversion, and partly as a practical means of supplementing their diet. Some outbuildings on Manoel Island provided 'sumptuous quarters' for two magnificent Middle Whites — and Wanklyn, ever the countryman, took a particular interest in their welfare. He was relieved when a near miss failed to prevent the safe delivery of two fine litters.

Pat Norman marvelled at the way Malta stood up to the bombardment. 'One of the fantastic things about the place is the rock of which the island is made. Sandstone is easily worked from the point of view of burrowing, but it is very resilient and tough for shock. This was born out lots of times and we experienced it once or twice at Lazaretto when a bloody great bomb arrived on top of the tunnelling and all that happened was a hell of a lot of dust, but no structural collapse. All the quarters were done by ourselves — all the submarines in harbour did the tunnelling with a few Maltese Boy Scouts.'[12]

Tubby Crawford saw little of Wanklyn when they returned to base. He would spend the first 24 hours discussing his patrol report with Simpson, checking over preparations for the next run. 'You never knew when you were going to be called out. Sometimes you just got in, loaded up the torpedoes and were sent straight off again, responding to a late intelligence report sometimes at just a few hours' notice. So when there was a gap, the COs were usually sent off to stay with friends in the country, who looked after them very well. I sometimes saw Wanks in the Mess, but I didn't tend to get a 'run ashore' with him, because he was more or less ordered by Simpson to go away and relax.'[13]

The Governor of Malta was generous with his hospitality. Wanklyn's letters at this time give 'The Palace' as his address: 'I am staying here for a few days' rest which I feel I have earned and begin to need,' he explained. 'His Excellency has been remarkably kind and has asked any submariners to come and stay when they can.'[14]

He passed his leisure hours jogging along the island roads in a pony and trap owned by his boyhood friend and now fellow skipper Anthony Collett. The sight of 'Sonny Boy' drawing 'the two tall naval officers with their big beards presented a striking turn-out,' one observer recorded: 'Lieutenant Commander Wanklyn takes an interest in the pig farm and likes to go shooting; but his greatest hobby is undoubtedly fishing. Perhaps the hours he has spent with rod and line in peaceful days have helped to develop that essential patience so necessary to a captain who excels, for the keen angler must know how to wait and strike exactly like the submarine captain.'[15]

The writer allowed that Wanklyn was normally 'quiet and serious'. But at a party he could rise to the occasion with a verve that was all the more startling for being unexpected. Then he and Collett would sing 'a little French song' to the accompaniment of 'Harmonica Dick' Cayley's mouth organ, 'bowing politely to each other at intervals in the traditional manner'.[16]

Wanklyn ashore was always smartly turned out — debonair even; at sea he wore 'the oldest jacket imaginable', with the gold rings hanging off the cuffs. It must have been pretty disreputable to excite comment among his fellows, whose standards of dress in their working environment were — as they remain — notoriously lax. One of his crew, Leading Seaman Charles Tuckwood, insisted that 'you could only tell Wanklyn was an officer if he had his cap on'. He remembered him walking along the jetty in an old pair of grey trousers 'with the biggest bloody hole in the backside'.[17] His beard, left untrimmed, had begun to acquire the ragged, patriarchal character it would assume in the memories of most who remember him. He had developed the habit of stroking it reflectively whenever a problem presented itself — almost the only sign of emotion he was to betray in moments of tension — and since the shortage of water on patrol kept washing to an absolute minimum, it quickly grew greasy and unkempt.*

Wanklyn's ease off duty could never be guaranteed. During daytime raids the submarines were dived in harbour, a practice which allowed them 'considerable immunity from damage'. They were manned by half crews taking turn about, but if a very junior officer was on duty when a heavy raid developed — and one towards the end of April raged on for six hours — the CO might be recalled to take charge.

And sometimes the boats were not dived in time. Tuckwood remembers when two were sunk alongside in a single day.

'It was a terrible sight. I was one of those who had to go and get the

---

* Wanklyn's record in the matter of his toilet at sea hardly bears comparison with that of the appalling Commander Shove in World War I. Even ashore he was usually seen with matted hair and a highwater mark above the collar. He had a pet rat which he kept in the sleeve of his monkey jacket. 'Ratto', as is the way of rats, would relieve himself copiously in his warm den — and Shove would 'shake the droplets out of his sleeve with apparent unconcern'. He summed up his own lamentable lack of personal hygiene on one occasion, remarking: 'Sub, I must wash. I can smell myself . . .'[18]

bodies out. They were just blown to piece, more or less. We were all sick. It was one of the worst things I've had to do in my life. People we'd known, too. One of the boats was stern down with the bows sticking up so we had to clamber inside at an angle to get at them. They weren't the complete crew, just a few on board playing cards where they shouldn't have been. There was no point in acting big in an air raid. Those Stukas came down so low you could see the pilot with his flying helmet and glasses. I saw one that close once, standing at the entrance to a shelter. Just curious, I was — but the Chief would hook you back in. The boats were spread out so they wouldn't be too much of a target, but it didn't do no good that day . . .'[19]

Newly introduced to the submarine world around this time was a sixteen-year-old who had the opportunity of watching Wanklyn in his rare periods of relaxation. By now, unattached young women — other than the native Maltese — were a rarity on the island. Only a handful of Service mothers and daughters were allowed to stay on. Melloney Scobell, the daughter of Major General Sir John Scobell, had joined her parents on his appointment as GOC (Troops) in September 1939. Having spent most of her life in India between periods of being 'hardly educated at all' at a succession of private schools in England, she was by her own account 'very ordinary, home-loving, well-behaved, strictly brought up and consequently rather dull'. This description scarcely accords with the family album photographs that show a slim, coltish figure in flowered summer frock determinedly steering a heavy Army bicycle through bomb-cratered streets. She was a splash of colour amid the yellow dust and desolation and soon found herself much in demand for what passed for social life in 'the most bombed place on Earth'. To their credit her parents allowed her considerable latitude, realistically concluding that she should be allowed to enjoy herself in an environment where no-one's survival could be guaranteed for long.

Until the Italians entered the war the principal centre of leisure activity for island 'society' had been the Sports Club at Mhasa. This then closed and put an immediate stop to those pursuits — polo, golf, squash and pony trotting — with which the more athletic of the privileged classes of Malta were used to amuse themselves.

'So we were left with tennis on the few private courts — and most of them had bomb damage — and sailing. Even the best swimming places were covered in barbed wire, but they still kept the Service Club at Sliema going and every Saturday evening they had a dance. I was there one night when I got stranded — my party went off somewhere and I had no means of getting home. Charles Oxborrow' (later lost in *Utmost*) 'took me home and later introduced me to Lieutenant Francis Ruck-Keene of *Upholder* and so I met David Wanklyn.

'Wanks had tremendous charm and charisma — you were never

there without being aware he was around. I thought he was rather shy in an austere sort of way, though. My age group thought of him as quite old, though he was only 30. But sometimes we'd all go and have a drink in *Upholder* and if he was in the party spirit he would be the life and soul. I seem to remember him strumming on a guitar if he was in a really hilarious mood and Dick Cayley, the commander of *Utmost*, would play with him on his harmonica and then we'd laugh and call them the 'Cayley Band'. He would fool about then, but most of the time he didn't join in parties very much — he seemed too tired most of the time. We all treated him with tremendous respect. He was capable of letting himself go and having a bit of fun but mostly in spurts and mostly at the base.

'I can't remember seeing him at any of the Sliema Club Saturday evenings. He was reserved and quiet but not in the last cold or cut off. You felt easy in his company — though perhaps we behaved a bit better than we did when he was not around . . .'

Despite her youth and privileged position, Melloney earned her moments of leisure by working shifts in the vast underground operations room at Lascaris, where she helped co-ordinate the island's anti-aircraft defences. Off-duty, she might ride off on the back of a motorcycle to a dance or a party. 'On the way home afterwards we'd find several bomb craters that weren't there before and sometimes we'd end up in the bottom of one and think it quite funny. But this party-going got much less as time went on and the privations bit deeper.'

Hardest of all to bear were the deaths of so many friends. While Wanklyn was resting up at the Palace, *Undaunted* and *Usk* were lost within a few days of each other.

'It was awful because you knew nearly all the people who were based there. We did a lot of sailing together in little dinghies and you'd be sailing with somebody one day and then off they'd go on patrol the next and you'd never see them again. We felt we had a duty to be merry and bright — you were letting the side down if you weren't. They were all going off into danger and we thought the best we could do for them was to give parties with whatever you could find in the way of food and drink . . .'

Chapter 17
The sinking of the Conte Rosso

Wanklyn's hunting ground now shifted to the SE coast of Sicily. *Unique* had completed a patrol off the southern approaches to the Straits of Messina where she had sighted an important convoy of five cruisers and various small craft, so Simpson considered *Upholder's* presence there well worthwhile.

She sailed on 15 May, steering ENE for the probable convoy route from Benghazi and then NW towards Messina. Soon after departure one of the loaded torpedoes developed a leak and had to be swapped with a re-load. 'This involved a major upheaval in the crew space and a certain amount of juggling in this confined area,'[1] Crawford noted. More bad luck followed three days later — during the forenoon watch a westbound convoy was sighted close to the land, but could not be brought within range.

Much more seriously, *Upholder's* Asdic set had broken down, thus robbing Wanklyn 'not only of a means of detecting the enemy, but also of a valuable aid in taking avoiding action during a counter-attack.'[2] A faulty washer had let in seawater and destroyed the insulation around a vital lead.

In the afternoon a signal arrived, advising that a convoy was expected to sail from western Italian ports bound for Patras. *Upholder* spotted it — a single escorting vessel with two tankers and a tramp steamer — early in the evening of the following day. A long way off track, Wanklyn nevertheless closed at speed and fired three torpedoes at 7000 yards. The ships were practically invisible against the land and he could not observe the result but a detonation was heard after about the right interval. Hearts beat faster down below — partly because of the foulness of the air, for the boat had been due to surface an hour earlier. Then the thud of the torpedo strike drove the discomfort from their minds. Wanklyn had scored again — and at a range of four miles.

The submarine sped away, registering a 4000 ton tanker as damaged. Within another two or three minutes the explosions from the other two torpedoes were heard, but Wanklyn guessed they had run ashore. During the next quarter of an hour six depth charges were heard, but they were way off the mark, at least a mile away.

There followed a break of some 36 hours in which nothing much happened. A hospital ship was allowed to pass by and then, just before noon on the 23rd, two more tankers were seen. Through the periscope on high power Wanklyn identified what appeared to be

French colours and was immediately faced with a difficult decision: were they operating under Vichy command, working for the enemy?

The name of the leading ship was *Alberta*. 'There is no French ship *Alberta* given in *Booth's Shipping*,' Wanklyn argued, '. . . but there is an Italian *Alberta*. The name of the second ship appeared to be *Damieni*, but this is not given in any list. All this left about 30 seconds to decide whether to fire or not. The ships were laden, steering a suspicious course for Frenchmen: the names produced a strong Italian flavour, and no information on neutral shipping had been received . . .'[3]

Wanklyn made up his mind. He fired three torpedoes at the rear tanker — 'bigger than the *Alberta* by about 1000 tons' and later confirmed as the Vichy tanker *Capitaine Damiani*, working under Italian charter.

'12.31   One torpedo hit.
12.50   Observed target settling by the stern: *Alberta* taking avoiding action; and the escort returning at full speed, dropping depth charges. One aircraft was searching overhead. Dived to 150 feet and retired to SE. The hunt continued all afternoon, 26 depth charges being dropped, but none much nearer than one mile.'[4]

The following afternoon 21 more depth charges were heard in the general area — but 'nothing in sight or sound', Wanklyn calmly observed.[5] Even so the ordeal was nerve-wracking as, with the loss of her Asdic, the submarine could not easily follow the movement of her attackers.

Upholder's patrol was drawing to a close and she retired south of the Straits, half-blind and with only two torpedoes remaining. Wanklyn could hardly have guessed that within four hours he would have completed the action that was to earn him the Victoria Cross — the sinking of the *Conte Rosso*.

Crawford saw her first: 'It was just getting dark and I was on watch and suddenly I spotted something, just a dark shape at first — and it was this monster liner, packed with troops bound for North Africa with about five destroyers around her. It was going to be a pretty dicey attack, because there was a fairy good swell and it wasn't easy to see.'[6]

There were in fact four very large two-funnel liners in the convoy. Wanklyn himself noted that they were 'strongly silhouetted against the afterglow of sunset' — it was the height of the swell that made observation difficult.[7] With only his periscope to rely on, he had to attack at point-blank range. What followed may best be described in the words of the subsequent citation, which remarked on the failure of the Asdic gear and took note of the failing light, pointing out that a surface attack would have been easily spotted:

'In spite of these handicaps, Lieutenant Commander Wanklyn decided to press home his attack at short range. He quickly steered his craft into a favourable position and closed in so as to make sure of his target. By this time the whereabouts of the escorting destroyers could not be made out. Lt Cdr Wanklyn, while fully aware of the risk of being rammed by one of the escort, continued to press on towards the enemy troopship. As he was about to fire, one of the enemy destroyers suddenly appeared out of the darkness at high speed and he only just avoided being rammed. As soon as he was clear he brought his periscope sights on and fired torpedoes . . .'[8]

The destroyer *Frescia* was then only 400 yards ahead. The senior officer on board spotted the tracks and fired off a Very flare — but was too late to save the *Conte Rosso*. Wanklyn dived to 150 feet and a minute later two 'mild explosions' were heard through the boat. Quickly the great ship of 17,879 tons went down, carrying 2,729 soldiers and crew — and the flag of the convoy Commodore, Rear Admiral Francesco Canzoneri. Almost at once the depth charge attack started and this time Crawford admits they had 'a pretty rugged battering'.

'With no listening devices you just heard the swish of the destroyer going over the top. It wasn't the first time we'd been depth charged but it was quite the heaviest and closest to date.'[9]

Through it all, Wanklyn's demeanour made the deepest impression on the other occupants of the tiny control room — 'they stood in the presence of greatness,' Sydney Hart would declare. 'It is on record that they saw canniness gleaming in his eyes. What impressed them strongly was his ineffable calm: his cultured voice gave no hint of his innermost feelings or thoughts. He was cool, calm, deliberate, they say: the perfect Englishman enveloped in an Englishman's unemotional calm . . .'[10]

Crawford says he gave a running commentary on the alarming sounds that entered the submarine's hull from the turmoil outside. 'He stood in the corner, stroking his beard, giving quiet orders to the helmsman to go this way or that — and it was just the general atmosphere of reassurance he generated that impressed the chaps more than anything. They said "Well, if the Captain says that's the sound of the ship breaking up, then that's OK." You obviously couldn't pull the wool over their eyes — but when it all comes out all right, quietly and quickly — particularly if you've had a success — then everyone tends to think "Well — jolly good!" Of course, not many of us had heard these noises before and it was very difficult to surmise what they were. You get the most extraordinary sounds under water.'[11]

'Nobody could assist the Captain other than those responsible for controlling the course and depth of the submarine. There was complete silence apart from a few quiet orders from Wanklyn, directing alterations of course, speed and depth in an attempt to throw off the destroyers, whose propellors could be clearly heard in the submarine as they passed over. As this happened, most of the crew involuntarily bent their knees and crouched in anticipation of the next deluge of depth charges.

'At one stage a peculiar noise such as might be made by a wire scraping along the hull caused all eyes to be turned towards the Captain, who quickly dispelled all anxiety by confidently stating that it was the noise of the ship breaking up. It was at moments like these that Wanklyn showed his greatness for, whatever doubts he himself had, he always exuded confidence, and this, of course, had an effect on every member of the crew . . .'[12]

'It lasted a couple of hours, perhaps — not a continuous battering. A destroyer came in and dropped a load and then moved off and listened for a while, trying to work out where we were. That night, with no Asdics operating, we had to be even more patient before we came up to look around. Once the destroyers had stopped swishing about, we allowed a good period to go by before surfacing.

'We didn't appreciate what the target was at the time — except that it was something pretty big. The joy was for the Captain, really, although we were all in it together, he was the one who made the final shot. A nice grin came over his face when he heard the torpedoes strike. I don't think he enjoyed the fact of killing, but he had a sense of having done his job. He was not one to jump up and down with joy — once the heat was off he just ordered a pot of tea . . .'[13]

At least 37 depth charges had exploded around *Upholder* — the last four being particularly close, leaving the men with 'pounding hearts' and 'almost shaking their teeth loose in their sockets' as the boat leapt and shuddered to the unholy subterranean cannonade. Despite his skill, groping in the dark with only his own ears and wits to guide him, Wanklyn was 'dodging death by hair breadths'.[14] When he finally crept away, those of his Ship's Company in other parts of the boat who had not the benefit of his immediate presence to reassure them must have heaved a collective sigh of relief. George Curnall admitted that he could not stop his legs shaking 'but did not let anybody notice it'. When they finally surfaced a little before 11 p.m. he noticed 'a terrible smell of fuel oil as I went up as lookout'.[15]

The VC citation concluded that the failure of the submarine's Asdic made it much harder for Wanklyn to get away, 'but with the greatest courage, coolness and skill he brought *Upholder* clear of the enemy and safe back to harbour.'[16]

Nothing succeeds like success — and *Upholder's* own faith in her Captain was now quite unshakeable. A legend had been born.

But sailors, by tradition, will always have some cause for complaint. In connection with the *Conte Rosso* one in particular — though it had nothing to do with Wanklyn — is worth mentioning. In

World War I bounty money at the rate of £5 per head was paid for all the enemy put out of action and if a large troop ship was sunk the lowliest submariner would collect a small fortune. At least 1300 soldiers perished in the *Conte Rosso* — but in the present conflict it was decided that all prize money would be distributed throughout the entire Navy. *Upholder* could otherwise have expected a hefty share and the submariner's contempt for those with 'safe billets' ashore who would partake of it may be readily appreciated. In the final reckoning, the reflected glory of that VC, together with a wide distribution of lesser honours, would be the most of the reward that the few surviving 'Upholders' would enjoy. More achievements lay ahead — for which official recognition did not in any case match the approbation of their peers. Wanklyn's finest hour was yet to come.

But he had begun to worry over the state of his crew's health. In six months away from England only six changes in complement had been necessary, 'two caused by accidents, two from ailments possibly attributable, one casual illness and one nervous complaint,' he reported, adding that all hands were keen to get away for a complete break. 'It is thought that this rest is most necessary, before the really hot weather starts, in order to build up the general health of the crew and to heal a few raw nerves.'[17]

The strain had been steadily mounting, despite everything the magic of Wanklyn's personality could effect and the depth charging that followed the sinking of the *Conte Rosso* had proved too much for one man, who suddenly dashed for the lower conning tower hatch and started unclipping it. He had had to be dragged away and held down — they were 150 feet down at the time. Wanklyn tactfully omitted this incident from his report, but when he returned to Malta he told Simpson the man should be returned to General Service as being temperamentally unsuited for submarines. It was, no doubt, a kindness on his part but he could hardly afford to do otherwise. The young sailor approached Simpson and begged him to reconsider, but Shrimp was bound to uphold Wanklyn's decision. 'The poor fellow was really distressed,' he remembered, '. . . but I reassured (him) that it was nothing for him to be ashamed of.'[18]

The risks of life at sea were one thing — accidents in harbour were something else again. Submariners in war took their chances with open fatalism, marked with their own peculiar brand of graveyard humour; it was less easy to accept casualties in which enemy action had no part. Tragedy of this kind met with *Upholder* soon after her return and slid a dark cloud over the triumph of the *Conte Rosso*. Torpedoes were being loaded when Crawford, sitting in the Wardroom, suddenly heard 'an enormous swishing noise'.

'I thought "God — they've opened the bow cap without the rear door being shut".' He raced forward to find that one of the torpedoes had begun to run as it was being loaded into the tube, giving off a huge gust of poisonous carbon monoxide. Petty Officer James Farley Carter, 'a first class experienced rating' in charge of the torpedo compartment, was overcome as he vainly tried to shut it down. Chris Read — the same who led the boarding party onto the *Arta* — went down with a line around his waist. He too succumbed to the fumes.

'By the time they were both brought up to the casing, artificial respiration was of no avail to Carter and Read was taken off to hospital. He had to be invalided out of the Navy later, but eventually recovered and became a padre.

'I don't know that we ever really discovered how or why it happened. There is normally a guard on the air lever which sets the thing running and presumably, either as they were taking this off or taking the clamp off it before doing the final loading, they must have tripped it — or they may not have had the clamp on at all — I don't know. Wanklyn wasn't even on board, he was resting. It was my responsibility. Carter was a jolly good TI, too — a great loss.'[19]

Preparations for the next patrol continued in an atmosphere of gloom. In the interval of about ten days that was customarily allowed, part of the crew were sent off to a rest camp in a remote part of the island. Meanwhile, re-storing the remedy of defects kept those left behind unrelentingly busy. *Upholder* was too valuable an asset to lie fallow.

Because of the friendship that existed between them the story has grown up that Wanklyn enjoyed special favour under Simpson's direction of submarines at Malta — that he would be the one chosen when a promising area of operations was identified. It has to be said that from all the evidence there is some truth in the accusation — though it in no way detracts from the record of Wanklyn's successes, which by now had risen to the point where he was regarded as one of the command's leading lights. That the Malta flotilla was 'a band of brothers', in the words of Nelson's ideal, likewise hardly presupposes that there was not a competitive edge to the camaraderie expressed in the Mess. Pat Norman says Simpson 'absolutely worshipped the man. That, I think, is possibly why there may have been undercurrents, in that the CO of the Flotilla gave preferential treatment to Wanklyn — because he thought he was so bloody wonderful. And he was, of course — his record of sinking ships was fantastic. But let's be fair, Shrimp was so good to us all.'[20]

It would be only natural if the growing admiration for Wanklyn were tinged with jealousy — though Mackenzie, for one, entirely refutes the allegation. 'I never met any resentment of Wanks' decorations, for instance. I have heard criticisms of others who had been highly decorated and which with hindsight people thought they didn't quite deserve — but never against him.'[21]

This unequivocal view has the value of being given not from the standpoint of any particular intimacy, Mackenzie was closer to

Tompkinson, whose own record would come close to matching Wanklyn's.

But while Wanklyn was rested during the first half of June, Simpson was reluctant to expose *Upholder* to undue risk in his absence. Accordingly he sent her out to cover the approach route to Tripoli from Messina under the temporary command of a new arrival as spare CO, 27-year-old Arthur Hezlet, who was at that time only half-way up the Lieutenant's list. 'Baldy' Hezlet, who had previously skippered the training submarine *H44* in home waters but had yet to take a boat out on war patrol in command, regarded this mission as 'a great compliment'.

'Wanklyn was already established as an "ace" and the leading submarine captain in Malta. Younger submarine officers like myself followed his actions completely. He did not press his ideas on other people but he would give them if asked. Anyway, he believed I was competent enough to take his boat out on patrol.'[22]

But Hezlet, despite being a 'fairly eager beaver', was not yet proven and he later discovered that Simpson had sent him out 'to some place right out in the middle of the ocean where I couldn't get *Upholder* into trouble, to make certain that she came back for Wanklyn to continue with!'[23] The only vessel of note he ran across during his entire 11-day outing was a hospital ship. Simpson rather shamefacedly admitted that 'perhaps it was over-optimistic to hope that much would be sighted by a single submarine operating a considerable distance from the port of departure or arrival'[24] but Hezlet took it in good part.

'The patrol area — halfway between Sicily and Benghazi — was chosen because the Flag Officer Malta thought it was a good place and he had been badgering Simpson to send a boat there for some time. Shrimp saw a chance to kill two birds with one stone and sent me to occupy it. We saw nothing.'[25]

The young Lieutenant concluded his report on a decidedly run-of-the-mill run with a sardonic comment on victualling: "Bread was bad after nine days at sea'.[26] He knew he had been used as a stop-gap and bore no ill-will. 'Remember, I was a totally unknown quantity and I don't blame Simpson or Wanklyn at all — anyway, Shrimp made up for it in my next patrol, which was in *Unique* off Tripoli, and that was a very different kettle of fish . . .'[27] On 20 August Hezlet carried out 'a brilliant attack' on a convoy of four liners with heavy sea and air escort, sinking the liner *Esperia* and putting 'so many troops into the sea that he was able to retire without any serious depth charging.'[28]

Chapter 18
'One cigarette all round — and one only'

Upholder sailed at short notice with *Unbeaten* on 24 June, following word that four more liners — taken to be loaded with troops — were on their way from Naples to Tripoli. Wanklyn hoped to make an attack before nightfall the next day, but despite picking up the sounds of an approaching convoy, heralded by occasional depth charge bursts, he saw nothing.

'There was no wind or ripple . . . and though day visibility was fair, the visibility at night was poor and tricky due to lack of horizon,' he wrote impatiently, adding 'it is remarkable that no aircraft at all were seen, although a periscope-depth patrol was maintained despite the calm sea.'[1]

Simpson later concluded that *Upholder* was about eight miles to the westward of the convoy's line of advance. The boat was recalled and arrived at Malta at dawn on the 27th, making this her shortest patrol and one of the rare occasions when she returned with nothing added to her 'Jolly Roger'.

The practice whereby submariners traditionally recorded their successes on a black flag on return from patrol took its cue from the Admiralty's early branding of the Submarine Service as 'a fraternity of pirates'. Max Horton flew such a flag as a joke when he commanded *E9* of World War I — and thereby incurred their Lordships' displeasure. But early in World War II a Jolly Roger was presented to *Osiris* when she sank an Italian destroyer in the Mediterranean. The idea quickly caught on and soon more submarines were marking the tally of their kills in this way. Now they are among the rarest of 1939-45 relics. The Royal Navy Submarine Museum has 15 of them, and there may be many more, hidden away in attics and 'ditty boxes' in the homes of Old Comrades who squirreled them away as souvenirs at the close of hostilities. They tell the stories of many famous exploits in patterns of red and white symbols sewn into the fabric around the familiar skull-and-crossbones motif. A red bar was used to denote a warship sunk on patrol, with white bars to indicate merchantmen. Cloak-and-dagger operations were shown as white daggers, gun actions as stars. The occasions when submarines acted as beacons for invasion forces were marked with designs depicting light houses or torches.

Some of the flags bear unusual symbols — there is the can-opener proudly included in *Proteus's* battle honours, recording the time when an Italian destroyer attempted to ram her and was herself torn open by one of the submarine's hydroplanes. They are generally very crudely made — though one, of rather superior quality, was sewn by nuns from a Malta convent — but this only serves to enhance their dramatic impact. *Upholder's* own flag is a replica of the original, which was lost when the boat was sunk. Once the badge of piracy, the black flag still reflects something of the submarine's lone-wolf, privateering role — to George Curnall it 'often seemed as if we had our own little private war going on.'[2]

A three-day patrol was easily endured but 'sleeping in between torpedo racks for weeks at a time without seeing daylight was quite a different matter', he says. Crawford remembers that *Upholder* was 'not as wet' as the German U-boats — he got 'absolutely soaked' on the bridge of a captured U-boat (renamed HMS *Graph*) in a flat calm passage from the Clyde to Londonderry. 'But they were still pretty uncomfortable. We had to have a canvas bird bath in the control room to stop the water getting into everything when we were surface running. If you sailed in lousy weather you got soaked as soon as you got outside the breakwater and you remained soaked for the rest of the patrol. There were absolutely no drying facilities so you were in damp clothes all the time and normally that was for about 12 days. We all had colds, but there were no great problems with health. Something like an appendicitis was an obvious bugbear — if you were right out on the enemy coast, what could you do? You couldn't operate on the chap — you just had to try and suppress it somehow.'[3]

Food was 'the one thing to enjoy' and the wartime submariner's relish for such rough-and-ready recipes as cheese 'oosh' would bring a blush of shame to the cheeks of their nuclear counterparts today, whose diet has moved the likes of Egon Ronay to praise. Maconachie's brand of tinned herrings in tomato sauce was a favourite: 'There was nothing fresh, everything came in cans,' Pat Norman remembers. 'It wasn't bad. Us and the fighter boys in Malta were the elite and we got the best of what there was, no doubt about it — while the poor wretched Maltese starved at one stage.' Even so, Wanklyn, who 'liked his food', had to put up with a dull and limited diet. It was as well he was fond of fish; it was often 'herrings one day, sardines the next and pilchards the day after that'.[4]

Commander Anthony Kimmins, the multi-talented film actor-writer-producer-director pressed into service as a war correspondent, has left what is practically the only first-hand account of life on board *Upholder*. It thus deserves to be quoted at length — though as a piece of reportage it is frankly propagandist. He observes that the experience of 'being cooped up in a steel shell with a cross section about the size of a London tube (train)' produced a number of odd side-effects:

'The amount of sleep you put in is quite amazing; it is largely because of the lack of oxygen when submerged. You don't notice it much at the time, but if you strike a match towards the end of the day, you will find that it just flickers and goes out. There is, of course, no exercise to be had in the terribly cramped quarters, and during the twenty-four hours you will probably move only a few paces — and yet you are always hungry and, oddly enough, by the end of a patrol you have probably lost weight.

'The routine seldom varies: sleep — eat — a spell on duty — sleep and eat. The only difference between day and night are that during the daytime, while you are running submerged and clear of the effect of the waves, it is all very still and quiet. At night, when you surface under cover of darkness to charge the batteries, you are rolling and pitching to the sea; there's the noise and the vibration of the diesels; and the conning tower hatch being open, you can smoke.'*[5]

Smoking while the submarine was submerged consumed too much oxygen to be generally allowed, but Wanklyn was apt to relax this rule in moments of stress. Charles Tuckwood says he was 'the only officer in the flotilla who would allow "one cigarette all round — and one only".' He would come down hard on anyone who tried to sneak an extra puff. 'He caught someone lighting one up from another once — and he didn't half lash him up, Wanklyn did. He got a month's pay stopped — but he asked for it. None of the other captains would let you have a fag down below. We used to do our smoking at night when the air came down the conning tower to clear it. And we really needed a fag then.'[6]

The periods spent on the surface provided the only opportunity to rid the submarine of her accumulated rubbish — 'gash', to use the Naval parlance. Strict precautions were taken to avoid leaving telltale traces of their passage for the enemy to find.

'You'd bring it all into the control room and ask the officer of the watch for permission to ditch gash. And then you'd haul it all up in tin pails we made ourselves and throw it over the side. The tins were stabbed full of holes so they'd sink and all the labels had to be taken off first. We took them back with us in a bag.'[7] (Today's submarines, which when on operations do not surface at all, overcome problems of waste disposal by shooting it out of the hull through a small tube inevitably christened the 'gash gun'. Empty tins are compressed and loaded into linen bags. Thus weighted down, they are carried safely to the bottom).

---

* Kimmins broadcast a description of a patrol in *Upholder* on the BBC Home Service on 20 February 1942 (see pages 137-138). This was written up for *The Listener* and the substance of his talk was widely used in magazines and newspapers at home and abroad.

Chapter 19
'I could literally hear
my knees knocking'

News of Simpson's promotion to Captain was brought to him in the Mess at supper time on 30 June. His reaction was curiously mixed. 'I was grateful, but I felt it was detrimental, or could be, to the very important position I held in the Wardroom of being an accepted member of the Mess in my own right, and not the "Captain" who should only enter the wardroom when invited, but had to be tolerated because of the conditions of service.'[1]

He was better pleased by 'a much more important local event' — the despatch of the first set of pigs to the Naval Victualling Yard refrigerators, this batch being followed by about a dozen each month against the day 'when we should really need them'.[2] Looking back on the formation of the Tenth Flotilla under his command, which would not follow until September, he thought the 'attendant rigmarole' was unnecessary.[3] No White Ensign ever flew from Lazaretto, with Stukas flying low over the base after dropping their bombs on the dockyard, the last thing he wanted was to advertise the place as a naval establishment. He would sensibly continue to eschew pomp and circumstance in favour of more pragmatic considerations — for this no doubt, his fellow comrades who survived the war may have cause to be grateful.

It was his practice to allocate patrol positions under a formula which allowed him fairly accurate knowledge of where a submarine would be at any particular time — something like: 'You are to establish patrol in the southern approaches to Messina in a vicinity of Latitude X and Longitude Y. If it is necessary to leave this position you should withdraw southward on Course Z a distance of up to 40 miles.'[4] The Captain would also know that he expected him to measure the risks he took against the probability of success.

Wanklyn had departed under orders such as these two days before. His first attack, against a single funnel liner early on 1 July, expended three torpedoes without result. He had fired from very close range, but the fish ran under due to 'the constant and drastic zig-zagging of the target'.[5] This was a procedure only recently adopted by Italian ships which presented a submarine with 'a most difficult attacking problem' that would shortly receive close attention from the Attack Teacher.

Upholder spent the next two days avoiding the attentions of a pair of destroyers who were obviously intent on clearing the way for an oncoming convoy. Early on the 3rd Wanklyn's patience seemed to have been rewarded with the sighting of a 4000 ton tanker hugging the coast. He ordered 'full ahead both' but broke off as the ship altered course around Cape Del Armi.

Three hours went by as *Upholder* moved slowly along the southern toe of Italy and then they picked out a few wisps of smoke close to Cape Spartivento. Three medium-sized merchantmen came into view, together with an armed merchant cruiser and a destroyer. Wanklyn dived and began his attack, switching off all unnecessary lights to save his batteries. At 11.25 a.m. the destroyer dropped a depth charge and Wanklyn was suddenly sure he had been spotted. The armed merchantman and the destroyer were both zig-zagging wildly 3000 yards outside the convoy line. A moment later he saw the destroyer turn straight towards him, racing ahead at 27 knots. He dived to 45 feet and altered course, returning to periscope depth once he heard the enemy warship pass clear to westward.

'11.42   In position 37 54′N 15 44′E fired three torpedoes at centre ship in convoy, a heavily laden, grey painted cargo vessel of about 5500 tons, carrying a deck cargo of wooden packing cases.

11.43-20 secs   Two heavy explosions at 20 seconds interval. Retired to Eastward at 150 feet. From distress signals intercepted it appears that the target was *Laura C* of 6000 tons . . .'[6]

The depth charges came crashing down immediately — 19 of them this time, shattering light bulbs as they burst with 'the sort of din that gets you more in the pit of the stomach than in the ears,'[7] as Kimmins would describe it. Wanklyn only noted that 'some were moderately close.'[8] (Thirty feet was in fact the lethal limit the submarine could endure.)

Once again they were spared and early in the afternoon they were able to watch the *Laura C* as she floundered, abandoned and alone with her upper deck awash. It did not seem possible that she could remain afloat for long.

The counter-attack continued later in the day. They saw an Albatross class submarine chaser approaching to the west, but she was well wide of her quarry as she dropped 27 depth charges in two 'brisk attacks' upon the horizon.

Nothing further of note occurred over the next four days and *Upholder* arrived at Malta at dawn on the 8th. 'This successful patrol was carried out with the usual determination and accuracy of torpedo fire that I have come to expect from Lieutenant Commander

Wanklyn,'[9] Simpson noted happily and six weeks later Cunningham himself was moved to add an approving footnote to the official report: 'HMS *Upholder*, under the skilful command of Lt Cdr M. D. Wanklyn, Royal Navy, continues to exact a steady toll of the enemy's shipping.'[10]

The boat now put in ten days of harbour routine — but Wanklyn was not disposed to rest on his laurels. Towards the end of this period he practised dummy attacks with *Utmost* and *Urge*, with Dick Cayley and Tommo Tompkinson — two friends and friendly rivals who were glad to benefit from each other's growing store of knowledge and skill. Each morning they would meet in the Staff Office to learn the latest news from the Staff Operations and Intelligence Officers and read a fresh batch of patrol reports. The interchange of information was invaluable.

'You spent a lot of time there picking each other's brains,' Mackenzie recalls. 'There was no formal 'wash-up'', but you certainly learned a lot that way. This practice was very exclusive to COs and spare COs waiting to jump into someone else's boat. Wanks would come in and you'd have half an hour discussing with him what he did in such-and-such circumstances or how he would deal with a certain problem. His comments were particularly prized, I remember. He was quietly spoken, but very clear in what he said. There would be no hesitation — without being overbearing or too adamant he would give you a straight answer.'[11]

10 p.m. Saturday, 19 July — and as the regular Sliema Club hop got under way *Upholder* slunk out of harbour as if she were a despicable pariah', clearing the boom in lonely isolation under cover of darkness.[12] She was off to play her part in Operation Substance, a plan to send a large convoy to replenish the beleaguered island and take away half-a-dozen empty merchant ships left languishing there for fear of air attack. Admiral Sommerville's powerful Force H based on Gibraltar would provide escort while the Fleet from Alexandria created a diversion to fool the enemy into thinking the convoy was intended to carry on through to the eastern end of the Mediterranean.

Upholder was stationed to guard the south of the island of Marittimo. The 22nd and 23rd proved blank days and Wanklyn decided to shift towards Cape St Vito at the western tip of Sicily, where he could still cover the route from Palermo.

This move soon paid off. Early on the Wednesday afternoon they found an eastbound convoy — a single Generale class destroyer escorting a laden 6000 ton supply ship. Wanklyn had earlier been forced to dive as the surface was flat calm and he found himself further off track than he had expected. He closed at full speed and fired three torpedoes at 5000 yards. Nearly four minutes ticked by until the now familiar 'ping' of impact was heard — followed immediately by the crash of an explosion. One of the fish had struck.

The sound of the destroyer's approach stilled the little cries of celebration. Retribution was close at hand as the deadly cannisters rolled off her deck — 17 of them spread over two hours. Wanklyn took the submarine down to 150 feet and retired to the north west while the destroyer attempted to carry out a hydrophone hunt — 'clearly stopping and starting, but never getting really close,' Wanklyn noted.[13] At 3.30 p.m. he returned to periscope depth and saw the target stopped and settling by the stern with the destroyer patrolling the seaward side, having broken off the counter-attack to give aid to the crew of the stricken ship. She sank an hour later.

Wanklyn now had 67,000 tons of enemy shipping to his credit, sunk or damaged — most of them supply ships, the prosaic but necessarily priority targets in the task to which the Malta submarines were assigned. Now, however, Mussolini's Navy was about to lose 'one of the jewels in its crown'[14] — the cruiser *Garibaldi*.

Early on the morning of Monday the 28th *Upholder* dived in thick fog to patrol the convoy route to the north of Marittimo. When the skies cleared in the evening she came across a pair of cruisers, each supported by Avieni class destroyers, the former maintaining a steady course while the latter zig-zagged on either bow. Asdic gave a speed of 230 revs — equal to 28 knots — so Wanklyn had to think quickly if the chance was not to pass him by. At 4000 yards he fired a full salvo of four 35 knot Mk IV torpedoes at 12 second intervals (he had been forced to place his last Mk VIII in reserve in order to keep a uniform salvo in readiness) and four minutes later heard two heavy explosions — with exactly 12 seconds in between.

The 8000 ton *Garibaldi* stopped dead in her tracks and, as one of the destroyers threw a protective smoke screen around the wreck, the other rushed straight towards *Upholder*, raining down depth charges from either side. It was a close call this time — some of them fell close by in the first 15 minutes of a barrage that lasted nearly three-quarters of an hour. Thirty-eight were counted off, but there may have been more. As the sea tore apart in the thunderous concussion and pull exerted by the resulting vacuum, the sounds merged into a continuous roar.

George Curnall thought his last moment had come. 'Once, when we were expecting to hear the next depth charge explode, we heard a destroyer pass right overhead and boy, we had our hearts in our mouths. I could literally hear my knees knocking . . .'[15]

Nothing could be seen through the smoke but the *Garibaldi* was undoubtedly written off for the time being. Simpson applauded Wanklyn's fast thinking and decision: 'I cannot recollect a previous instance of a 28 knot target being hit by torpedoes,' he marvelled as he forwarded another set of names for awards — his third recommendation for *Upholder* in three months.[15]

Wanklyn returned to Malta on the last day of the month to find that Operation Substance, despite some losses, had been a great success. Six large merchantmen laden with essential supplies had gained the sanctuary of Grand Harbour a week before. On the 25th, however, the submarine base itself had been threatened by an Italian human torpedo — one of the famous two-man chariots known by their originators as 'Maiale' ('pigs'). These slow-speed craft driven by frogmen were part of the specialised Decima Flottiglia Mas (Tenth Light Flotilla) whose exploits alone give the lie to the popular myth that suggests a certain lack of resolution on the part of Italy's fighting men. In this instance, one had made for Manoel Island as part of a concerted attack on the convoy carried out by eight explosive motor boats — water-borne kamikazes piloted by a single man in an ejector seat that would afford him a slim chance of survival by throwing him clear before the moment of impact. It was a supremely courageous but utterly suicidal enterprise — Malta's harbour defences were by now of a strength and pitch of alertness unknown elsewhere in the Mediterranean and they blew every one of them out of the water in the space of two minutes, killing most of their crewmen. The pair that rode the chariot were lucky to escape with their lives — it broke down and they were forced to abandon it and were captured as they tried to swim ashore in St George's Bay, two miles away from their target.

Young George Curnall had found the attack on the *Garibaldi* and its aftermath distinctly trying on the nerves. During the return from Malta Wanklyn had to weave his way through a minefield.

'You could hear the wires pinging on the side of the sub. Once again he got us through but all in all it was a rather harrowing experience.'[17] He needed his spell at rest camp, but there not for the first time in his life, his quick temper got the better of him — with immediately disastrous results that in the end would be his salvation. 'I and a few friends were jogging along the road to the camp for a swim. Only having bathing trunks on, we didn't have our minds on anything other than a few days' freedom and relaxation. There were a few military types drinking in the garden of a club and we heard a voice bellow out: "Don't you salute an officer?" On looking round I saw they were Army officers. One in particular I replied to, saying "I haven't got a cap on" and he got really nasty, saying "Bloody eyes right, then!"

'I realised — as well all did — that he was half-drunk, so I jumped the wall and whacked him one — and was immediately surrounded by MPs . . .'

Curnall was carted off to the cells as cockily unrepentant then as he remains to this day. 'I thought he deserved it, no-one respects a drunken officer. That's where the difference lies. If that'd been Wanklyn, and he was nobody's fool, you would have had eyes right out of respect and he would probably have said "On the double, lads" or something with a bit of humour. Anyway, I ended up with a court martial . . . Wanklyn came to visit me in the cells. We had a chat and he told me he had tried to get me off, but the Army wouldn't have it. I think it was a Colonel I hit . . .'[18]

Service discipline brooked no extenuating circumstances and he was rewarded with a 30-day stretch in the notorious military prison at Corradena, where he found himself the sole naval inmate among a mix of Army miscreants, civilians and Italian prisoners of war. He noted with pardonable irony that the latter were exempt from hard labour under the terms of the Geneva Convention.

'Your job all day was to break up rocks for shelters for the Eyetie POWs — while they sat around sunbathing. If you stopped for a minute the MP would fire a rifle above your head, hitting the rock behind. I saw old Maltese drop with exhaustion and I thought to myself "We're sinking the Italian ships month after month and here am I breaking up bloody rocks to protect *them* from the air raids.'[19]

Even the most innocent rebellion against this harsh regime was visited with savage reprisal and George was perhaps too innocent for his own good: 'I managed to have a bit of a break when they put me in the staff cookhouse. After being used to eating green bread and cheese, I had a bit of a gorge with steak and tomatoes — but when night came I was sick in my cell, not being used to such luxuries.'[20]

The prison authorities were not disposed to take a charitable view — indeed they came down hard: 'Wanklyn wouldn't have believed it if I had told him — all over a piece of meat and a few toms.'

George was defiant to the last: 'I put a bow tie on when I came out of prison but there was a Marine at the gate and he said "Get that bloody thing off or else you'll be back inside".'[21]

On his release on 1 September he was drafted to spare crew and joined *Ursula* in the middle of October.

Chapter 20
'All the dogs in Sicily were barking'

Heartened by his success in the Marittimo area, Wanklyn was anxious to try his luck there again. But when *Upholder* sailed on 15 August he had a more specific target in mind. It had been noticed how vulnerable the coast-hugging rail systems of Italy and Sicily were to sea-borne attack and the Malta submarines were now beginning to land train wrecking parties. Altogether in 1941-42 twelve operations were mounted — one submarine actually surfaced to shoot up a train loaded with troops as it passed along the Calabrian coast.

Now it was Wanklyn's turn to embark one of those collapsible rubber 'Folboat' canoes that Michael St John had cursed back at Loch Long, together with a pair of 'cloak and dagger' men — Lieutenant Walker of the Hertfordshire Regiment and Corporal Bryant Bird of the Beds and Herts. In addition to the hazards of their own mission ashore, they would experience all the horrors of submarine warfare in the space of a single 12-day patrol.

And so, jammed to capacity in the heat of high summer, *Upholder* made her way to Sicily. Three days later she reached her patrol area to the north of the islands of Marittimo and Levago. Wanklyn had word of two slow-moving convoys expected in the area but missed them both and decided to move off to Cape St Vito where just after breakfast on the 20th he found a small cargo vessel and a trawler. He fired two torpedoes at the former, later identified as the *Enotria*, and one hit home a minute later. As the little ship staggered under the blow and dropped quickly out of sight, the trawler hastily unloaded four depth charges and beat her way back west to Trapani. It could not have been much of a homecoming — later in the evening Wanklyn saw an air raid in progress there.

Moving back to Marittimo and back again to Cape St Vito to watch for another expected convoy, *Upholder* once more failed to make contact. Wanklyn decided that the slow convoys were keeping close to the Sicilian coast while the fast ones moved several miles to the west of Marittimo. Simpson judged it likely that 'the enemy had lately learnt wisdom' and was frequently changing convoy routes near focal points.[1] Who could blame them? Operating without benefit of 'anything approaching the British Asdic . . . or RDF (Radar), blind on the surface at night and relying solely on their hydrophones' the Italians were struggling with the courage born of desperation to supply their armies in North Africa, in the face of attacks by aircraft and submarines out of Malta which their own air force had claimed to have rendered 'completely inoperative'.[2]

Evidence of the Italians' mounting concern was presented to Wanklyn on the afternoon of Friday the 22nd with the sighting of a flying boat patrolling to the eastward. Five minutes later three tankers appeared, approaching the submarine on a westerly course with a destroyer each in escort. *Upholder* was right ahead of the leading ship — dazzle painted in mauve and khaki with 'four enormous drums secured to the boat deck'. Wanklyn fired a full salvo at her. 'At this moment,' he noted, 'the flying boat was crossing to the disengaged bow of the convoy after passing close overhead and the starboard wing destroyer had dropped back to hustle the rear ships.

'16.32   Two torpedoes hit. Retired at speed to north west.

16.35   Counter-attack by two destroyers started. Forty-three depth charges were dropped in eight minutes after which there was a pause for reloading. It appeared that the destroyers were using throwers and dropping patterns of four and five charges. It was impossible to avoid the attack for, with one destroyer approaching on either quarter there was nowhere to go. Fortunately, due to the speed at the start of the run, the last patterns fell about 200 yards astern. The destroyers turned and dropped their reloads on the return journey. Total number 61. Damage insignificant.'[3]

It had been, even so, a dramatic illustration of Italian determination and growing expertise. As usual, Wanklyn's comments on the effects of counter-attack were a masterpiece of understatement. The thoughts of his fellow travellers, as they bent their heads under a shower of shattered light bulbs and cork chippings from the submarine's pulverised insulation, their vision blurred as their world shook and trembled, must have been less than sanguine. Corporal Bird still remembers the total tally of depth charges spread over the entire patrol: 'There were 108 in all, only seven poor ones in the first attack. My action station was in the fore-ends amongst the torpedoes. I asked Wanklyn for a more interesting position and he granted me the place right next to the control room where I could hear all that was going on. He was a man who inspired everybody — "on the ball" the whole time . . .'[4]

Bryant Bird too, had come under the spell. The crew might be forgiven for believing they had charmed lives by this time but Simpson did not put their survival down to pure chance: 'Although, admittedly, good fortune attended the moments of firing, it is noted that at the moment the torpedoes left *Upholder*, the flying boat was retiring on the disengaged side, and the destroyer on the engaged bow had returned to the rear of the convoy. This accurate appreciation of the enemy's movements shows the care with which Lt Cdr Wanklyn studies each problem of attack.'[5]

Daytime visibility was 'phenomenal' on the 23rd and 24th but there was a tendency to coastal mist at night and around dawn, through which Wanklyn was worried a convoy might pass undetected. But when he did make another sighting, forty miles to the NW of Sicily at 10.20 a.m. on the second day, he cursed his misfortune. It was a 'miniature armada' — a Cavour class battleship with two cruisers in line ahead in close order escorted by six destroyers. And he only had two torpedoes left.

At a range of over three miles with the ships making 25 knots there was little chance of much of a bag — and the come-back would be ferocious . . .

Wanklyn raced into the attack and less than a quarter of an hour later fired the last two shots in his locker at the rear ship. The minutes ticked by and he heard 'one explosion very like a torpedo' followed immediately by the expected deluge from the destroyers.[6]

Fortunately none of the 32 charges counted came very close and Wanklyn moved off quickly to the NNE, hoping to shadow a damaged ship turning for Palermo. An hour went by and he raised his periscope — nothing in sight. He could only put a six inch gun cruiser down as a 'possible'.

It was time to set about the 'other business'. Early on the afternoon of the 25th he came to periscope depth off Cape San Marco to survey the coast for a suitable position from which to make the attack on the railway. He chose the first bay to the east of Palermo, about three miles east of Sciacca. At 9 p.m. the submarine surfaced seven miles offshore to charge her batteries and just before midnight the Folboat was brought onto the casing. Walker and Bird moved up from the fore-ends clutching their Tommy-guns — demolition charges hung about their waists, black grease masking the white of their faces and thick rubber soles muffling the tread of their feet.

'On the bridge, just before we took off, Wanklyn said he thought we were about 800 yards from the shore.' Bird thought his usually spot-on judgment of distance had failed him this time. 'I can remember saying "What!?" Our trip to shore was very quick — I would estimate you could more than halve that. Anyway, the beach was made for Folboats, there were no rocks. We quickly carried our boat etc. into some scrub land, hid it between some bushes and moved off inland.

'After going no more than about 300 yards, small arms fire started. Lieutenant Walker fell into a hole which we thought must have been a slit trench. By this time people were shouting and I think all the dogs in Sicily were barking . . .'[7]

On the bridge of *Upholder* consternation reigned. A few feet away two rifle bullets smacked into the water. To Wanklyn 'it seemed certain that the party had been killed or captured.'[8] He would now have been entirely justified in making his escape — E-boats posed an immediate threat from nearby Sciacca. But to Bird's everlasting gratitude he waited. In the pitch darkness, with no means of knowing what was going on ashore, he waited for over two hours.

Meanwhile Bird was satisfied it was the submarine and not themselves that was being fired on ('It don't take long to get that message') though the knowledge that his ticket home might at any moment be removed did nothing for his peace of mind.

'I'm sure what happened was that *Upholder*, as soon as she dropped us, quietly withdrew from being so close to shore. Meantime she had been spotted, and by the time they fired at her she was a bit out of range. Had we been seen ourselves, we would have been sitting ducks.'[9]

The shots came from a house about 300 yards to their right but whether the submarine had been picked up by official coast watchers or merely by a family guarding their vineyards was never discovered. Walker and Bird decided to press on. Half-a-mile from the beach they hit upon a well-made road where they had expected to find the railway. Thinking it could not be far off, they made a stiff climb inland, doggedly struggling up 500 feet to the crest of a hill which they discovered sloped steeply away on the far side to a wide, level valley. Below, they could see the glint of water — perhaps a small lake — and a train running to the east with all the carriage windows lit. It was fully a mile away, too far for them to do the job and meet their schedule. Silently they swore at the charts they had studied so carefully — they had been hopelessly inaccurate.

There was nothing for it but to bury their demolition charges and head back for the beach — but would *Upholder* still be waiting for them and would their means of escape have been cut off anyway by this time? During the march uphill they had heard more dogs barking and several more shots fired at intervals, followed, just after 1 a.m., by a fusillade of ten or fifteen sharp reports.

Bird was relieved to find that their luck had not totally deserted them. 'To our very good fortune they hadn't even found the Folboat. When we tracked *Upholder* down she was somewhere about a mile out at sea.'[10]

It was past 2 a.m. when Wanklyn saw the blue-shaded light of their torch winking the recognition signal. 'The relief from anxiety was very welcome,'[11] he wrote. Needless to say, it was doubly so for Walker and Bird. 'Had she gone without us — well, we understood how dangerous it was for a submarine to wait about close to land. Those E-boats were very fast . . .'[12]

He soon discovered, as he had guessed earlier, that Wanklyn had indeed gone inshore closer than safely allowed in order to make their landing easier. 'After getting on board again, one or two of the crew told me they had touched bottom when we started to go ashore.'[13]

The mission had been a failure but several other ventures of this sort had been crowned with spectacular success. A month earlier Tompkinson's *Urge* had landed a team which blew up a long tunnel five miles south of Taormino. Simpson estimated that this and other submarine-launched attacks led to constant patrols by 'day and night by men either singly or in pairs at intervals of about two miles . . . over a distance of possibly 800 miles'[14] along the railroads of Sicily and the mainland. 'Thus for a negligible effort we estimated that up to 2,500 Italian men were fully employed doing nothing.'[15] It was reckoned that many troops and well over 1000 tons of war material travelled southwards every day and 'to put this out of action for only 24 hours constituted a success nearly as good as the sinking of a ship.'[16]

Simpson was understandably peeved when the Commander-in-Chief signalled him a mild reprimand on an occasion when a convoy was missed because one of his submarines was away train wrecking, reminding him that 'Convoys are your primary target'.[17]

Only two days after returning from patrol *Upholder* was ordered back to sea with *Ursula* to intercept a fast convoy southbound from Tripoli. The minefields in this area had recently been extended and had lately carried off *P32* and *P33*, two new additions to the Malta flotilla. Following the sinking of *Union* in late July by the Italian torpedo boat *Circe*, this added up to three submarines lost in four weeks, 'a bitter set-back' for Simpson, in spite of the mounting blitz his boats were carrying on against the Italian troop-carriers. In addition to Hezlet's attack on the *Esperia*, Tompkinson had also put the 23,000 ton *Duilio* out of action.

Just a few hours before Wanklyn sailed, 'Tommo' had already made a successful attack on *Upholder's* quarry, possibly sinking 'a very large two-funnel liner' five miles to the south of Capri.[18] Since it was apparent that the convoy would pass via Messina, *Upholder* was sent to intercept just after midnight on the 30th. After establishing communcation with *Urusla* she was set to guard the eastern approaches to Tripoli some eight miles to the ENE. The day passed uneventfully and then, early on the Sunday morning, after diving three miles north of their patrol position, they heard the sound of light surface forces patrolling in *Ursula's* area. As visibility increased, Wanklyn saw a torpedo boat and two E-boats. With an important convoy on the way their presence was hardly surprising but *Upholder* had dived just in time to avoid detection. Wanklyn altered course and ordered 'silent routine'. He changed course again an hour later, having sighted two bombers and smoke from two ships on the horizon, and moved northward to close.

The sea was glassy calm as the convoy came into view. Three big liners — *Neptunia*, *Oceania* and *Marco Polo* — were sailing in two columns escorted by at least four destroyers. Wanklyn knew the range on firing would be 'very great unless the enemy zig-zagged drastically towards us at the vital moment' — and so it proved. At between 6-7000 yards he loosed off a full salvo, spread over three ships' lengths, at *Neptunia* and *Oceania* which were then half a length apart. All missed. As one of the destroyers was heard to increase speed, Wanklyn concluded that the tracks had been spotted — an assumption borne out by the flurry of depth charges that followed in the next quarter of an hour. He moved to the north and headed for home and so, on 1 September *Upholder's* 13th patrol came to an end. Not so unlucky, after all — they were safe to fight another day. But the crew were glad to put 'Number 13' behind them, submariners, as much as any seafaring fraternity, are superstitious to a degree. The crews of *Oceania* and *Neptunia* were not to know that their own luck would not hold out for long.

Chapter 21
'The most skilful attack ever made'

The day after *Upholder's* crew returned to a welcome fortnight's break, the *London Gazette* announced awards to eleven of their number. Crawford received the Distinguished Service Cross; Engine Room Artificer Fred Frame, Leading Seaman Gordon Selby, Leading Telegraphist Gilbert Cummins and Leading Stoker Cliff Chapman were each decorated with the Distinguished Service Medal; and Lieutenant Christopher Read and Petty Officer Jim Carter were Mentioned in Despatches — the latter, of course, posthumously. Wanklyn got his first DSO and so, as the morning editions took up the tale and printed his photograph, the public at home had their first sight of him. The strong, full-bearded face smiling up from the breakfast table had just the right blend of integrity and resolution they wanted to see in a British submariner. This was no cold-eyed killer — to many he was the image of the sailor on the packet of Players' cigarettes. (Nazi propagandists, in contrast, preferred that their U-boat men should look vaguely homicidal. The official portrait of Dönitz is lit in such a way that the eyes blaze with a savage glitter and the effect is positively maniacal. To Airey Neave, who served the indictment of the War Crimes Tribunal on him at Nuremberg, the actuality was less impressive. The eyes were 'a disappointing shade of grey' and he seemed 'reticent and shy'.[1] At Spandau Dönitz would be a model prisoner.)

It was the sinking of the *Conte Rosso* that would eventually earn Wanklyn the highest award for gallantry. But this had not been announced and meanwhile the month of September was to produce *Upholder's* most spectacular success as Wanklyn conducted 'what was arguably the most skilful attack ever made by a submarine commanding officer'.[2]

Upholder, *Upright*, *Ursula* and *Unbeaten* left Malta on the 16th to have another crack at the fast troop-carrying convoy which *Upholder* had failed to embarrass two weeks earlier. The liners had reached Tripoli unscathed and to Simpson it was 'reasonable to suppose that the enemy would try this route again at any rate once more, since it had proved successful on the first occasion'.[3] His surmise proved correct when he got 'hot news' that three liners had teamed up in Taranto. He summoned all the COs then in harbour, Wanklyn, Wraith, Woodward, Hezlet and Tompkinson, to a conference in his cabin.

Simpson judged that *Ursula* and *Urge*, operating five miles north of Ras Hilal, might attack about half an hour after sunrise, so that the light would be sufficient to make their runs submerged. The other three submarines were to be placed well to the eastward, spread ten miles apart with *Unbeaten* five miles to the south, *Upright* five miles to the north and *Upholder* on the expected course of the enemy, so that they could carry out a night attack. Thus Wanklyn, as the senior officer, could keep in touch with his consorts and keep them more or less in position.

Tompkinson alone demurred, placing scant reliance on 'sudden schemes devised on a signal just received'.[4] He asked to be counted out and Shrimp at once agreed. It is an illuminating instance of the rapport that existed between these men that Simpson could readily accept what others might view as rank insubordination and find no fault. 'I knew very well that Tompkinson . . . would be the first to volunteer if he was feeling rested and relaxed; obviously he was tired and on edge and had the guts to say so. It was just this relationship between myself as a member of the Wardroom and a brother officer which was so invaluable to me in assessing the possible.'[5] He knew that his COs 'needed to be studied and their idiosyncrasies respected'.[6] 'Unlike Wanklyn,' he noted, 'Tompkinson did not accept all my ideas as either good or reasonable ones.'[7] He took this in good part — and indeed valued his 'mature criticism' — but he was not to be moved from a plan which he believed to be 'safe and effective'. And so it proceeded, with *Ursula* taking 'long stop' alone.

Upholder's crew did not greet the sudden end to their holiday with much enthusiasm. Charles Tuckwood was having a quiet drink in a bar on Sliema Front when the summons came.

'A naval patrol came by and this Petty Officer fished out a bit of paper and read "The following boats' crews report back immediately to base" — and he gave out our name. Everybody moaned. But when we got back to the boat they were just shoving in a few vittles, so we could tell we weren't going far, though they didn't tell us exactly where until we got out of harbour, of course. Wanklyn said: "Well, we're on a very tricky job this time — it's a big troop movement out of Naples for Libya and you know how our Army are having a rough time of it now. We've got to stop them at all costs." So everybody looked at one another and said "Oh God . . .".'[8]

From the outset, Wanklyn found himself under an appalling handicap. His gyro compass broke down and could not be repaired, so he was dependant on his magnetic compass which could not guarantee the same certainty of manoeuvre.

Tubby Crawford was on watch at 3 a.m., drenched with spray on a 'pretty bumpy night' with the submarine trimmed down so that only her conning tower showed above the surface, when 'we got a message from Woodward in *Unbeaten* saying "They're coming, boys!" '[9]

Upholder, moving at 10½ knots which was the best speed she could manage, was lurching and swinging wildly in the long swell as the convoy appeared, silhouetted against the light of the rising moon. The helmsman struggled to keep on course, with only the erratic magnetic compass to rely on. It was still too dark for a submerged attack — such a fast moving convoy, seen to be heavily escorted, could only be attacked from long range, outside the destroyers' protective screen.

Crawford looked round to find Wanklyn had joined him on the bridge. 'Then we sighted these monsters coming along. The night sight we had was pretty rudimentary — just a thing with a line of sight you had to move along depending on how fast you thought they were going. You just had to look along that and say "fire" and with the submarine bows moving from side to side on the waves it was a pretty dicey business. I don't know if the liners were on each other's quarter, but Wanklyn got a period when two of them overlapped and with the yawing of the submarine he fired one at them to the bow and the next one to the stern and then he came back to the middle. Anyway, he got four fish off and hit two of them.'[10]

Wanklyn's astonishingly skilful timing had accurately covered the target. Once again, as he learned later, *Oceania* and *Neptunia* had crossed his path and this time he had made no mistake. Two explosions were heard, the first wrecking *Oceania's* propellors right aft and bringing the 19,405 ton liner to a stop. The next tore a mortal wound squarely in *Neptunia's* side. At once the third ship, identified as the *Vulcania*, sped away at stop speed while the destroyers crowded round to pick up survivors from the packed troop carriers.

It was this that saved *Upholder*, though Crawford naturally expected the usual response. 'After a night attack like that one slips down quickly. I told the look-out to get below and started going down myself. Wanklyn looked round and said "Where are you all going?" I said I thought we were about to dive and he hesitated for a bit and then said "Yes — we will dive". But he was quite keen to stay up and see the result of the thing, I thought . . .'[11]

Crawford's prudent advice prevailing, they retired to the south and reloaded, surfacing after half an hour had passed to view the results of their handiwork.

> '04.45   Sighted one large vessel stopped in the position of the attack and escorted by only one destroyer. A second ship was making to the westward at about five knots with another destroyer in attendance. The third ship was well out of sight . . .'[12]

What happened next, as *Upholder* closed in to finish off the stricken *Oceania*, was perhaps the most remarkable episode of the entire attack. Tubby Crawford: 'Just as we got to a suitable range we were put deep by a destroyer — and by that time we were too close to come up again and fire from the same side. So Wanklyn said the only thing to do was to go right under her and come up the other side and then turn around and fire. Unbeknownst to us, at the same time Woodward in *Unbeaten* had been closing from the eastward and saw this lone wrecked liner sitting there. He must have thought he was on to a good thing and he was just lining up to fire on that side when he saw the target disintegrate and go down — we just beat him to it.

'In a way one might say it was a bit naughty of him to come into our patrol area — there was always the chance of a collision. But that's one of the risks one takes. I gather he was just in the position to say "fire" when Wanks' torpedoes exploded. It must have given him quite a jolt!'[13]

Wanklyn noted that the ship sank in eight minutes — 'with many popping noises reminiscent of the end of the *Conte Rosso*.' He attributed these 'to watertight compartments crushing as the ship sinks into deep water'.[14]

Other destroyers coming up at full speed were just in time to pick up survivors but the loss of life was great. The diary of an Italian prisoner of war, who had been travelling in the *Vulcania* and was later captured in Cyrenaica, recounted the death throes of the *Oceania* through the testimony of a friend who was one of the few who managed to escape:

'. . . the ship listed badly, and in three minutes had vanished leaving nothing but wreckage and foam behind, a frightful sight which left all who beheld it stunned. Alfizzi, who was still on board when the explosions took place, told us that the scenes in those three minutes were past description. He just managed to save himself by jumping overboard. Most of the drowned were Germans (who were in all the ships in the convoy) because they insisted on taking their kit and rifles with them on to the destroyer, and were taken by surprise by the last two torpedoes.'[15]

Including his earlier attack on the *Conte Rosso* Wanklyn had now accounted for 60,000 tons of liner shipping conveying troops to the battlefront — and Hitler complained bitterly to Mussolini about the poor protection given to the Afrika Korps reinforcements on passage. *Upholder* had helped to drive the wedge between the two dictators deeper still. Raw's report to the Commander-in-Chief Mediterranean on the combined operation applauded the teamwork of all the participating submarines which 'left nothing to be desired'. But he reserved his most glowing praise — in which Cunningham concurred with equal warmth — for Wanklyn, 'whose devastating accuracy at 5000 yards range in poor light and with his ship yawing badly was almost unbelievable and shows the highest skill, not altogether unexpected in this most able officer.'[16]

Yet on his return to harbour Wanklyn's fellow COs found him 'morose and disgusted'. On being asked why he should behave like this after so successful an attack . . . he replied that it was only luck, as he had fired by eye. This purist was never satisfied unless he had done the perfect attack where luck played no part![17]

This observation is given by Commander F. W. Lipscomb in his standard work *The British Submarine*. He does not give the source on which it is based, but it suggests a picture of excessive modesty that, while it cannot in any way be evidenced as false, still jars the eye. Too much self-deprecation excites the same suspicion as against one who 'doth protest too much'. Simpson allowed that Wanklyn was 'not a better attacker than many others in normal circumstances' but that 'wherever he was sent the enemy appeared, and noteworthy targets, too'.[18] And if, as has been noted, he deliberately favoured Wanklyn in this respect, allowing him to 'turn fleeting opportunities into complete success',[19] he also averred that his protege's self-effacing style made him 'loved and respected by all'.[10] It would be understandable if this much-quoted diffidence produced deeper 'undercurrents' than those hinted at by Pat Norman, though Simpson was sure that no-one grudged him his now firmly-established ascendancy — which was in sharp contrast with the 'rivalries which existed in flotillas during the First World War'.[21]

In any case, for the next six weeks or so Wanklyn's uncanny knack of being in the right place at the right time temporarily deserted him. *Upholder's* meteoric career now entered a period in the doldrums. Her next patrol, north of Marittimo and stretching to Cape St Vito between 23 September and 2 October, was unique only in that not a single target was sighted. They fared no better two weeks later when searching the Kerkenah Bank in company with *Urge*. Air reconnaissance had reported a merchantman and a tanker northbound from Tripoli but they did not cross their path and the two ships may have returned there.

Wanklyn had to face up to another disappointment on his return from this depressingly empty trip when he learned that Crawford was shortly to be taken from him. He was being sent home to do his own Perisher and would soon reappear on the Mediterranean scene to win his spurs in command of *Unseen*. 'I am very sorry to lose him,' Wanklyn wrote his wife on 6 November — nursing a 'fat head' after giving him a farewell dinner the night before. 'He has done marvellous work and is a great friend.'[22]

Tubby was to carry the letter back with him and Wanklyn expressed a wish that he was returning in its place. 'All my thoughts are going anyway and it's only a matter of time till I follow them in person. How I long to see you and Ian again; your letters give me a wonderful picture of him, growing up so fast . . .'[23]

While the call of home was strong, his sense of frustration at his recent inactivity welled over: 'I haven't had a shot for some time now but we shall shortly be in a good position again.'[24] This can hardly had reassured her. *Upholder's* next patrol would be her seventeenth — the point at which it was generally reckoned that most submarine crews were played out. Alistair Mars noted that 'very few lasted longer than 12 months'[25] and this would be accepted — unofficially at least — as the limit for an operational tour in the Med. Of necessity at this time, however, some were extended and *Upholder* was not to be spared. As the months wore on, the continued strain and privations took their toll on the men's health, though morale remained high. Mackenzie was shocked at the extent of his own deterioration when he finally got leave at the end of 1942. 'It wasn't a healthy existence — one did tend to get rather pale. You never saw true daylight other than through a periscope. I remember being taken shooting three days after I got back to Scotland. Lord Lovat, the great Commando leader, was a family friend and he invited me over for some rough shooting over some of the most rugged and steepest country I've ever walked across — and my God it brought it home to me just how unfit I was. It must have run us down. The supply people went out of their way to give us better rations than the rest of the Navy got, but there was a hell of a lot of tinned stuff.

'I can remember going on patrol with canned asparagus — you know, real gourmet foods. But every Mess in the boat except the Wardroom put it straight in the gash bucket. They just didn't fancy it.'[26]

Chapter 22
'A sight granted to few submariners'

Upholder sailed on the evening of 7 November with the inexperienced Lieutenant Brian Band as temporary First Lieutenant. They were on the look-out for supply ships southbound for Benghazi — but early the following morning the Coxswain, Chief Petty Officer John Swainston, spotted a U-boat at 4000 yards. It was, Simpson noted approvingly, 'a particularly fine sighting, since the moon was low and at any moment *Upholder* would have run across the moon's rays beam on to the enemy'[1] — thus making her the target instead.

The officer of the watch was another (unrelated) Norman, 21-year-old temporary Lieutenant J. H. Norman, RNVR, likewise an officer of very slender experience who was making his first trip as Wanklyn's 'fourth hand'. He acted 'immediately and correctly', turning towards the enemy, stopping engines and going slow ahead on the electric motors before Wanklyn joined him on the bridge.[2]

Upholder dived at once, out of the unwelcome spotlight of the bright moon, and Wanklyn altered his firing course as the enemy moved to starboard. Visibility was 'excellent' and he closed on a target which appeared to be 'a Perla, Sirena or Argonauta class submarine, having a long flat casing, square-looking bridge without periscope standards and a gun on deck'.[3] He fired four torpedoes at 1500 yards — a submarine was too valuable a prize to risk anything less than a full salvo. Within a few seconds there came the sound of a single, massive detonation. The engine noise stopped. Four minutes went by and Wanklyn raised the periscope. The submarine was still in sight but stopped. Hastily, he altered course towards her and reloaded another torpedo, but just before 4.30 a.m. the U-boat disappeared. He heard a light explosion, followed by a chilling, rumbling sound. Muffled noises passed down *Upholder's* starboard side, disappearing just abaft the beam.

'At this moment the periscope passed through an oil patch and, by the plot, *Upholder* was within 200 yards of where the torpedo hit,' Wanklyn wrote in the log.[4] They had heard the death rattle of one of their own kind from close quarters and it left an uncomfortable echo. In less than a quarter of an hour the reload was ready, only there was no need for it now. At 4.37 a.m. *Upholder* came to the surface and ran back through the area — 'but no survivors were seen or heard.'[5]

Towards evening, when they were back in their patrol position, a signal came through advising that Force K — the cruisers *Penelope* and *Aurora* with the destroyers *Lively* and *Lance* — would be passing through that night, on its way to attack a large enemy convoy ferrying men and supplies to North Africa. Simpson neglected to inform Wanklyn that the British ships had been ordered not to attack any submarine, which he later admitted might have saved him 'some subsequent anxiety'. Wanklyn for his part, was only too glad to have removed the threat of the U-boat, which had almost certainly been posted to intercept them. But when they came in sight just before midnight he sensibly dived to 80 feet. As the ships passed over he noted with relief that 'no Asdic impulses were heard, so the vivid visions of a pattern of 14 depth charges were quite unjustified.'[6]

While fearful of the awful possibility of being the victim of a tragic 'own goal', Wanklyn was anxious to hold on in the track of Force K and assist in any subsequent melee — which was just practicable if the enemy convoy made no more than eight knots. He surfaced twenty minutes later and, as the sounds of a distant cannonade came across the water he was privileged to 'a sight granted to few submarine commanders'.[7] Having set course towards the flash of the guns, during the next hour he saw six ships set ablaze away to the south east. Just before 2 a.m. one blew up and two enemy destroyers were seen fleeing to the northward. Force K had struck a swift and devastating blow — yet another convoy would not reach Rommel.

Wanklyn moved closer to the scene to clear up any stragglers. Three darkened ships were seen moving close to the floating bonfires and he dived to attack a destroyer, but in the lurid flicker of the flames it was difficult to make any positive identification and, as he did not know whether *Lively* or *Lance* were still in the area, he decided to stand away to the northward and wait for dawn.

First light revealed the trio to be two Avieri and one Turbine Class destroyers and he moved confidently to attack the nearest of these — the *Libeccio*, lying stopped to the south west of Taranto. The others were heading the wrong way to pose any immediate threat and Wanklyn fired a single torpedo into the sitting duck. After a short and ineffective counter-attack — five charges were dropped but only the first fell close — *Libeccio's* companions hastened back to her aid, one circling the damaged ship while the other went alongside. Wanklyn watched 'a large number of men' being taken off, waited for three-quarters of an hour, and then returned to finish her off. *Libeccio* was sitting low in the water. He had three torpedoes left and he considered expending one on the already stricken ship and earmarking the remainder for the other two. But when three aircraft arrived at the scene he prudently decided to withdraw deep and watch developments — in any case, he had still not fired a single shot in his allocated patrol area.

At 8.50 a.m. 'a terrific explosion' reverberated through the boat.

'It was probably caused by one of the merchant ships blowing up, and not by a depth bomb, as the submarine was not lifted at all,' Wanklyn concluded calmly.[8] Two hours later he raised the periscope and found two cruisers and two destroyers five miles away to the north east. He closed on the damaged destroyer, now under tow but soon afterward saw the cruisers rushing down and concentrated on these instead. As they zigged away, he turned in to fire.

'11.08   Fired three remaining torpedoes at rear cruiser from a range of 2500 yards. Salvo was spread over 1½ lengths to allow for errors in speed and the probability of a zig. One destroyer was stationed on the starboard helm (the far side) of the target, the other was well ahead to port. One torpedo suffered a gyro failure, and was heard to pass overhead.

11.11¼   Two torpedoes exploded about 25 seconds apart.'[9]

It had been, Simpson judged on studying the reports, another 'brilliant attack'.[10]

'The fact is that Upholder positioned itself so as to fire from 2500 yards on a 120° track at a high speed, screened, zig-zagging target and unquestionably got all his data accurate,' he wrote.[11] The first torpedo had passed ahead and hit an Avieri class destroyer forming the port wing screen. While the second, the gyro failure, tore around 'in delirious circles'[12], dangerously close to Upholder herself, the third shot down the same track 25 seconds later and hit the remains of the destroyer which had been stopped by the first. The twice-smitten ship sank at 11.19 a.m. 'Had not the second torpedo been a gyro failure,' Simpson reasoned, 'there is little doubt that two hits on a Trento class cruiser would have been secured, since the first torpedo to hit would have immediately reduced the cruisers' speed and thus allowed the second one to hit aft.'[13]

Upholder's crew had at the time been more preoccupied with the gyro failure's threat to their own survival. It might be assumed, wrote Sydney Hart, that as the Asdic rating picked up 'the whistling scream of it as it raced around, with very little imagination the crew convinced themselves that they, too, could hear it. Finally it swung around and disappeared . . .'[14]

Later it was found that the last four torpedoes fired had not had their gyro relay valves cleaned since 21 September — an oversight which 'probably accounted for the gyro failure which robbed Upholder of greater success'.[15] It might equally have sent her to the bottom in place of its intended target . . . Even so, it had been a supremely victorious weekend at sea — just 87 hours in which Wanklyn had accounted for 'one U-boat and one destroyer sunk beyond dispute and another destroyer damaged so badly that her survival was problematical'.[16]

Chapter 23
'VC — but mother in tears'

Sydney Hart relates that *Upholder* left Malta on Tuesday, 25 November to begin her eighteenth patrol with her crew animated by 'a complete and almost mystical confidence'[1] in her commander. But for Pat Norman, filling in as First Lieutenant on this occasion, it would be 'a shattering experience'.[2]

They drove through a stiff gale on the way to their billet south east of the Straits of Messina and dived in position at dawn on the Thursday. Breakfast was being cleared away as they came across their first target — a big, brand-new tanker moving westwards with a pair of destroyers. At 7.30 a.m. Wanklyn approached from the south west, hoping for an alteration of course to the northward to bring his target in closer, and ten minutes later the enemy duly played into his hands. But for once Wanklyn's keen eye failed him. He fired a full salvo from 2800 yards, allowing a speed of ten knots, which was the approximate speed given him by the plot but he had badly underestimated. The destroyers were zig-zagging broadly, their screws churning at 200 revolutions, and Simpson thought more reliance should have been put on this data than on the range plot — but if the enemy had been doing 14 knots, say, she could not have been hit. (The tanker was later sunk by Force K south of Kerkenah.)

In the small hours of Saturday Simpson ordered a new disposition of three submarines across the Gulf of Taranto. The Italian battle fleet was about to leave to attack a westbound convoy heading from Egypt to Malta. *Upholder* was given the westernmost position and arrived on station at dawn the next day. Twenty-four hours of patient waiting passed without incident. Then, around 4.30 on the Monday morning, as *Upholder* chugged slowly along the surface, the look-outs discerned eight dark shadows heaving through the Stygian gloom — three cruisers and five destroyers. As Wanklyn closed, the enemy zigged straight toward him, with the nearest destroyer bow on at about 3000 yards.

Watching from the bridge, Pat Norman was gripped with sudden, cold terror. 'I was just petrified — there were enemy ships all around. But David had no nerves at all. He was absolutely cool and calm. He started to attack on the surface, he was going to do the whole bloody thing on the surface, I thought, weaving in and out of the destroyer escort. Everybody was on tenterhooks . . . "What the bloody hell is going on?" we were asking ourselves — "Look, there's a destroyer over there and another over there!" and so on. But he continued apparently unmoved. It was a dastardly situation . . .'[3]

At the last moment, as it seemed to Norman, Wanklyn gave the order to dive — though in the pitch darkness of the early winter morning nothing could be seen through the periscope and the attack now had to be carried out by pure science — relying on the chancy information provided by the Asdic bearings. Norman announced 'Seventy feet'. The minutes ticked by — four, five, six minutes.

'Fire one! Fire two! Fire three! Fire four!'

The salvo streaked away, aimed for the last cruiser in the line but almost immediately the hydrophone sounds of the target disappeared and then reappeared on a reciprocal bearing. The propellor noises could be clearly heard in the torpedo compartment and it was obvious that the ship had passed nearly overhead. The torpedoes, having no chance to gain correct depth, must have passed clean under her.

With all his teeth drawn, Wanklyn could only remain on station for reconnaissance, but he was unable to establish wireless communication with Malta — probably due to the screening effect of the high land near Cape Colonne — and after three fruitless attempts decided to head for home. There were mitigating circumstances for this failed patrol ('one of the few occasions David missed,' as Pat Norman observed.)[4] Simpson felt that 'in view of the fact that he only had one officer on board who had been to sea with him in *Upholder* before' (Sub Lieutenant J. H. Norman) 'it was natural that the Commanding Officer's efforts were somewhat divided between the periscope and supervision of attack instruments.

'The second attack on the cruisers was a very good effort which failed through no cause within (his) control.'[5]

The award of the Victoria Cross was first announced on the BBC's 6 p.m. news bulletin of Thursday, 11 December. Admiral Max Horton had written to Betty the day before from his headquarters at Northways, London: 'I want to be the first to congratulate you — everybody in submarines will be equally delighted as I am for we know better than others the measure of his sustained courage and skill.' Thoughtfully, he added a postscript: 'When I saw your husband some six weeks ago he was looking very well and both he and his officers and men were in splendid spirits.'[6]

This last was welcome news indeed — Betty, as the newspapers were quick to remark, had not seen him for almost a year.

Tubby Crawford, by now deep in the throes of his Perisher at Blockhouse, had already had an inkling on his arrival home, gleaned from his return interview with Horton. Once the glad tidings were made official he at once penned a warm letter to the wife of his former CO — they had not met and would not do so until many years had passed — in which he dwelt exclusively on the domestic scene ashore at Malta, intuitively picking out the details she would wish to know. There he had enjoyed, he assured her, 'the best ten months I have had in the Service and I think the only thing lacking from a married man's point of view is his wife and family'.[7] That and boiled sweets, he concluded with cheerful inconsequentiality — an 'always popular gift' if she wanted any ideas for a Christmas parcel.

She received a gleeful telegram from her husband two days later — though its arrival came as a nasty shock; telegrams in wartime usually only meant one thing: 'Betty darling I have got two tails and they are both wagging hard.'[8]

Lying in bed with a cold at her parents' home at Meigle, she first had the news by telephone from London. The record of her husband's achievements was a revelation. 'Letters gave no news because he wasn't allowed to say anything. He would sometimes remark "We got a fish today" if he'd sunk something and I knew that was what he meant.'[9]

Now the Press descended on her in earnest, eager to lend homely colour to their portrait of the new hero.

'We allowed the photographers to come and Ian was made to get into bed and pretend to look as if he had woken up with his father's VC — it was lunchtime, really . . .'[10]

The next day's papers were splashed with photographs of the young wife, smilingly keeping the home fires burning while two-year-old Ian stared, blank and uncomprehending, at the camera; his father was by now the dimmest of memories. Betty was 'terribly excited' by the news but could only add that she 'gathered from his letters that he had been rather busy lately'. She begged that there should be 'no fuss' about the award: 'Naturally we are very proud. We only wish we could have him home with us again . . .'[11]

'VC — but mother in tears' the *Daily Mirror* proclaimed,[12] while the *London Evening News* carried a photograph of Marjorie Wanklyn and her daughter wreathed in smiles. The *News Chronicle* took the opportunity to interview them at their London flat. After reading the Admiralty's statement describing her son's 'coolness and skill', Mrs Wanklyn reportedly exlaimed: 'How like David. Never to be flustered and so determined — that is him all over. But I know he would never endanger the lives of his men — he loves them all too much for that. He has an extraordinary mathematical mind. That is why he is so good with torpedoes — every one is a hit.'

Obligingly, she searched her memories for early intimations of greatness, recalling David as a little boy 'scarcely three years of age, seen in tears in the garden because he could not get the stones he was trying to balance to stand upright, but never losing either his temper or patience'. She wound up with the fond, classically feminine hope that her son would be sent home to receive his decoration so she could show off 'a new fur coat and a new hat'.[13]

Later reports, notably in the *Gloucestershire Echo*, which was able to highlight Wanklyn's connections with Cheltenham and Charlton

Kings, were able to draw on an interview he had given to the *Times of Malta*. In this he overcame his habitual reserve to the extent of admitting he had been 'exhilarated by the news' which had certainly come as 'a wonderful surprise' when he was woken up by a knock at his cabin door at 6 a.m. and expected an order to go to sea. Otherwise the *Times* had to work hard to flesh out the story. 'Some quiet rivalry exists among the submarines of the Flotilla in assessing who has caused the enemy to expend the most (depth) charges,' the interviewer warbled on. 'Asked what quality was most needed in submarine warfare for success, Britain's submarine Ace replied: 'That's a nasty one, so I will use a long word: "Imperturbability".'

He became expansive only in describing *Upholder's* debt to her cook — no specialist, just an ordinary Able Seaman selected on the basis of some accidental culinary talent picked up along the way whose 'ability and ingenuity, particularly when the weather was rough, were a matter of special interest' to the ship's company and their welfare.[14] It was a fine tribute to one of the unsung heroes of submarine life and struck an immediate chord of approval among the cognoscenti.

It was the seventh VC to be awarded to the Royal Navy in the war and the first to the Submarine Service. Privately, Wanklyn declared he felt it 'belonged to Malta'. Tompkinson, however — 'a gay personality with a gentle nature who hated war and despised its rewards' — told Simpson he was glad Wanks had got the VC. 'He's earned it, it suits him'.[15] Such, perhaps, was the general view — recognition, since it more easily devolved upon a single personality, was here well-bestowed.

The blaze of publicity which attended the award's announcement would not be rekindled until nearly a year had passed and *Upholder's* loss was finally made official — fully four months after the event. In the meantime, Wanklyn's celebrity made him an obvious public relations target and it was for the duration of his next patrol, from 12-21 December, that Commander Anthony Kimmins of the Admiralty Press Department took passage to the central Ionian Sea. Unlike the voyage of his German propaganda counterpart Lothar Büchheim — whose experiences as a war correspondent in a U-boat eventually led to the international best-seller *Das Boot* and a highly successful TV series in 1984, Kimmins' trip unfortunately produced nothing in the way either of defensive or offensive action to give spice to his descriptions. An important convoy movement from Taranto had been anticipated and Simpson was tempted to throw everything he had got across a route which air reconnaissance had shown was in frequent use by Tripoli-bound enemy transports. He was able to send all nine submarines of the Flotilla to sea at once and five were already on patrol when Wanklyn, again as Senior Officer, sailed in company with *P34*, *P31* and the Polish submarine *Sokol* — under the command of the redoubtable Boris Karnicki.

Until nightfall, fighter escorts protected the little armada and the patrol line was established at ten-mile intervals soon after dawn on the 14th. But as the day wore on the RAF observers found no sign of any southbound enemy movements and it was decided to disperse the submarines. *Upholder* moved south of the toe of Italy and began her task there early on the 16th, spending the next four days successfully avoiding being spotted from the air, where several slowly circling Savoia 79s kept watch, and from the sea, where armed trawlers, destroyers and E-boats forced them to keep their heads down. Kimmins was forced to fall back on the powers of his imagination to recount the routines of attack and counter-attack that might otherwise have befallen her.

Upholder arrived back at Malta at 8.30 a.m. on 21 December at the end of an entirely undistinguished outing. 'Snow White and the Seven Dwarfs' — the prize sow from the base sties and her latest offspring — were the first to grunt them a welcome and Kimmins' report, later broadcast on the Home Service, ended with an appropriately mundane domestic footnote: '. . . a dilapidated motor van pulled up on the roadway above and a massive bearded figure leant out from the driver's seat. It was the officer in charge of the pigs on his way to the slaughter house to put an end to half-a-dozen of the fattest. He wasn't looking forward to that at all. Odd, because only a few days before he'd sunk a transport and put an end to any number of Huns . . . and he'd had no qualms about that!'[16]

Even so, Kimmins claimed to have enjoyed himself. 'It had been a wonderful experience,' he would write in a rather jarringly cosy memoir of his various assignments. Typically, he remarked that life down below 'seemed to encourage that same frankness that one finds when grouped round a camp fire under the stars, or sheltering in a mountain hut and looking down on a glacier.

'In a cruiser or any surface ship I could have served with Wanks and his crew for months and become little more than acquainted, but down there in the depths of the Mediterranean we really got to know each other. We discussed life, our experiences, our innermost thoughts and our fears with a frankness which would have proved horribly embarrassing in any normal circumstances.'[17]

He recorded his host's repugnance for the inevitable loss of life that attended a successful action — though he must have got his information secondhand: 'Wanks, I know, hated killing, and when he had sunk a supply ship he would toss and turn in his bunk for nights afterwards, trying to shut out the picture of the death and suffering he had caused . . .'[18]*

---

* Anthony Kimmins went on to write, produce and direct several classic British post-war films, including *Mine Own Executioner*, *The Captain's Paradise* and *The Amorous Prawn*. He died in 1964.

Chapter 24
'A pretty close call'

Wanklyn was allowed a short rest as 1941 drew to a close and Pat Norman took command on 29 December for a day's exercises with *Urge* and the trawler *Beryl*. He confessed to some unease, although he was not entirely an unknown quantity: 'I didn't want to let the ship's company down — they adored Wanks and here was I, a bloody stranger more or less, taking them to sea. They didn't know whether I was as good as their man. It's always a touchy situation . . .'[1]

As they moved off, he was not to know that *Upholder's* very survival would lay in the balace before many hours had passed.

To his relief, the exercises were concluded without incident, but the last leg of the trip home was visited by the sudden shock of ambush from the air, an event unique in *Upholder's* annals and for good reason sharply clear in Norman's recollection nearly half a century later.

'Malta was heavily mined at that time by the Italians, so one's arrival was through a swept channel from the 100 fathom line, which was the normal procedure to escape the attentions of the Luftwaffe, and we surfaced literally a quarter of a mile off the entrance to Sliema Harbour. Just as we got up I had a look around — we could almost make out the people ashore, we were so close — when my signalman said to me: "Aircraft over Valletta." I said: "That's all right, probably a Hurricane or something." But it wasn't — it was an Me 109 with another one in quarter line from him.'[2]

It was 4.30 in the afternoon. *Upholder*, *Urge* and *Beryl* were attacked simultaneously. *Urge* managed to dive in time, but *Upholder* was just reading a warning message from the shore signal station when the first enemy fighter hurtled towards them.

'I kicked the signalman down the hatch, shouted 'Dive! Dive! Dive!'' and pressed the tit of the klaxon . . . Down we went with the top hatch still open because I was still outside. I was half in, half out, shutting the hatch, when a cannon shell went off just behind my head on the bridge and knocked me clean out.

'I don't remember any more except that the signalman grabbed hold of my legs, pulled me down and went up himself and shut the hatch, by which time the submarine was three-quarters down.* And all this while the boat was heading towards the harbour with barely

---

* Norman's own account differs from the official report, which has him shutting the hatch himself.

room to turn. The First Lieutenant' (Lieutenant James Drummond, later lost in command of *Sickle*, had taken over from Brian Band) 'did a U-turn dived, which was brilliant work, and went out to sea again — and there was bugger-all room to do that . . .

'I was semi-conscious, because I remember the Coxswain giving me chloroform or something. Drummond, bless his heart, brought her back into the harbour dived — which was again quite a thing — and surfaced alongside Lazaretto.'[3]

Norman had received flesh wounds in the back of his head and right arm and had a whole cluster of cannon splinters in his back. He was lucky to be alive.

'I recall being carried out of the submarine onto the brow with all my brother officers thinking I was a gonner. They were all looking a bit miserable and I made the usual heroic gesture to cheer them up — you know, "Anybody got a cigarette?" That rebuilt the atmosphere . . . I was wheeled up into the temporary sick bay we had in a cave underneath the Lazaretto, where the doctor started cutting bits of metal out of me.

'David came in while this was happening — and the gallant VC took one look and spiralled onto the floor! I think part of the trouble was, if I'd been screaming in agony it would have been all right, but I'd been so doped up with anaesthetics and Christ knows what and there I was lying on my stomach trying to smoke a cigarette and apparently untouched by the doctor's ghastly machinations. It must have been a macabre sight. Poor old David — it didn't do him any good, really . . . The doctor swore at him — "Bloody spectators!" he said and he was wheeled out of the theatre.

'He came to see me lots of times in hospital and I apologised for nearly bending his boat. It had been a pretty close call.'[4]

After this attack on *Upholder* the practice was initiated whereby submarines dived before entering or leaving harbour — 'a tricky operation even when carried out by skilled commanders.'[5]

The air raids had been stepped up in the closing weeks of 1941 — 'just enough to make a Christmas greeting for an unhappy New Year' Simpson noted gloomily.[6] Still, thanks in part to Wanklyn's careful husbandry, there were now over a hundred fat porkers in the freezer, which Boris Karnicki was adept at turning into a variety of succulent Polish-flavoured seasonal dishes, and it was hoped the deep caverns hewn into the rock would ensure the base's survival even if the Lazaretto itself was pulverised.

News from abroad was bad. The Japanese had bombed Pearl Harbour at the beginning of the month, and though Governor Dobbie assured the beleagured islanders that Singapore was safe — and said it 'with complete confidence, since I was the officer responsible for installing the guns'[7] — the Royal Navy was soon shocked by the loss of the *Prince of Wales* and the *Repulse*. Dobbie's words would soon return to haunt him, but meanwhile the Tenth Flotilla felt able to move confidently into the New Year. The tiny force of submarines had done much to boost morale of late. Tompkinson's *Urge* had put the Italian battleship *Vittorio Veneto* out of action with a single torpedo on the 14th, which helped counter concern over the mounting toll of civilian deaths. Over 50 died in the bombing during the last ten days of the month and there were to be another 80 casualties in January and over 200 in February. And the 'real months of horror' were yet to come.

But the success rate of the submarine force was in large part to blame for the intensification of the aerial bombardment. The enemy concentrated heavily on the anchorages and on the dockyard and *Upholder* was fortunate to escape their attentions. During his two-day visit to the Flotilla in late October, Horton had told Simpson he would try to limit the period of service of Malta-based submarines to one year and with this in mind Shrimp twice tried to persuade Wanklyn to return home for a well-earned rest. He would not near of it — *Upholder* was not scheduled for refit until after her twenty-fifth patrol and he was determined to take her home himself.

Wanklyn was blessed with a unit that had brought him great reward and trusted, respected, even loved him. He felt that he could not leave them behind in another's hands. And besides, there was no real sign yet that *Upholder* was 'played out' — indeed, she seemed to be gathering strength for a new onslaught.

Chapter 25
Second U-boat —
the Amiraglio St Bon

During the first four bitter months of 1942 two submarine attacks commended themselves to Simpson in retrospect as having shown 'a particularly high degree of skill'.[1] The first of these was carried out by Wanklyn at the beginning of the New Year.

He had put to sea in the early evening of 31 December — all thoughts of Hogmanay resolutely pushed aside — bound for a patrol area north of the Straits of Messina. His orders were to search for targets along the shipping route north of Sicily. To begin with he was 'dogged by a series of setbacks'.[2] Just before 5.30 on the morning of the 2nd he sighted a submarine zig-zagging some four miles distant and dived to close in bright moonlight but half an hour later his target was identified as HMS *Una* and the attack was hastily broken off. On the morning of the 3rd he found three brigs and an armed tug off Cape St Vito. They were not worth a torpedo and air activity was too intense to allow gun action. Near midnight, north of Cape Gallo, he fired three torpedoes at a 4000 ton cargo vessel. The range was only about 2400 yards but all his fish missed and for once he could offer no explanation. A single explosion was heard, and since the escort vessel had been seen moving off towards Palermo, leaving the merchant vessel unguarded, Wanklyn could only assume that one of his torpedoes had run to port and detonated on the Cape. By the time he had reloaded, his target was well away.

Upholder went east of Palermo, where she found another likely victim, the Italian coaster *Sirio*, nicely in position nearly right ahead. '. . . even so, there was lots more trouble in store,' Wanklyn wrote[3] and certainly the attack which followed would be one of the most traumatic he ever logged. It was 5.37 a.m. on the 4th as the submarine dived below a canopy of dazzling starshine — and no sooner was she down than the torpedo in No 1 tube began to run hot, causing complete loss of trim. Wanklyn fired No 3, which he had thought was the one at fault until the trouble persisted, and No 1 immediately after. One of the torpedoes hit the bottom and exploded underneath the submarine 'with a terrific concussion', shaking the boat as severely as the worst depth charging she had known.[4] It was as well there were 500 fathoms of water beneath *Upholder's* keel at this point, or she might have been the cause of her own destruction.

Nothing daunted, Wanklyn continued the attack, crossing the bows of the *Sirio* to the south side to ensure good visibility without land behind the silhouette. He fired the other two tubes, aimed individually at 1000 yards, and one torpedo hit amidships. Yawing heavily, *Sirio* continued on for fully ten minutes, stopped briefly to lower two boats, and then proceeded fitfully towards the coast. Wanklyn loaded his last torpedo. As his prey turned westwards he surfaced to give chase, hoping to engage her with his 12-pounder deck gun — but the damaged Italian at once opened up with her two Breda automatics and *Upholder* was forced down again. Soon the plucky little vessel picked up speed, her 9 knots outdistancing *Upholder's* submerged 5½, and was last seen rounding Cape Zaffarano with a tug in company. She deserved to make her escape and Wanklyn was impressed by her handling 'good enough to suggest at least German control,' he decided.[5]

The darkest hour just before dawn the following day found *Upholder* preparing to dive 15 miles NW of Messina, and as Wanklyn came to the bridge the look-out drew his attention to a dark object approaching rapidly dead astern. At first he thought it was a trawler and immediately gave the order to dive but a few minutes later the unmistakeable bulk of a massive two-gun submarine crossed the circle of his periscope. Wanklyn had not wasted a moment — something had rung an alarm bell in his brain and he had dropped below in the very nick of time, for the U-boat was now zig-zagging wildly. It seemed likely she had spotted *Upholder* first so why hadn't she dived, too?

Wanklyn had just one shot left and he prayed it would not let him down. Ordering full speed he wheeled around 180 degrees, hastily estimating the target's speed at 15 knots — for the revs were too fast to count — and chose an arbitrary track angle, aiming for the conning tower.

His luck — or good judgment — had returned. Half a minute later he saw the torpedo smash in just before the forward gun, throwing up a towering waterspout. It was the first strike he had waited to watch and its sudden violence was appalling. With a roar and a huge gout of flame the U-boat disappeared before his eyes. *Upholder* had claimed her second submarine — and Wanklyn had earned an automatic bar to his DSO. All that remained on the surface was a wide patch of blazing fuel oil. By the time *Upholder* surfaced this had burnt out and it seemed impossible that anyone could have survived the holocaust that had so quickly passed — but three heads were spotted, bobbing in the greasy scum. As the survivors were hauled, shocked and trembling, on to the casing, the last of the trio to be rescued promptly collapsed. He had to be roped and hoisted to the conning tower and then lowered into the boat down the ladder which his compatriots had managed unaided before him. This took time, while *Upholder* lay dangerously exposed — and the threat of imminent attack was close by. The unconscious Italian was halfway down the trunking when the rope jammed in the casing and at that very moment the Asdic operator picked up the sound of revolving propellors. Fully a quarter of an hour passed before *Upholder* was able to dive and head off to the south of Vulcano Island off the NE tip of Sicily.

Once they had been cleaned up and dried off, Wanklyn found his prisoners willing to talk. The U-boat, they revealed, was the *Amiraglio St Bon* of 1500 tons — nearly three times the size of *Upholder*. They identified themselves as Lieutenant Como, Torpedo Officer — the last to be taken aboard, now fully recovered — Petty Officer Telegraphist Valentino Chico, and Torpedoman Ernest Fiore. The two ratings had been on watch when the torpedo struck. Como confirmed that they had indeed sighted *Upholder* first and had laid their forward gun as *Upholder* dived. They had been on passage from Messina to Palermo to have a small leak repaired, which had prevented her diving and thus sealed her doom. The captain and the other two look-outs had also been on the bridge and he had seen his captain swimming away — 'but he must have collapsed in the water'.[6]

To most questions Como, a 24-year-old native of Pola who had served only six months in submarines, gave evasive answers 'while still seeming friendly and talkative'. He admitted that listening watch on hydrophones had been maintained while running on main engines — 'but at no time was *Upholder* heard'.[7] The *St Bon* was a brand-new boat, having left the builders four months since, and had only just completed her work-up. Como had previously served in destroyers — in 1938 he had visited Plymouth in the *Commerigo Vespucci* he said. It appeared he had little love for his German allies: Most were confined to the embarkation ports and 'the Italian people had no wish to embrace them,' he said.

Chico, a 21-year-old Sicilian, agreed that their Axis partners were 'heartily disliked'. Like Como, he had had only six months in submarines, having done his training at the German school at Bordeaux. He added — comfortable in the knowledge that for him the war was over — that he didn't think much of his own officers either. They had little consideration for their men, he said — 'on a long patrol only the officers were allowed water for washing'.[8]

The third of the trio, Fiore, a bricklayer from Reggio who had had a short spell as a regular and had been twice recalled from the reserve, was only too keen to get back to the building trade.

Wanklyn gleaned some useful intelligence from his conversations with his three, in the end, cheerfully compliant POWs. In particular, they confirmed the sinkings of five Italian submarines and the continued existence of one, hitherto believed destroyed. *Upholder* made her way homeward, surviving a nasty encounter with a Junkers 88 which dropped a stick of bombs about 200 yards on her starboard quarter around breakfast time on Thursday the 8th, and arrived safely in port two hours later, her Jolly Roger proudly emblazoned with her latest U-boat kill. Smiling faces lined the casing — 1942 had got off to a lucky start. Did they but know it, the three Italians were the luckiest of all.

Chapter 26
'A foul lake of wrecks'

Upholder was granted only six days' respite before being put to sea again, and this was largely taken up with maintenance. In any case, by now rest and relaxation of any kind were practically impossible. On the day she sailed, 14 January, there were fourteen air alerts in the space of nineteen hours.

'The towns and villages lay much in ruins. The heavy limestone blocks of which the houses were constructed were vast heaps of rubble. Whole streets were blocked and areas cut off.'[1]

The courageous *Daily Mirror* reporter Bernard Gray — who had smuggled himself into the island in a bomber arrived from England and was later lost while working the same trick in a submarine bound for Egypt which never arrived — life in Malta seemed unendurable, far worse than anything he had experienced in the London Blitz. During one raid he described the din of 'the world's most formidable barrage' as successive waves of aircraft, 25 at a time, moved above him. 'We could not see or hear anything . . . stones were falling, shrapnel coming down like rain and planes dropping from the sky. It was terrifying, and more planes were coming in. We saw very little of this wave because of the clouds of dust which now enveloped us.'[2]

It was against this background that the weary crew of *Upholder* lived and worked, to this grim welcome that they returned after the long days on patrol. There was no let-up, just one set of tensions replaced by another. Often they must have wished they were back at sea, for there seemed little to choose between the expectations of either situation. The great harbour was now a graveyard fringed by docks, wharves and storehouses reduced to unsightly piles of grey rubble — 'a foul lake of wrecks and more than ever a dangerous gauntlet to run'.[3]

As they edged their way through this mess in the dismal shadow of the early winter evening, their relief at leaving such chaos behind would be mixed as usual with apprehension as to what lay in store for them ahead — and wonder at what fresh scenes of destruction would greet them if they should be lucky enough to return.

Upholder was to take up the central position of a line of three submarines across the entrance to the Gulf of Taranto, providing cover against the heavy naval forces there that were threatening a British convoy bound for Malta. *Una* and *Torbay* were set ten miles either side of her. At dawn on the 16th *Upholder* was on station. A hospital ship was seen but nothing more for the next four days and orders were received to break off after dark on the 20th. In the afternoon a northbound motor vessel escorted by a destroyer was spotted far to the westward. Wanklyn expected either *Una* or *Torbay* might have been in a position to attack, but neither reported seeing them.

Simpson was by now determined that *Upholder* should have a normal rest period — and though he had news of a southbound convoy leaving Taranto he decided that his 'brightest star' should not be deflected from her passage home, since submarines had already been despatched from Malta direct to the eastward approach route to Tripoli. When *Upholder* arrived back at base at dawn on the 24th he made his second attempt to persuade Wanklyn to return to England. Met with the usual resolute refusal, he insisted that he hand over command to Pat Norman for at least one patrol. Thus Wanklyn was able to enjoy a full month's break.

On 8 February, replying to a letter from *Upholder's* 'godmother' — her sponsor, Mrs Phoebe Thompson, the wife of a Vickers director who since launching the boat nearly two years before had maintained a close interest in her fortunes — he described his latest country retreat as 'very pleasant and comfortable', so ensuring that he would be 'thoroughly fit for the next round'.[4] This was a white lie if ever there was one; bombing raids were now reaching a peak of fury. Only the day before Malta had trembled under 17 attacks within 24 hours. Very soon the *Times of Malta* would report: 'For some eighty days now there has been a period of almost continuous alerts. With few respites, days and nights have been enlivened with the sound of tense air battles, anti-aircraft guns in action, and the whistling and crash of bombs.'[5] A week later the Regent cinema in Kingsway, Valletta's main thoroughfare, received a direct hit, killing a large number of civilian and Service patrons.

Yet Wanklyn carried on painting a bright picture for the news-hungry Mrs Thompson: 'We have had a little more fun this year already, so I hope we can continue the good work till some of the "new boys" take our place.'[6]

Upholder was doing just that. Even as he wrote Pat Norman was adding to her score some 40 miles to the south of Pantellaria and opening up the impressive personal account he was later to build up in command of *Una*.

He was by now 'fully recovered' from his wounds — in exactly the time Simpson had predicted, although after only five weeks he must still have been suffering from some residue of the legacy of the cannon burst that had come so close to ending his career. By the end of his patrol, *Upholder's* twenty-second, there would no longer be any doubt as to his competence. On the first day of February he had departed for the area between Marittimo and Palermo on the north coast of Sicily with an American officer, Lieutenant Ruble, USN, embarked as an observer. It was a rough passage and he was obliged to slow down on the surface as the heavy head seas threw torrents of spray down the hatch into the control room. Part of the way led through a minefield and here Norman's nerve was 'racked to the utmost' by the need to act upon the Asdic rating's quiet pronouncements on the returning signals from the mines and their mooring cables.[7]

On the fourth day they were dived six miles west of Cape St Vito in the Gulf of Castellammare when a Navigatori class destroyer appeared in the 'magic eye' of the periscope. Norman summoned his attack team. A moderately heavy sea and swell prevailed, tending to lift the submarine and hindering depth-keeping at periscope level. As Norman prepared a salvo of three, he was uncomfortably aware that the moment of discharge, temporarily lightening the boat before the empty tubes flooded, was the most dangerous moment of all.

He fired his fish at 1300 yards, and whether or not the submarine had broken surface, the hydrophone effects immediately signalled an alteration of course on the part of his intended victim, indicating that she was beginning to comb the tracks of the torpedoes before they could have reached their target. It was just after 2 p.m. and over the next hour ten depth charges were counted, falling around the submarine as she crept slowly to the northward towards the Messina Straits. She was still in harm's way an hour further on as an armed trawler threw down another seven charges in her wake, but by evening the attack had died away and *Upholder* came to the surface again.

There was a short-lived frisson of excitement in the small hours of the following day while they were patrolling the convoy route between Cape Gallo and the Castellammare Gulf. The look-out had reported an enemy U-boat and preparations for attack were well under way when the target was discerned to be nothing more sinister than a volcanic outcrop; 'the error was gently pointed out by Lieutenant Ruble, United States Navy,' Norman noted shamefacedly.[8]

Another 'U-boat' spotted hugging the shore of the Cape just after noon together with a number of small ships, turned out to be an Orsa class destroyer. She was the only vessel within range but two minutes after the sighting an aircraft passed 'very low and close'[9] and Norman hurriedly broke off the attack and dived deep. Sure enough, he had been seen — the destroyer turned back, hurling depth charges. None of these fell close, but the sounds of patrolling surface craft were picked up throughout the day and it was not until 10 p.m. that Normal felt able to surface, having slowly withdrawn to the north near the island of Ustica.

The next day passed without incident. Late in the evening Norman received orders to intercept a merchant vessel steaming at 14 knots towards Cape St Vito and shortly after midnight saw a mass of flares falling on the far side of Levanzo Island. He presumed this to herald an aircraft attack on his target which a later signal confirmed. The sea was flat calm under a clear sky and he dared not stay on the surface to find out for himself. All day long, as he moved towards the Gulf, the skies were thick with aircraft and a full 24 hours went by before he found his opportunity — a small diesel merchantman in ballast, moving east together wtih a destroyer. After recording the days of dross in close detail, Norman described the attack that was to finally bear fruit with spare simplicity:

'1739   Fired three torpedoes at merchant vessel.
1740   One torpedo hit. Retired to westward. HE (hydrophone effect) of merchant vessel ceased.'[10]

And so the armed trawler *Aosta* was added to *Upholder's* tally. Norman logged the subsequent attack by her escort with equal brevity — though reading between the lines that plot the hour-long ordeal that followed, the submarine was not let off lightly. They heard the destroyer starting and stopping, her lethal load breaking into 'hundreds of fragments which rattled like shrapnel' against the hull as Norman halted and moved off again in turn, playing the horrid cat-and-mouse game that no amount of skill could guarantee against the deal of chance.

But his luck was in because suddenly the destroyer sped off to the east at top speed. Perhaps she had used up all her depth charges and felt vulnerable to attack herself. When *Upholder* surfaced a few minutes later she found the sea and sky empty once more except for the seagulls feeding on the litter of dead fish thrown up by the bombardment.

Through the next four days the submarine ploughed doggedly on with nothing to occupy her but the continuing bad weather and heavy seas, in which Norman found he was often unable to keep periscope depth. But he had earned Simpson's approbation for a 'well-conducted patrol'. Only the press of air activity had robbed him of the chance of better success.

It was dawn on Friday the thirteenth when *Upholder* arrived back in Lazaretto Creek, 'by repute, an inauspicious day for somebody,' Simpson wrote.[11] About noon he was near the base front gate when the klaxon sounded and he ran for the nearest shelter off the men's messdecks. One of the month's 236 recorded air raids was about to begin. A few minutes later a Stuka screamed down, dropping a bomb in the creek — a near miss which 'shook the whole building'.[12] At 2.30 p.m. another raid produced parachute mines. Two exploded at the western end of the Lazaretto and brought down the roof — which was constructed out of two-hundredweight stone slabs — over the messdecks. Eight more fell on Manoel Island, killing three men and completely demolishing the barracks. 'The walls remained like empty shells, reaching thirty feet towards the sky.'[13] A fortnight later the Flotilla's officers moved into an empty heavy oil tank eighty yards away from the ruins, their few sticks of furniture salvaged from the wreck set up in the odd dry spots on an uneven floor, each little 'island' connected by duck boards lying across glutinous pools of oil and water. In this 'stinking cavern' the base would continue to operate for two more months. Simpson himself was lucky — though his day cabin had lost its roof, his sleeping quarters, containing his clothes, had survived. For four weeks, however, all the officers and ratings messed together 'under the stars or the sun', retiring to the deep shelter to sleep.[14]

In terms of the sheer discomfort imposed by this troglodytic existence the transition from life at sea to life ashore was now barely discernable for Wanklyn and his men. He found relief in penning a letter to his wife, discussing plans for his long-anticipated return in language that suggested nothing of the circumstances in which he was living. He might have been a businessman abroad, offering advice against an uncertain schedule of sailing times and leaving the final arrangements to her own judgment.

To her suggestion of a cottage in Scotland he responds: 'Take it for June and July. We must have a separate pied a terre while I have my leave, at least. As I have no idea what job I shall get I cannot foresee further than that; but if it is building' (another submarine) 'again, you will be with me as before . . . if you find something more attractive — up Glen Sla say — try and get it instead. But certainly take something.'

Betty should expect to be waiting in London for him on 1 June and he promised he would cut off his beard before she saw him again — 'but probably not till I can get at a barber. You won't get too prickled, darling . . .'[15]

Chapter 27
'Report farm casualties'

Believing that a large convoy would shortly try to force its way to Tripoli from the east, Simpson planned a strong submarine concentration off the Libyan coast. *Upholder*, with Wanklyn back in harness, sailed on the evening of 21 February, the last of four submarines departing at half-hourly intervals. Four more were already near Homs at the Western end of the line. *Upholder's* group was to take up position near Misurata, further along to the east.

Head seas delayed *Upholder* on both nights of her passage and it was not until 7 a.m. on the morning of the 23rd that she was able to dive about 12 miles north of her station. Wanklyn had been forced to abandon the precaution of zig-zagging in order to keep to his schedule and the look-outs on the bridge had passed the hours of darkness drenched and miserable against the lashing spray. Visibility remained poor at 5000 yards maximum and although he saw no ships Wanklyn spotted a Cant flying boat which he assumed was part of the convoy's air cover. Sure enough, the submarine soon picked up the sounds of fast ships to the south, moving rapidly westward, but these eventually turned north and back east; they must have been the convoy's cruiser escort, returning to port after parting company.

Shortly before he arrived in his ordered position, he began to hear the distant rumbling of a long series of depth charges — one or other of the submarines in line had been detected. Still no ships had passed through *Upholder's* area. By 9 p.m. the concentration was dispersed and she set course for the western approaches to Tripoli to cover the route near Zuaga. Here, around the same time the following night, Wanklyn found two ships and immediately gave chase — but broke off once they were identified as destroyers. There was no point in risking his luck against dedicated submarine hunters when bigger prizes might still be at hand. Even so, he stayed on the surface and followed them towards Sidi Blal. He picked up a contact early on the 26th and started to attack, mistaking the distant object for a submarine — and when he realised his error he was so close that he could see the sparkle of a cigarette end thrown from the bridge of a destroyer. In the gloom they might as well have been Roman candles and Wanklyn blessed the carelessness of the Italian watchkeepers as he dived to avoid detection.

Yet they were not so idle, after all. Through his periscope Wanklyn found not one but a pair of destroyers and 'both appeared to be suspicious, remaining stopped and pointing'.[1] Twenty minutes later he felt himself to be in the clear and surfaced but — found them lying only 1000 yards to the northward and so quickly dived again. The submarine was enveloped in a deathly hush. Suddenly, shockingly, the pin-drop silence was broken by an unearthly grating noise, seemingly generated by some kind of transmission emanating from the watchers above. The men had never heard its like before. Hearts beat faster as they men debated inwardly on the possibilities of a new secret weapon in anti-submarine warfare — there were always rumours . . . Wanklyn climbed into the conning tower where the noise seemed to intensify to a grinding screech 'like a squeaky hinge'.[2] Fortunately the contact, supposed to have been gained by some form of Asdic, was not held and Wanklyn was able to withdraw without difficulty. The mystery was never solved.

Three more destroyers appeared during the day, moving in and out of Tripoli. Wanklyn left them alone as being 'targets unworthy of the possibilities of the area'.[3] They passed a quiet night and when the light of dawn filtered over a calm sea he decided to reconnoitre Zuaga again. By 9 a.m. he was watching the activities of a pair of minesweepers, combing the searched channel there as far as Marsa Sormon and back. But in the afternoon a sandstorm blew up over the coast, making further reconnaissance impossible, and he moved back east.

Soon the keen ears the Asdic rating picked up a faint contact. As the periscope swung onto the bearing Wanklyn took in the bulky outline of a merchantman — despite the dazzle paint covering her superstructure and the hazy mist that enveloped her, he could tell she was a big one, 5500 tons at least. Dodging her single destroyer escort he fired three torpedoes at 2800 yards. Two hit — his judgment of course, speed and distance were clearly unimpaired by his month-long lay-off. The destroyer increased speed and started depth charging, but was soon forced to turn her attention to her fast ailing companion. The *Tembien*, 5584 tons, went down in twenty minutes, the sounds of her death-agony clearly heard in the submarine that slew her, now lying doggo at 70 feet.

Wanklyn watched the destroyer return to Tripoli and felt safe in surfacing and retiring to the north east. He dived again to reload his salvo — a task practically impossible on the surface where the pitch and roll of the boat could easily lead to a fatal accident. And now he encountered another difficulty which Simpson would identify as a serious problem of supply — 'one warhead, 20 years old, was too swollen to enter the tube'.[4]

It was something all the Malta-based submarines had to cope with. High explosive deteriorates with age and the closely-besieged island had to make do with stockpiles of ancient weapons. Small wonder that some failed to reach their targets — and it was another nagging worry to the crews that they might be carrying any number of highly volatile passengers. More careful checks were clearly needed to weed out the more obvious duds and Simpson noted that 'steps are being taken to ensure that warheads are gauged more carefully before embarkation.'[5]

As it happened, there was no further opportunity to test what was left of *Upholder's* arsenal. The period 28 February–3 March was simply logged: 'blank days with rough seas and poor visibility'[6] and Wanklyn took her back east along the coastal route to re-enter Malta on the 5th — with just one more bar stitched on her now crowded Jolly Roger.

By now the threat of starvation — long-anticipated and from time immemorial the prime sanction of siege warfare — was looming over Malta. Food was almost the main preoccupation of all the inhabitants — 'to the exclusion of almost everything, except self-preservation'.[7] New regulations were introduced governing the sale of bread and flour, although actual rationing was held off for the time being. Meat was in such short supply that no unguarded animal was safe — though the Maltese, in common with most Mediterranean southerners, were not big meat eaters. Simpson wrote: 'How glad I was at this time that all those porkers were available to our flotilla and base staff to keep us fully energetic'.[8] It was fortunate indeed that such a sizeable stockpile had been laid up in cold storage, for it was during March that a heavy bomb wiped out the little farm in the quadrangle of the wrecked Lazaretto — thus far miraculously untouched. The sow and her latest litter — Wanklyn's pride and joy — together with around 100 rabbits, the property of many doting individual sailors who regarded them more as pets than as potential meals, were mourned, as is the way of sentimental men far from home, with a depth of grief that seems disproportionate, but touching all the same. The Commander-in-Chief himself was moved to inquire by signal: 'Report farm casualties'. More practically Simpson replied that they were 'mincing down satisfactorily'[9] but he had to advise one submarine to delay her return from patrol for two days while the debris was cleared up. Another loss was 'one irascible turkey cock, whose bad temper was attributable to sympathetic sailors who would soak dried peas in their tot of rum and then feed them to him'.[10]

Upholder's expectations of a rough homecoming had been realised to the full. On the day she got back several attacks on Manoel Island cut off all electric light, telephones and water mains. The next day dive bombers narrowly missed *Una* and *P36*, peppering the latter with splinters. Half an hour later a second wave of bombers hit the fuelling lighter lying near *P39*. This caught fire and sank and the submarine base was dowsed in shale oil, *P39* being severely damaged in the process. Simpson pointed out that around a thousand air raids had taken place during the Flotilla's 14 months of operation and that this was their first major casualty — but from that day onward all submarines were kept dived during daylight hours at deep water berths.

And so *Upholder* spent the interval of waiting for her next sortie lying on the bottom, manned by half-crew.

Chapter 28
'No mean achievement'

The days were lengthening towards the arrival of Spring as *Upholder* departed at dusk on the 14th for the Gulf of Taranto, with orders to prevent enemy surface forces intercepting a Malta-bound convoy. She was soon forced to dive to avoid an E-boat, seen heading south at high speed. 'This may have been *Xmas*, who was known to be at sea', Wanklyn observed, patiently waiting for the sound of her engines to disappear before resuming his journey.[1] A full two days' passage ended with fresh instructions to divert to Brindisi above the eastern heel of Italy, for the convoy had been delayed. Wanklyn welcomed the chance to try his luck in the Adriatic, which he had long been pressing for, but first he had to pass through the venomously hostile Straits of Otranto, where he could expect anti-submarine forces in abundance.

Sure enough, just after noon on the 17th, two destroyers were spotted racing south at 25 knots and it was late in the evening before he could surface and plot his way for the searched channel leading to the port — in peacetime a familiar embarkation point for the Orient, now a highly alert focus for the comings and goings of war. A pair of auxiliary minesweepers were found there the following morning, busily working over the port roads. In the early afternoon Wanklyn watched as an insignificant little sloop passed into the harbour and then turned his attention to a merchant vessel which, though small, seemed to merit the presence of a surface escort and a couple of aircraft circling above. He was tempted to attack, but the range was too great and he allowed that she was not worth the trouble anyway. But he agonized again when she came to anchor in the outer harbour and 'gave a possible sitting shot through the boom gate, which must have been open continually for small craft.'[2] He manoeuvred to take advantage of this opportunity and was suddenly spoiled for choice. A small Perla Class submarine with a single anti-submarine vessel was coming in, presumably on their way back from a day's exercises. But again range could not be closed within 3000 yards and he held his fire. His sense of frustration mounted as the afternoon lengthened, producing a succession of tugs, minesweepers, brigs and schooners moving in and out of the harbour but still nothing worth a torpedo.

Finally the hours of waiting were rewarded. Just after 5 p.m. a second submarine appeared, steering south at 12 knots. *Upholder* was fine on the bow. Wanklyn turned her onto a parallel course as he found his target, apparently a small submarine of the Settembrini

Class, zigging towards him. Four small sailing craft now threatened to complicate his task. These were lying right above him at this point and he was compelled to make a gentle, retiring turn. The manoeuvre — 'executed most brilliantly'[3] — required great delicacy in order not to disturb the water with his passage and give the game away. *Upholder* just managed to steady on track again in time to fire.

As he raised his periscope, Wanklyn found the range had closed to 550 yards and he ordered a full salvo, fired at eight second intervals. At that distance success would soon be signalled loud and clear and the first shattering blow of impact was quickly followed by another. Through the still-raised periscope Wanklyn saw the smoke cloud of the second explosion soar up after the first, rising above the stern just as the conning tower slipped below.

There was no immediate comeback. Wanklyn had time to photograph the black pall that marked the grave of the submarine (later confirmed as the *Tricheco*) but within the hour the southern Adriatic was alive with small craft. He counted eleven in all, including an E-boat, hunting for survivors without making any sort of concerted attack on the aggressor. *Upholder* was able to reload her tubes unmolested and at 8.45 p.m. she surfaced and sped to the eastward. Soon she ran into another E-boat patrol, however, and was forced to dive to run clear. A tense hour followed, the E-boat keeping close company all the while. Minute by minute they expected a shower of depth charges that would signal detection and the batteries were now alarmingly low. Eventually the stalker gave it up, but Wanklyn let another hour go by before surfacing. Fresh air flooded in to the stale compartments of the submarine, quickly restoring the jaded spirits of the oxygen-starved crew. But the batteries needed much longer to regain their strength and for nearly six hours *Upholder* was obliged to sweat it out, dangerously exposed, while the generators ran at full power.

As the sun rose above the eastern horizon, Wanklyn dived close inshore off St Cataldo Point, hoping to find a target for his gun. He needed to keep his four remaining torpedoes in reserve for bigger game — but even a humble fishing boat had its uses for the enemy. Such a chance presented itself at breakfast time on the 19th when he sighted four small craft — the diesel trawler *Maria* and three fishing smacks.

Seconds after the conning tower erupted from the sea 100 yards from the *Maria,* Wanklyn emerged from the hatch and gestured to her shocked crew to abandon ship. He fired warning shots over her companions, signalling them to keep their distance, and in this interval four men from the *Maria* — half her crew — managed to launch a cobble boat while the remainder jumped into the sea. Seven more shells, all but one scoring hits, soon finished the little trawler off. She caught fire and settled with three gaping holes at the water line.

'During this action,' Wanklyn noted, 'two brigs, one towing the other, were sighted very close inshore: but as the gun action had already lasted 15 minutes it was considered unwise to give chase.'[4] By now it was broad daylight and at any moment the sea and sky might be blazing with the heat of revenge. He dived and pulled away to the eastward — where he was glad to see two of the fishing smacks, one flying an ensign, return to pick up the trawler's crew. As night fell he surfaced to complete his passage through the Straits of Otranto.

Word arrived that the delayed convoy had finally sailed from Alexandria and he was ordered to return to his position off Taranto by midnight the following day. He was there by 5 p.m. but two whole days were to pass with nothing to record but the distant sounds of a patrolling E-boat and a destroyer. The morning of 23 March brought a severe south-easterly gale. Heavy rain and driving spray made visibility 'very poor[5]. With news of an action by the 15th Cruiser Squadron it was known that a Littorio Class battleship and several cruisers were at sea and *Upholder*, now joined by *Proteus* and *P36*, was instructed to move as close to Taranto as safety allowed. The battleship was said to have been damaged and pulses quickened with the prospect of a major prize — if only the elements would allow a clear shot.

But the storm raged on throughout the day and when, just after 5 p.m., the sound of 'heavy HE moving west fast' pinpointed the arrival of their quarry, little could be seen[6]. Wanklyn closed on the bearing at full speed and it was another quarter of an hour before the target finally appeared — a bouncing, tantalising blur splashing over the eye of the periscope. 'Only the bridge and funnels were seen fully and these only as dull shadows.'[7] She was making a good 20 knots.

Two minutes later Wanklyn fired a full salvo of Mark IVs from a range of about 4000 yards — too hastily, perhaps, but the target was only in sight for four minutes altogether and it was a long shot he had to take. In any event, she zigged just after the torpedoes left the tubes and none hit. Simpson felt that the less powerful Mark IV weapons would not have been equal to the task anyway and the incident illustrated for him the disadvantage of carrying them at all.

'*Upholder* unloaded one salvo of Mark VIIIs and one of Mark IVs but since on sailing the first object of the patrol was interception of heavy Naval units, the Mark VIIIs were loaded into the torpedo tubes: thus, due to change of plans, this powerful salvo was fired at a U-boat and when subsequently the battleship was sighted, only Mark IVs remained. These were quite correctly set to a 12 and 14 foot depth setting in case the battleship was not seen, but a 6 inch cruiser proved to be the target.'

These torpedoes' depth settings could not be changed without withdrawing them half-way out of the tube and so *Upholder's* striking power against the battleship was 'most severely reduced'.[8]

Simpson felt bound to add that just to have kept the submarine at periscope depth in those heavy seas had been 'no mean achievement'. Much of the credit for this, of course, lay with *Upholder's* latest — and, as it turned out, last — First Lieutenant, 22-year-old Lieutenant Francis Ruck-Keene. 'Ruckers' had come back to the boat at the beginning of December at Wanklyn's particular request. He had been appreciative of the young man's quality during his brief secondment early in the summer of 1941, about the time when Melloney Scobell had formed an attachment to him of a more personal nature. 'Such a combination of character and good looks is all too rare,' someone later wrote to her. After their meeting at a party that shortly followed her introduction to the submarine base she had lost interest in the general social life and had hopes that they might become engaged. Wanklyn had played his part in smoothing the way for their romance. He had been, she would remember, 'very sweet to Francis and me'.[9] But in January, as the air raids intensified, a flying boat had taken Melloney out of Malta. She would never see him again. *Upholder's* next patrol would be her last.

Chapter 29
'Count the days,
they are not so many'

The *Upholder*s were a close-knit crew — all but a handful had been with Wanklyn throughout the submarine's life. Among those who had gone their separate ways, Christopher Read had long been invalided home. Tubby Crawford was in command of the training submarine *H50* in home waters and would shortly bring *Unseen* to the Mediterranean to follow in his mentor's footsteps with a surety that would twice earn him the Distinguished Service Cross. Gordon Selby, the Second Coxswain, was now asked if he would care to move a step up the ladder and join *P39*. 'I was in two minds because *Upholder* would be going home soon, but the temptation to go as Coxswain was too strong.'[1] Thus, at the last moment, fate intervened.

Some months earlier it had fallen to Selby to conduct the feisty, pugnacious George Curnall to the cells. On *Upholder's* return from her penultimate patrol Charles Tuckwood would likewise rail at the dead hand of an authority against which there was no appeal — but in which Providence again took an interest. Every submariner had to present himself for a medical examination after a spell at sea. The poor conditions they endured may have been a matter of necessity but the Admiralty could not afford to take too many risks with the men's health — trained submariners were in short supply. A somewhat delicate matter intervened to save Tuckwood . . .

'The doctor said: "I see when you were born they didn't make a very good job of your circumcision — I think you'd better go and have it done again." I said: "Can't it wait till I get back home, surely? I've had it for twenty-odd years now — another few months won't hurt." He said: "You do as you're told — be outside sick bay at 08.30 with your gear." And that was that. I was really worried about going into hospital because I knew the boat was supposed to be going home after the next trip. I went to see Wanklyn at the base and told him the story — but there were only two men the captain couldn't appeal against, and that was the padre and the doctor, and he said: "Well, you'll have to go and have it done, Tuckwood, and I'll see that when we go home you will go with us".'[2]

There would be just one more departure from *Upholder* — a passenger embarked for her final patrol who would leave her at sea a few days before the end.

Captain Robert Wilson of the Royal Artillery was fast becoming one of the most celebrated of the elite band of 'special commandoes'. Thirty years old, slightly built, he had the matinee idol good looks of the young David Niven — who was himself at the same period proving his worth as a real-life hero in uniform away from the silver screen. With his neat cravats and clipped moustache, 'Tug' — as with all other Wilsons in military life he was inevitably known — appears in all his photographs as the very image of the dashing officer-type of the period. A typical 'Pongo', one might suppose, who should have been an anathema to the determinedly off-beat fraternity of submarine officers with whom he cast his lot.

But there was nothing Blimpish about Tug Wilson. He had made his first submarine trip out of Malta the previous Spring in *Triumph* and had happily come to terms with the informal discipline of submarine life, taking to its routines, as his biographer Rex Woods would observe, with little difficulty.[3] He had lately been awarded the DSO, an unusually high honour for an officer of his rank, on the strength of an impressive series of sabotage jobs directed mainly against the Italian railway network of the type described earlier.

Wanklyn had recognised a kindred spirit and the pair had become fast friends. For his part, Tug would say that 'to have known Wanks, both on duty and off duty, was in itself something of which any man would be very proud.'[4] They had never had the opportunity to serve together on operations however, and Wanklyn seized upon it with joy when it finally came. Tug had been called home and Simpson asked him if he was willing to undertake a vital mission on the way. This latest submarine trip — his tenth — involved the landing of a couple of important agents near Carthage in the Gulf of Sousse. *Upholder* was chosen for the job, although Wanklyn had asked for another chance at the rich pickings he had found off Brindisi. The sinking of the submarine *Tricheco* would earn him the second bar to his DSO but Simpson fretted that he had taken too big a risk. The attack had been 'highly dangerously'[5], he felt, and he was determined to pack him off in the opposite direction, where the temptation to test his mettle might not be so strong.

The deep fatigue now gripping the entire crew was apparent to all but themselves, it seemed. One of them wrote a letter to his mother complaining of a bad head cold: 'with that and the foetid atmosphere here (I) don't seem to have taken a decent breath for days.' But he concluded optimistically, 'the more blitzed we get, the more luck we seem to have against the enemy's ships.'[6] They could have had no inkling that that famous good fortune of theirs would shortly run out, although the present job was hardly routine. Another Army man had been embarked with Wilson. Bryant Bird watched his 'best mate' Lance Corporal Charles Parker go on board and was struck by a terrible premonition: 'None of our gang liked the spy jobs much — something always went wrong . . .'[7]

He might easily have gone in his place — at Wanklyn's request. But 24 hours before he had been detailed off for a mission with Boris Karnicki in *Sokol*, which in the event was cancelled at the last moment. And so another — albeit honorary — *Upholder* was left behind.

The two agents, whose mission was to gain information on the sailings of enemy transports from Africa to Sicily, would have to make their way ashore through rough surf and on recent experience Wilson knew a Folboat might easily capsize anyone unused to its ways. He requested an inflatable rubber dinghy for them from the RAF, which he proposed to tow in his canoe to the edge of the turbulent water surrounding the coast. It had to be inflated on deck, of course, and this made a fearful noise over the moonless sea as they arrived at their appointed billet on 9 April. Eventually Wilson had dinghy and Folboat lashed together on the narrow casing and as the submarine's main vents were opened to settle her lower in the water they were easily floated over the side. He paddled slowly away, straining against the pull of the dinghy with its cargo of spies and the modern paraphernalia of their ancient trade.

Soon he was lost to sight and the lookouts waited anxiously, forced to remain stopped on the surface against his return. But Wilson spotted the dark outline of the submarine's conning tower first as he made his way back, having successfully set his charges on their way. 'Pongo approaching!' he called softly through the gloom, 'operation successful'.[8] Wanklyn turned on the bridge, relieved to see his friend safely back, and quickly ordered the Folboat stowed before moving off to a rendezvous with *Unbeaten*.

She was waiting two miles west of the Lampion Rock off the island of Lampedusa and by the time they contacted her during the early hours of the 11th, the sea had roughened considerably. It had been planned that Wilson would transfer to *Unbeaten* and travel in her to Gibraltar on the first leg of a long voyage home to a well-deserved leave. But now this option looked decidedly risky. *Unbeaten* had been damaged during an air raid while lying on the bottom of Lazaretto Creek. Her torpedo tubes were badly twisted and she was operationally useless. But she was still more or less seaworthy and it had been decided she was fit to travel home for repairs. Wanklyn now offered the Army man the alternative of finishing the patrol with him — Simpson would arrange to fly him home, he said. Wilson only hesitated for a moment: 'Much as I love your company, David, I'll cross over to her and take my chances, if it's all the same to you.'[9]

It would be a fateful decision, and he might have regretted it a few moments later as he paddled his Folboat over to *Unbeaten* and heard her First Lieutenant shout down, only half-jokingly: 'Piss off, Tug — we've got two feet of water in the fore-ends and the batteries are gassing. You'll never make it to Gib.'[10] But he was well-used to

'Trade' humour by now — and, as he later informed Sydney Hart, he was himself troubled by no sense of unease over leaving *Upholder* behind. With him, however, he carried what was to be Wanklyn's last letter to his wife — and this was imbued with an odd strain of lyricism that is lacking in his earlier, quietly prosaic correspondence. In a strange passage of pure fantasy he suggests they go bathing together on his return to port:

'Would you like to come to Anchor Bay with me on Wednesday, or perhaps Sunday would be better?' he offers. 'I can't produce a car these days but perhaps someone would lend us bicycles for the day . . . Last week the flowers were lovely, masses of tiny wild iris, the orange blossom in full bloom and all the gardens a mass of colour.'

He then makes an abrupt switch — unintentionally hilarious in the context — to an account of the pigs' sufferings: 'one complete litter buried and three other tiny suckling pigs squashed. Two more were electrocuted the other day but were bled in time and made good pork . . .'

'Well, darling,' he concludes abruptly, 'count the days, they are not so many. Only 59.'[11]

He had written the letter the night before the rendezvous with *Unbeaten* — 'You would be amazed if you knew just how this one is going to reach you'. It would arrive home a few weeks later.

Wanklyn and *Upholder* now pass out of history and into legend. What follows is mostly conjecture. The only certainty is that on the afternoon of the following day they were moved, together with *Urge* and *Thrasher*, to set up a patrol line to meet yet another convoy heading out of Tripoli. The three submarines were expected to be in position early on the 15th. Sometime the day before Wanklyn may have fought his final duel — and the record would show his supposed last opponent to be worthy of the name.

Chapter 30
'A giant among us'

By a curious irony Capitano di Vascello the Barone Francesco Acton was descended from an old English family that could trace its roots much farther back than Wanklyn's own — from the beginning of the 14th century the main branch had its seat at Aldenham Hall in Shropshire. Sir John Acton, 6th Baronet (1736–1811), after distinguishing himself in the naval service of Tuscany, was to reorganise the Neapolitan Navy and rise in succession to be Minister of Marine War and finely Prime Minister of Naples during the Napoleonic era. The Fleet he built up — perhaps 120 of sail by 1798 — was later placed under the orders of Nelson.

Francesco numbered among his forebears several high-ranking officers of the Italian and Neapolitan navies. He was the son of Admiral of the Fleet Alfredo Acton, one-time Commander-in-Chief of his country's naval forces and the Italian representative to the Naval Conferences held at Washington and London in the inter-war years, who had been the Commander of the Combined Italo-British Cruiser Task Force during the battle of the Strait of Otranto of 15 May, 1917, when he flew his flag in HMS *Dartmouth*. Acton Senior had subsequently been decorated with the Military Order of the Bath. Francesco, born 24 August 1910, joined the Naval Academy at Livorno in 1926 — just a few months after Wanklyn entered Dartmouth. For a while, indeed, his career would almost exactly parallel Wanklyn's own. He opted for submarines about the same time and between 1934-39 was assigned to various patrols in the Mediterranean and Aegean in addition to others further east, to the Red Sea and Indian Ocean. Unknowingly, their paths might well have crossed during Wanklyn's spell in *Shark* during the Spanish Civil War. Perhaps his impeccable connections helped secure his appointments as Flag Lieutenant and Aide-de-Camp to the Commander-in-Chief 2nd Naval Squadron between 1939 and 1940 — but he later took part in most of the major Italian naval operations in the Mediterranean, was cited four times in the Joint Forces Bulletin and awarded no less than ten decorations. In September 1941 he was appointed Commanding Officer of the destroyer *Pegaso*, one of the most active units employed in escort duties to North Africa.

On 14 April 1942 *Pegaso* was in a group of destroyers guarding a convoy from Naples at Tripoli. At 3.47 p.m. they came under attack from 'numerous English dive bombers'.

'Shortly after this, at 16.15, one of our reconnaissance aircraft sighted a submarine. The sighting was subsequently confirmed by the sighting of a periscope. Given also that the submarine was detected by echo sounder, I proceeded immediately to attack the individual submarine using heavy depth charges. She disappeared following the prompt attack and echo sounder contact, and given the importance of escorting the convoy to its destination and ensuring its continuous anti-submarine and anti-aircraft protection, I resumed escort duty.

'Studying war reports and locations of operations conducted by submarines lost in the said period, we believe that *Pegaso's* operations of 14 April 1942 were launched against HMS *Upholder* . . .'[1]*

The sounds of a prolonged and heavy depth charging were carried across the Gulf of Sirte to both Tompkinson in *Urge* and Mackenzie in *Thrasher*. Sydney Hart was serving in *Thrasher* at this time and recalled that the Asdic operator twice tried to make contact with *Upholder* — at 8.30 p.m. on the 14th and 2.30 p.m. the following day — but without success.[2] The official view, endorsed by Simpson's later dispatch, agreed that this was probably how *Upholder* met her end.

But was it? Several of Wanklyn's brother officers preferred to believe, as some continue to maintain, that he struck a mine. For many, perhaps, the legend was too strong; it could not allow him to be the loser in a single, one-to-one contest. Simple bad luck was easier to understand and accept. Mackenzie, for one, still inclines to this view — but he had some evidence of his own to justify it.

'It's an odd thing — they always say he was depth charged and sunk by the Italians, but I don't think their records prove that unequivocally. We heard incessant depth charging going on most of the day and he was or or less in the next-door billet. We thought "Poor old Wanks — he's getting a hell of a bollocking." And then we went on our way. We were recalled to Alex and he to Malta and in one of the routine broadcasts we all listened in to, the morning he was due back, there came a message addressed to *Upholder* from SM10 saying "the radar put you six miles off Delamara Point" as though he had actually got home. And then maybe he was mined coming up the swept channel. That's what I always thought . . . I just wonder if he was sunk when they said he was or whether the radar had picked up something else. I've always had that doubt. So many of the Tenth Flotilla were lost from mines — they were being mined every night in the search channel and we had very few minesweepers so they couldn't really guarantee keeping it clear.'[3]

Michael St John is another who holds to the mining theory. He points out that it was common for boats to disappear on their last scheduled missions.

'People cut corners — they became desperately concerned with

---

* *Pegaso* was scuttled after the Armistice with Italy.

ever having a blank patrol. They would go out, some of them, for eight or nine patrols and come back with something in the bag each time, and then on the last patrol they were sent to what was supposedly a safe area — and that wouldn't be good enough. They cheated, they took risks in order not to come back empty-handed. Tubby Linton, another distinguished submarine VC, was coming back from a trip in a completely blank area of the Tyrhennian Sea when he intercepted a signal not addressed to him talking about a convoy leaving Maddalena. It was within striking distance so he diverted himself — and what he'd forgotten, which was what he should never have done, was that he hadn't been sent the latest "box" intelligence about new minefields . . .'

In Wanklyn's case, however, St John could only conclude that he must have been the victim of 'a frightful turn of fortune. I can't ever see him getting agitated on that score. I suppose the answer is, if you go on long enough — well, it's the law of averages . . .'[4]

When the news filtered through to Tubby Crawford, who was running escort groups out of Londonderry in *H50* (which had known Wanklyn, it will be remembered, six years before) he was equally fatalistic.

'Losses were so high at that time that if two of you sailed on patrol the same day the chances were that one of you wouldn't be coming back. You knew a chap like Wanklyn was always looking for the enemy and it was a toss of the dice which way it came out. So I wasn't surprised — just desperately sad.'[5]

His grief was reflected throughout the Submarine Service. Arthur Hezlet spoke for all the younger generation of submarine captains who had gained inspiration from Wanklyn when he wrote that his loss 'affected me more than any other incident I can recall during the war'.[6]

Others whose lives Wanklyn had only briefly touched were likewise moved to the depth of sorrow. Tuckwood looked up from his hospital bed to find a glum-looking Commando sitting beside him. 'A Sergeant from Nottingham, he was. I said "What's up with you then?" and he said "Well, I don't know how true it is — but you don't know how lucky you are . . ." It was quite a few minutes before he could tell me, he was that full up — he knew all the blokes, like I did. Anyway, he told me the rumour that the boat was lost and that set me off, too. And he came up a few days after and said "It was right — it's official . . ." '[7]

The destruction of *Upholder* and her gallant crew signalled the end — at least temporarily — of submarine operations out of Malta. Within a few days, following the elimination in the air and on the ground of most of the island's defending Spitfires, Simpson was forced to admit that his situation was untenable and he planned to evacuate to Alexandria. The Flotilla departed over the fortnight from

26 April. *Urge,* having sailed on the 27th, became overdue and it gradually became certain that she too must be added to the roll of those units 'still on patrol'. 'Lieutenant Commander E. P. Tompkinson, DSO and two bars, and his brave company had survived their close friends in *Upholder* by only two weeks,' Simpson mourned.[8] When *Olympus* met the same fate on 9 May — twelve survivors swimming six miles back to shore east of Valletta — Shrimp was close to despair: 'In three weeks about half my fine command had been killed,'[9] he wrote. All the personal effects of *Upholder's* crew had been stowed in her for return to their families, so these too were lost.

Betty Wanklyn was staying with her parents at Meigle when the news that her husband was missing was broken to her by the Chaplain from the nearby naval base at Dundee. To add to the strain of her bereavement, she was obliged to treat the information as confidential — 'to deny vital information to the enemy' — until the official announcement by the Admiralty, which would not follow until nearly four months had passed. Indeed, as Simpson write to her on 11 May, it had been 'largely for his safety that so little had been published to date of his astonishing successes'. He assured her that this consideration had much preoccupied him during *Upholder's* final series of operations — 'thinking not only of him and you but of his great value to the country. In February I asked David if he would care to go home since I could arrange it, but very naturally his ambition was to bring *Upholder* safely back with him. I had little reason to suppose this was tempting providence, he was so superbly confident.'

Scrupulously honest as ever, with himself as with anyone else, he could not hide the fact that he had privately welcomed his decision. 'As my most able captain and devoted friend I was most loath to part with him earlier than I had to — I only suggested it after feeling that his value to the Royal Navy and the whole country was such that I disliked the attendant responsibility.

'I have lost a friend and adviser who I believe I knew better than my brother . . . His record of brilliant leadership will never be equalled. He was by his very qualities of modesty, ability, determination, courage and character a giant among us. The island of Malta worshipped him. This tribute is no overstatement.'[10]

In the 16 months that *Upholder* had operated in the Mediterranean, Wanklyn had sunk two U-boats and damaged another, damaged a cruiser and a destroyer, and sunk or damaged 19 supply ships totalling 119,000 tons. These successes alone would qualify him as the top British submarine ace of the war, but there was, as Simpson observed, something more to his stature than was demonstrable by mere statistics. In a later tribute from the Admiralty, personally addressed to his widow, further remarks of Simpson's were quoted, dwelling on those qualities of leadership which had brought 'automatically the loyalty and maximum effort from all who served with him. As an example of this, during the past year, two or three worthless scamps have been drafted to *Upholder*, never again to appear at the Defaulter's table. Wanklyn had exceptional intellectual ability and judgment far beyond his years.'[11]

Simpson now revealed, however, that Wanklyn, after operating through March 'with his usual brilliance' had asked him if the redocking of *Upholder* could be changed with another submarine so that he could remain on the station a further two months and 'add to his bag'.[12] In this, perhaps, his judgment was finally at fault. Simpson had noticed his growing tiredness and refused the request.

For all the eulogies that the immediate aftermath of his death produced, it might have been expected that Wanklyn would soon be passed off as yet another sad casualty of a Service that knew grief in abundance. Yet the Lords of the Admiralty, normally so taciturn in such matters, also recognised that they had lost someone special. On 22 August the communique that officially proclaimed the news — reported in a blaze of publicity with photographs of Wanklyn and his friend Tompkinson, whose death was also announced — was a rare departure from the usual straightforward expression of regret:

'It is seldom proper for their Lordships to draw distinctions between different services rendered in the course of normal duty, but they take this opportunity of singling out those of the *Upholder*, under the command of Lieutenant Commander Wanklyn, for special mention. She was long employed against enemy communications in the Central Mediterranean. Such was the standard of skill and daring set by Lieutenant Commander Wanklyn and the officers and men under him, that they and their ship became an inspiration not only to their own Flotilla but to the Fleet of which it was a part, and Malta where for so long the *Upholder* was based.'[13]

'I think they did that because of the name *Upholder* had made and Wanklyn himself had set such a fine example of leadership,' said Tubby Crawford. 'He was looked up to — and they were such a fine team. Tompkinson and so on were respected, but I think Wanklyn was the tops.'[14]

The rest of Wanklyn's brother officers thought the same and determined to have a permanent reminder of him. In November his mother received a letter from the Wardroom mess president at HMS *Dolphin* informing her of their decision to commission the Royal Academician Harry Morley to paint his portrait. Never having met his subject, Morley had to build up the picture from photographs and information given by his family and the men who had served under him.

'It would have been very easy for me to make mistakes in detail,' he confessed. 'For example, one always thinks of naval men as having ruddy, weather-beaten complexions. But I was told that submarine men don't see much sunlight and they are not exposed very often to the weather.' This last was not, one must presume, a notion any submarine watchkeeper who had spent many nights on a storm-swept open bridge would agree with — but Morley was correct in inferring that Wanklyn's face, 'like most submarine officers', was rather pale.'[15]

And so he painted him, pale and full bearded on the conning tower, staring keenly at the horizon, his hands resting on a pair of binoculars — but here in one detail the artist was indeed mistaken. The hands belonged to a friend of his, a picture restorer who worked in a nearby studio, and they were, as befitted his trade, quite small and delicate. 'David's', his sister gleefully pointed out, 'although likewise capable of both gentleness and precision, were enormous — like great bunches of bananas.'[16]

In spite of this (possibly fortunate) defect the finished portrait was well received by family and Service alike — although Wanklyn's mother actually preferred the preliminary sketch, in spite of its having awarded him a cauliflower ear which he also did not possess in life. This she was able to buy for the token fee of a halfpenny and it now hangs in the Submarine Museum at Gosport. The portrait itself was first shown at the Royal Academy Exhibition on 1 May 1943 and now enjoys pride of place in the Wardroom at HMS *Dolphin* — the Submarine Service's Alma Mater.

Betty's own gift to her husband's memory reflected the quiet conviction of his religious belief. Learning that the font in the chapel at *Dolphin* was not in keeping with its surroundings — the whole internal architecture is of plain English oak with no decoration beyond the colour supplied by the badges of submarines set around its walls — she asked the Dockyard carpenters to construct a replacement, eventually installed to complement the place's 'peaceful simplicity and source of inspiration'.

Her first concern had been for the widows and children of the crew. But she was dissuaded from the idea of setting up a special fund, Rear Admiral R. B. Darke — who commanded HMS *Dolphin* throughout the war — having assured her that 'all necessitous cases'[17] would be dealt with through the Royal Benevolent Trust, to which all submarine flotillas contributed through a special Submarine Dependents' Fund.

In truth, her own situation was hardly comfortable. She was left with a modest pension based on her husband's pay, with £36 allowed for her infant son, and she was soon forced to find employment. She took a job for a while 'as a sort of nursery governess' at Shaftesbury in Dorset, and it was from here that she travelled up to Buckingham Palace on 2 March 1943 to receive her husband's decorations from King George VI. Three-year-old Ian was among half a dozen sad-faced little boys whose photographs, taken immediately after the investiture, were spread across two pages of the *Daily Mirror*. They had been unable to match the dutiful smiles offered by their mothers and perhaps the pictures, as they so often are, were most honest than the text that accompanied them. Of Ian it was said: 'His father is dead. But all he can understand about the VC, DSO and two bars which the King has given to Mummy is that they are pretty things and are nice to hold.'[18]

For Betty the ceremony had been an ordeal — as the ever-solicitous Tubby Crawford had anticipated. He had kept up his correspondence with her (though they would not actually meet for over 30 years) and ventured the hope that it had not been 'too nerve-wracking — I'm sure the King and Queen were very kind to you.'[19]

As it happened, all the King had asked her was the date David left Dartmouth — 'and it was so embarrassing because I didn't know . . .'[20]

While in London she stayed with a friend who fell ill with measles. Her employers at Shaftesbury would not allow her to return in case she passed the infection to their child and she was invited to stay at Tonbridge with Lady Campbell, whose son had been a page at her wedding five years before. Thence she moved to Chesham, to a gardener's cottage belonging to some friends, and eventually a flat was provided for her in London through the Officers' Families Fund. Somewhere along the way Crawford lost touch with her. She attended the unveiling of various memorials through the years — her husband's name, for want of any location more closely connected with him, was inscribed on the simple stone at Meigle. In 1957 she was invited to launch the submarine *Cachalot*. It was not until 19 March 1975, when she arrived at HMS *Dolphin* for the inauguration of new sports and accommodation blocks there, one of which was named for her husband, that the two finally met. In November that year Crawford and his wife took her to Malta for the dedication of a window and plaque comemmorating the Tenth Flotilla at St Paul's Cathedral in the island's capital.

Ian Wanklyn entered Dartmouth in 1958. His naval career took him to Malta in the carrier *Ark Royal* — where he was photographed by the *Times of Malta* conducting a tour of the ship for the island's Ladies' International Society. It would be one of his last appointments. In 1977 he left the Navy to take a business management course and is now marketing director of a company specialising in hospital equipment. In 1971 he had married Penelope Malins, the daughter of Captain Charles Wickham Malins, DSO, DSC* — a distinguished destroyer commander who had twice been decorated for sinking enemy submarines in the Mediterranean. Betty Wanklyn, now settled at Bexhill-on-Sea, has three grandchildren who come to stay with her in the school holidays.

Crawford was taking *Tireless* to the Far East when the war ended.

His last submarine command before his return to General Service was *Artemis* in 1950–51. He was eventually promoted Captain and was placed on the retired list in 1968 after a happy return to Malta as Commodore Superintendent. He was then for 12 years the Flag Officer Submarines' Publications Officer at Gosport, having his home nearby in Southsea. On 14 November 1989 he attended the launch of the second of the new Upholder Class submarines, named for his own wartime command, *Unseen*.

Of the other *Upholder* survivors, the Rev Christopher Read now lives at Dornoch in Staffordshire. George Curnall married his childhood sweetheart and took up carpentry after the war. He left his turbulent youth behind him and progressed in the building trade to become a site agent. One of his grandsons has joined the Army Maritime Regiment and the other, at the time of writing, is also hoping for a career at sea. 'It must be something in the blood,' says George.

Gordon Selby's submarine career continued through the war. He now lives in Ingleside, New South Wales. Through the Australian Submarines Association he maintains close links with his wartime colleagues. He met the wife of his most celebrated skipper for the first time in 1986, at a lunch given by Crawford after the launch of the new *Upholder*.

Charles Tuckwood, spared her predecessor's last dive by what for him was truly 'the kindest cut of all', returned in 1945 to his pre-war job as a milkman at Enderby, Leicesteshire, where he lives to this day.

Pat Norman completed 19 patrols, including 15 in his own highly successful command, *Una*. After the war he commanded a frigate in the Far East and was First Lieutenant of the new battleship *Vanguard*. He learnt to fly and saw service in carriers before being promoted Captain in 1954. His last job was as Captain of HMS *Ganges*, the legendary boys' training ship at Ipswich. He left the Navy in 1964 and was appointed Deputy Director of the British Wood Preserving Association. The harbour at Poole, where he now lives with his second wife Marion, is lined with his experiments with non-durable timbers. His grandson has returned to the family Army tradition as an officer in the Royal Electrical and Mechanical Engineers.

Michael St John, successfully completing his Perisher after leaving *Upholder* at the end of 1940, took command in succession of *L26*, *Tuna* and *Traveller*. The latter was lost in the Gulf of Taranto while he lay sick ashore at Malta with dysentery. His last submarine was *Totem* — later sold to Israel, she mysteriously disappeared during her delivery voyage. He left the Navy in 1955 to run a light engineering company. Married with three children he now lives in peaceful rural seclusion at Heyshott in West Sussex, where he spends much of his time tape recording books for the blind.

The rest of Tug Wilson's eventful career is detailed in Rex Wood's biography *Special Commando* (William Kimber 1985). The last man to see Wanklyn alive made his tenth and final folboat expedition in September 1942 — 'which earned him a Bar to his DSO but also landed him in an Italian prisoner-of-war camp'. Twice he tried to escape and on recapture the second time narrowly avoided execution by the SS, who suspected him of being either a Communist or a spy. He was finally sent to Oflag 79 near Brunswick where he endured nearly a year of privation and anxiety under 'the added risk of being hit by Allied bombs — American by day and British by night.' The camp was actually hit on one occasion and three officers were killed. Under this incessant pounding the supply of Red Cross parcels dried up and by the time of his liberation on 12 April 1945 his weight had dropped to eight stone. He went on to serve in Palestine and Korea, where he earned a Mention in Despatches, and was Commanding Officer of the 37th Heavy Anti-Aircraft Regiment when he returned to Malta en route for Suez in 1956. Lieutenant Colonel Wilson later took voluntary retirement to become Army Careers Officer for Warwickshire — a post he held until 1973. He now lives with his wife Marjorie in Leamington Spa.

Corporal Bryant Bird was demobbed on 26 March 1946 and was later self-employed as a blacksmith and farrier. He went into semi-retirement after his 65th birthday at the end of 1984.

Several of Wanklyn's contemporaries who survived the war went on to achieve high rank. Hugh Mackenzie was Flag Officer Submarines in the early 1960s and Chief Polaris Executive from 1963 until 1968 when he retired as a Vice-Admiral. For ten years he directed the Atlantic Salmon Research Trust, of which he is now vice-president. He is also vice-chairman of the Salmon and Trout Association — 'likely the sort of thing Wanklyn himself might have done'.[21]

Hezlet had preceded 'Rufus' Mackenzie as Flag Officer Submarines, after which he too was promoted Vice Admiral. His last job before his retirement in 1964 was as Flag Officer Scotland and Northern Ireland. His book *The Submarine and Sea Power* (1967) was quickly complemented by a companion volume, the equally authoritative *Aircraft and Sea Power*.

Shrimp Simpson got his flag together with the customary CB — rather scant reward, some have observed, for his efforts described here and in his own memoirs. A few months before their publication in 1972 he died suddenly in New Zealand, where he had spent his last years as a sheep farmer. The book was written 'as a duty and as a tribute to my men of the Tenth Submarine Flotilla at Malta, of whom more than half were killed in action'.

At the end of July 1942 the Flotilla had been able to reassemble at Lazaretto but by then only four veterans of its finest hour were left,

Pat Norman's *Una* among them. Reinforcements from Gibraltar — including *Unbroken*, Alistair Mars' famous command — made up the numbers. Simpson handed over to Captain George Phillips in January 1943 and the 'Fighting Tenth' continued at Malta until November that year, when it moved to Maddalena in the Straits of Bonifacio — ironically the former base for the Italian Tenth Submarine Flotilla. After the Allied landings in southern France in August 1944 the base was closed down and the Flotilla dispersed.

Simpson was Commodore 'D' Western Approaches for the last two years of the war and afterwards had his introduction to the country where he was to make his home when he was appointed First Naval Member and Chief of the New Zealand Naval Staff. He was Flag Officer Germany and Chief British Naval Representative on the Allied Control Commission and retired as Flag Officer Submarines in 1954 — but he had truly reached the pinnacle of his career over a decade before. Vice Admiral Sir John Roxburgh would note that 'few officers (and Shrimp was only a Commander at the time) can have been given such an unfettered directive to operate an important command as he was in January 1941 by Admiral Cunningham from his headquarters in Alexandria: "If you don't get results and don't dispose your forces to suit me I will soon let you know. Until then you have a free hand to act as you think best to achieve your objective." The results Shrimp achieved with his submarines at Malta undoubtedly prove what a sound leader he was.'[22]

Would Wanklyn have moved on to reach distinction beyond his wartime exploits? Crawford remarks that 'no-one, pre-war, had marked him as a future First Sea Lord. He was a perfectly ordinary, straightforward, good officer, though he had all the right qualities for senior rank. He certainly showed his leadership. Perhaps the war situation brought it out or it was there all the time. I think probably the latter was true, but the war emphasised it. He wasn't a pushy sort of chap . . .'[23]

It may be that in peacetime a certain lack of political drive would have denied him the ultimate laurels of Flag rank. In his prosecution of the tasks required of him by the exigencies of war no-one could accuse him of diffidence, though his tenacity in attack time and again overcame the sort of difficulties others might have considered to pose an unacceptable risk. His professional ability usually won him through — although Crawford again observes that he was 'no innovator',[24] merely a superb practitioner of accepted tactics.

These speculations are inevitably inconclusive but not definitely idle. A leading graphologist who has had the opportunity to explore Wanklyn's correspondence inferred, without the benefit of any other insights, that he was dealing with 'a very complex character — so complex, in fact, that if two people were asked to describe him their descriptions could vary to such an extent that a third party might wonder if they were describing the same person'.[25] His conclusions are set out in Appendix 2. It is easy to view such a study as a curiosity, although psychologists recognise the value of handwriting as an illustration of personality. In this case the examination throws up a number of points that give weight to the observations of the witnesses to character quoted here and others that appear so much at variance with the received view that one would expect them to be vehemently discounted. Whether, for instance, Wanklyn was driven by an inferiority complex that 'lay at the root of his quest for power'[26] may be worth pursuing. But did his ambition 'blind him to the sensitivity and needs of others so that he could easily become oblivious to their feelings, needs and limitations'?[27] I don't think so — nor, I suspect, would many of his familiars describe him as 'starchy', certainly not 'to those whom he considered his inferiors'.[28] He got on rather better with them, according to those who were his social equals — and markedly less well, from all the evidence, with most of his superiors. This does, perhaps, suggest that a degree of insecurity may have been part of a contradictory make-up that, on the surface at least, always gave the impression of the utmost confidence.

Wanklyn's early life was unsettled and as the younger brother, both at home and at boarding school, the competitive instinct must have been instilled in him early. Taken to an extreme, this could well have driven him to the sort of behaviour that could 'swing dramatically from reckless bravado to sulky broodiness'.[28] There is evidence enough for both extremes. For the first, one might cite the early morning attack on 1 December 1941, begun on the surface in the midst of a densely escorted convoy, that so petrified Pat Norman; for the second there is his curious attitude to the result of what was probably his most notable achievement — the attack on the liners *Neptunia* and *Oceania*, which left him 'morose and disgusted' with what he viewed as a lucky strike in which skill had played no part.

If he was, according to the basic assessment of both the graphologist and of Crawford, with whom he had a close working relationship, primarily a conventional personality whose ideas were unoriginal, contributing little to the furtherance of submarine warfare, what explains his appeal in a Service that hugs to its bosom a whole gallery of colourful, quixotic characters?

There was something other-worldly about him — and a certain naivety that, set alongside a lucky instinct, a sometimes dazzling operational expertise and a genuine, pastoral care for the individual, made for an irresistible combination. It was the men, the ordinary seamen, who thought of him as 'one of us', rather than his fellow officers. Simpson, who of the latter probably knew him best, has noted that he was less assertive than, say, Tompkinson at the conference table. And it is in that green baize jungle that reputations are consolidated in the administrative power struggles that honest men are proud to despise. Popular heroes — and Wanklyn was one, within his sphere — often fail in this regard, but this seldom costs them the respect and affection of either those who served with them or who follow on in the same tradition.

Leonard Hussey wrote of Sir Ernest Shackleton some lines that distill the essence of leadership at a personal level — and mirror so exactly the feelings of those who served under Wanklyn that they may deservedly be repeated here in his name:

'. . . he expected perfection in no man; but he was quite willing to overlook what was bad and just remembered the good in everyone. He had a way of compelling loyalty. We would have gone anywhere without question just on his order . . . Now that he has gone, there is a gap in our lives that can never be filled.'[30]

The Admiralty communique that announced the loss of *Upholder* concluded with a simple epitaph that has remained above her unknown tomb ever since — the best-known valedictory in the annals of the Submarine Service:

'The ship and her company are gone, but the example and the inspiration remain.'[31]

Appendix 1

Still on patrol —
the crew of HMS Upholder

Officers: Lieutenant Commander David Wanklyn, RN
Lieutenant P. R. H. Allen, RN
Temporary Sub-Lieutenant J. H. Norman, RNVR
Lieutenant Francis Ruck-Keene, RN

Ratings   Petty Officer Telegraphist William Anderson
Leading Telegraphist Leopold Blake
Engine Room Artificer Norman Board
Able Seaman Thomas Brown
Engine Room Artificer Charles Burgoyne
Acting Leading Seaman Robert Davidson
Able Seaman George Foster
Acting Chief Engine Room Artificer Frederick Frame
Ordinary Telegraphist Edmond Gregory
Stoker Petty Officer Frederick Gregory
Acting Leading Stoker Alfred Heath
Able Seaman Gwilym Hughes
Able Seaman Francis Lane
Acting Petty Officer Frederick Martin
Able Seaman David Miller
Stoker Second Class Edward Munday
Telegraphist Patrick Newlands
Leading Seaman John Partleton, RFR
Leading Stoker Frederick Perkins
Acting Leading Stoker John Rowe
Acting Leading Seaman Lambert Saunders
Stoke First Class Ernest Self
Leading Signalman Rex Simmonds
Able Seaman George Smith
Able Seaman James Smith
Petty Officer John Swainston
Acting Leading Stoker Fred Topping
Leading Seaman William Turner

To *Upholder's* Roll of Honour must be added the name of Lance Corporal Charles Parker of the Beds and Herts Regiment, who embarked with Captain Wilson for her final patrol, remaining on board after the latter transferred to HMS *Unbeaten*. It was thanks to the efforts of his friend Corporal Bryant Bird that he finally joined the list of her company in the Ministry of Defence archives on 22 May 1986.

Analysis of handwriting by Alexander R. Tulloch MA, AG (Dip), Director of Research, the Academy of Graphology, London

(The following study is based on a series of letters written by Lieutenant Commander Wanklyn which span the period of his command of HMS *Upholder*. It was reasonable to suppose that the strains of a long and largely uninterrupted campaign might have been shown up in a graphological examination — and my sole purpose in commissioning it was to chart the progress of any physical or mental deterioration they might have brought about. To those who from personal observation have testified to the strength of character of the subject the fact that, as I am assured, no such decline can be traced will come as no surprise. It is a remarkable document, nonetheless, for having presented a number of conjectural opinions which seem to me entirely apposite — though perhaps as many appear to be definitely insupportable. Mr. Tulloch's conclusions are bound to be controversial; they are reproduced here in their entirety.)

'Basically a conventional personality whose thinking processes were rapid but unoriginal. He had the capacity to concentrate on a given problem but could easily be carried away if his feelings were aroused and this could have a negative effect on his judgment. In fact, his judgment was not particularly good and he was more of an "action man" than a thinker with a constitutional impetuosity which frequently caused him to throw caution to the wind and adopt a "devil take the hindmost" approach. He was a very passionate man (in all senses of the word) who would drive himself — and others — to the limit and beyond. The combination of a tendency to "live on his nerves" and a driving ambition could blind him to the sensitivity and needs of others so that he could easily become oblivious to their feelings, needs and limitations.

'He was determined and aggressive and frequently possessed of a diminished ability to see the other person's point of view. This was emphasised by a starchy and reserved attitude, particularly to those whom he considered his inferiors, and a pronounced ability to cut himself off emotionally from others so that he could operate without hindrance and concentrate on getting the job in hand completed.

'He was not an easy man to get on with and inspired respect and awe rather than love or affection. Very few people would have been able to get close to this writer and his stubborn, obsessional and ruthless ambition made him a loner disinclined to seek, or feel relaxed in, the company of others. He could also be pedantic, suspicious and very inscrutable.

'The aggressive nature of this writer makes it easy to see how he would have been able to "discover himself" in wartime. Living under the constant threat of danger would have been no problem for him. On the contrary, the war would have provided him with a natural outlet for personality traits which he might otherwise have found difficult to channel. His energy, drive and impetuousness could easily produce the "hero" who thrived on dangerous, risky missions. Add this to his genuinely felt, intense patriotism and conservatism and we see a man who would be more than willing to risk, and possibly sacrifice, his life for his country. On the other hand, however, such tendencies could lead to problems in peacetime and may have produced problems of social adjustment.

'Psychologically, the writer was not without his problems. His behaviour could swing dramatically from reckless bravado to sulky broodiness. He was predominantly an introvert who kept things very much bottled up inside him. There was also a rebelliousness in his make-up existing alongside a basic desire to live according to the rules and a respect for law and order, traditions and principles. This was not unconnected with other anxieties he experienced arising from the conflict between powerful, instinctual urges and his personal morality and self-discipline. The fight between the Angel and the Beast in this man produced a repressed and inhibited personality with more than his fair share of emotional problems.

'There is also evidence in the handwriting that the outlet his anxieties found in acts of military bravado was, to a certain extent, a "cover up" for an inferiority complex. He was driven by the need to prove himself and by consuming aspirations. Also, his outwardly self-confident and/or assertive personality concealed a sensitivity which few would have detected in him. Evidence of this is provided by his pronounced tendency to take relatively mild criticism very much to heart and an inability to easily forgive or forget. An inferiority complex was also at the root of his quest for power and prestige and generated in the writer a conviction that life is nothing more than a series of struggles emanating from an environment which he perceived as being essentially hostile.

'On a more positive note the writer had a profound sense of responsibility and was an "upright member of the community". He could be severe, but always fair and straightforward with a pronounced sense of justice.'

Bibliography

BRADFORD, Ernle *Siege: Malta 1940–43* Hamish Hamilton, 1985

CAMERON, Ian *Red Ensign, White Duster* Muller, 1959

CIANO, Count Galeazzo Diaries 1937–38

COMPTON HALL, Commander Richard *Submarine Warfare — Monsters and Midgets* Blandford Press, 1985

COCKER, M. P. *Royal Naval Submarines 1901–1982* Warne, 1982

COOK, Graham *Silent Marauders* Hart Davis, MacGibbon, 1976

EDWARDS, Jill *The British Government and the Spanish Civil War* Macmillan, 1979

HART, Sydney *Submarine Upholder* Oldbourne Book Co. Ltd., 1960

JACKSON, Gabriel *A Concise History of the Spanish Civil War* Thames and Hudson, 1974

LIPSCOMB, Commander F. W. *The British Submarine* A. & C. Black, 1954

MACINTYRE, Donald *The Battle for the Mediterranean* Batsford, 1964

MARS, Commander Alistair *British Submarines at War 1939–1945* William Kimber, 1971

MASTERS, David *Up Periscope* Eyre and Spottiswoode, 1942

SIMPSON, Rear Admiral G. W. G. *Periscope View* Macmillan, 1972

STAFFORD, Commander E. P. *The Far and the Deep* Arthur Barker, 1968

THOMAS, Hugh *The Spanish Civil War* Hamish Hamilton, 1977

TURNER, J. F. *VCs of the Royal Navy* George Harrap, 1956

WOODS, R. *Special Commando* William Kimber, 1985

Source References

Copies of letters and transcripts of interviews have been deposited with the Royal Navy Submarine Musuem

Chapter 1 'A fitting and a most humbling occasion'
1. *Barrow Evening Mail*, 2.12.86
2. *Daily Mirror*, 3.12.86

Chapter 2 Out of Argentina
1. *The Buenos Aires Standard*, 7.3.1897
2. *Illustrated London News*, 28.8.1875
3. Letter from Peter Wanklyn to Mrs E. Wanklyn, 18.12.86
4. Miss J. Wanklyn, interview with the author
5. Ibid
6. James Pope-Hennessey *Queen Mary* George Allen and Unwin, 1959

Chapter 3 Wanklyn Minimus
1. Miss J. Wanklyn op cit
2. Ibid
3. Letter from Peter Wanklyn, op cit
4. Miss J. Wanklyn, op cit
5. Ibid
6. Letter from Jack Wanklyn to Peter Wanklyn
7. Ibid
8. Miss J. Wanklyn, op cit
9. Ibid
10. Surgeon Captain Frank Golden, interview with the author

Chapter 4 'Very much his own person'
1. Letter from Jack Wanklyn, op cit
2. Miss J. Wanklyn, letter to the author
3. Letter from Lt Cdr Dick Raikes to the author, 31.1.87
4. Ibid
5. Mrs E. Wanklyn, interview with the author
6. Miss J. Wanklyn, interview with the author
7. Sydney Hart *Submarine Upholder* Oldbourne Book Co. Ltd., 1960
8. Vice Admiral Sir Peter Gretton, letter to the author, 17.2.87
9. Miss J. Wanklyn, op cit
10. Ibid
11. Letter from Jack Wanklyn, op cit

Chapter 5 'A mode of warfare which those who command the sea do not want'
1. Rear Admiral G. W. G. Simpson *Periscope View* Macmillan, 1972, P24
2. Cdr Richard Compton Hall *Submarine Warfare — Monsters and Midgets* Blandford Press, 1985
3. *Chatham Evening Post*, April 1975
4. Rear Admiral G. W. G. Simpson, op cit, P54
5. *Illustrated London News*, October 24, 1931
6. Sydney Hart, op cit, P24
7. Captain C. P. Norman, interview with the author
8. Ibid
9. Miss J. Wanklyn, op cit
10. Mrs E. Wanklyn, op cit
11. Ibid
12. Ibid

Chapter 6 'Franco's lot were the worst'
1. Gabriel Jackson *A Concise History of the Spanish Civil War* Thames and Hudson, 1974, P144
2. Hugh Thomas *The Spanish Civil War* Hamish Hamilton, 1977, P734
3. Jill Edwards *The British Government and the Spanish Civil War* Macmillan, 1979, P101
4. Hugh Thomas, op cit P739

5. *Janes Fighting Ships* 1936
6. Count Galeazzo Ciano *Diaries 1937–38*
7. Gabriel Jackson, op cit P148
8. Count G. Ciano, op cit
9. Captain C. P. Norman, op cit
10. Ibid
11. Ibid
12. Ibid
13. Ibid
14. Ibid
15. Mr. W. Curtis, interview with the author, 7.5.87
16. Captain C. P. Norman, op cit
17. Jill Edwards, op cit P105
18. Hugh Thomas, op cit P743
19. Miss J. Wanklyn, interview with the author, 31.3.87
20. Mr W. Curtis, op cit
21. Jill Edwards, op cit
22. Gabriel Jackson, op cit P148
23. Jill Edwards, op cit P127

Chapter 7   'Very close to him, in his problems'

1. Mrs Stella Danvers, interview with the author
2. Mrs E. Wanklyn, interview with the author
3. Ibid
4. Ibid
5. Ibid
6. Ibid
7. Captain C. P. Norman, op cit
8. Captain Jock Bethell, quoted by Captain G. W. G. Simpson, op cit
9. Rear Admiral G. W. G. Simpson, op cit
10. Vice Admiral Sir John Roxburgh, Foreward to *Periscope View* by Rear Admiral G. W. G. Simpson
11. Cdr Michael St John, interview with the author
12. Rear Admiral G. W. Gay, letter to the author, 12.2.87
13. Rear Admiral G. W. G. Simpson, op cit
14. Ibid
15. Ibid
16. Rear Admiral G. W. Gay, op cit
17. Rear Admiral G. W. G. Simpson, op cit
18. Mrs E. Wanklyn, op cit
19. Collection of Mrs E. Wanklyn
20. Mrs E. Wanklyn, op cit
21. Rear Admiral G. W. G. Simpson, op cit
22. Rear Admiral G. W. Gay, op cit
23. Ibid
24. Cdr E. P. Stafford, USN *The Far and the Deep* Arthur Barker, 1968
25. Cdr Richard Compton Hall *Submarine, The News*, Portsmouth Special Issue
26. Cdr E. P. Stafford, op cit

Chapter 8   'Our chances weren't going to be very good'

1. Vice Admiral Sir Hugh Mackenzie, interview with the author, 5.2.87
2. Captain Pat Norman, op cit
3. Captain G. W. G. Simpson, op cit
4. Vice Admiral Sir Hugh Mackenzie, op cit
5. Ibid
6. Cdr Dick Raikes, letter to the author, 31.1.87
7. Mr F. Matthews, letter to the author, 5.4.87
8. Ibid
9. Ibid

Chapter 9   'Little chance of shooting up a Hun'

1. Mr F. Matthews, op cit
2. Vice Admiral Sir Hugh Mackenzie, op cit
3. PRO ADM
4. Mr F. Matthews, op cit
5. Ibid
6. Lt Cdr M. D. Wanklyn, letter to his mother 6.11.39

7. Lt Cdr M. D. Wanklyn, letter to his mother 2.1.40
8. Vice Admiral Sir Hugh Mackenzie, op cit
9. Lt Cdr M. D. Wanklyn, letter to his mother, 2.2.40
10. Lt Cdr M. D. Wanklyn, letter to his mother, 15.2.40
11. J. Philip-Nichols *Happy Days in H32, Ships Monthly*, July 1979
12. Ibid
13. Ibid
14. Lt Cdr M. D. Wanklyn, letter to his mother, undated
15. Mrs E. Wanklyn, op cit
16. Rear Admiral G. W. G. Simpson, op cit
17. Ibid
18. PRO ADM 199/1828
19. Ibid
20. Mrs E. Wanklyn, op cit
21. Cdr Dick Raikes, op cit
22. Mrs E. Wanklyn, op cit

Chapter 10   'An almost intuitive perception'

1. Mr G. Curnall, letter to the author, 31.1.87
2. Cdr M. St John, interview with the author, 10.3.87
3. Captain M. L. C. Crawford *Profile Warship 16 — HM S/M Upholder* Profile Publications Ltd, 1972
4. Sydney Hart, op cit
5. Captain M. L. C. Crawford, op cit
6. Mrs E. Wanklyn, op cit
7. Cdr M. St John, op cit
8. Lt Cdr M. D. Wanklyn, letter to his mother, 9.10.40
9. Mrs E. Wanklyn, op cit
10. Miss J. Wanklyn, interview with author, op cit
11. Cdr M. St John, op cit
12. Miss J. Wanklyn, op cit
13. Cdr M. St John, op cit
14. Ibid
15. Ibid
16. Captain M. L. C. Crawford, interview with the author, 19.1.87
17. Ibid
18. Sydney Hart, op cit
19. Donald MacIntyre *The Battle for the Mediterranean* B. T. Batsford, 1964
20. Cdr F. W. Lipscomb *The British Submarine* A. & C. Black, 1954, P168
21. Rear Admiral G. W. G. Simpson, op cit

Chapter 11   The Illustrious Blitz

1. Rear Admiral G. W. G. Simpson, op cit
2. Ian Cameron *Red Ensign, White Duster* Muller, 1959
3. Ernle Bradford *Siege: Malta 1940–1943* Hamish Hamilton, 1985
4. Ibid
5. Ibid
6. G. Selby, notes compiled for the author, 5.12.86
7. Rear Admiral G. W. G. Simpson, op cit
8. Captain M. L. C. Crawford *Profile Warship 16 — HM S/M Upholder*, op cit
9. Ernle Bradford, op cit
10. Ibid
11. Ian Cameron, op cit
12. Rear Admiral G. W. G. Simpson, op cit

Chapter 12   By guess and by God

1. Sydney Hart, op cit
2. Vice Admiral Sir Hugh Mackenzie, op cit
3. Richard Compton Hall *The Professionals*
4. Ibid
5. PRO ADM 236/48
6. Sydney Hart, op cit
7. PRO ADM 236/48
8. Ibid
9. Vice Admiral Sir Hugh Mackenzie, op cit
10. Ibid
11. PRO ADM 236/48

12. Vice Admiral Sir Hugh Mackenzie, op cit

Chapter 13   'Obviously a very disappointed man'
1. PRO ADM 236/48
2. Sydney Hart, op cit
3. Captain M. L. C. Crawford, interview with the author, 19.1.87
4. Sydney Hart, op cit
5. PRO ADM 236/48
6. Ibid
7. Ibid
8. Ibid
9. Ibid
10. Ibid
11. Ibid
12. Ibid
13. Ibid
14. Ibid
15. Ernle Bradford, op cit
16. Ibid
17. Richard Compton Hall *The Professionals*
18. Ibid
19. PRO ADM 236/48
20. Ibid
21. Ibid
22. Ibid
23. Ibid
24. Ibid
25. Ibid
26. Rear Admiral G. W. G. Simpson, op cit
27. Captain M. L. C. Crawford, interview with the author, 19.1.87

Chapter 14   Plain butchery
1. Rear Admiral G. W. G. Simpson, op cit, P128
2. Ibid, P128
3. Ibid, P129–30
4. Captain C. P. Norman, op cit
5. Rear Admiral G. W. G. Simpson, op cit, P130
6. Captain M. L. C. Crawford *Profile Warship 16 — HM S/M Upholder* P83

Chapter 15   'The spell is broken'
1. PRO ADM 236/48
2. Captain M. L. C. Crawford *Profile Warship 16 — HM S/M Upholder* P86
3. PRO ADM 236/48
4. Captain M. L. C. Crawford *Profile Warship 16 — HM S/M Upholder* P87
5. Sydney Hart, op cit, P58
6. The Rev C. Read, letter to the author
7. Ibid
8. Sydney Hart, op cit, P59
9. Captain M. L. C. Crawford *Profile Warship 16 — HM S/M Upholder* P86
10. PRO ADM 236/48
11. The Rev C. Read, op cit
12. PRO ADM 236/48

Chapter 16   'The oldest jacket imaginable'
1. Lt Cdr M D Wanklyn, letter to Peter Wanklyn, 10.5.41
2. Alistair Mars *British Submarines at War 1939–1945* William Kimber, 1971, P169
3. Ibid
4. Ibid
5. Captain C. P. Norman, op cit
6. Captain M. L. C. Crawford, interview with the author, 19.1.87
7. Captain C. P. Norman, op cit
8. Lt Cdr M. D. Wanklyn, letter to Peter Wanklyn, 10.5.41
9. Lt Cdr M. D. Wanklyn, letter to his mother, 11.5.41
10. Read Admiral G. W. G. Simpson, op cit P136
11. Ibid P122
12. Captain C. P. Norman, op cit
13. Captain M. L. C. Crawford, interview with the author, 19.1.87

14. Lt Cdr M. D. Wanklyn, letter to his mother, 11.5.87
15. David Masters *Up Periscope* Eyre and Spottiswoode, 1942 P171-72
16. Ibid
17. Mr C. F. Tuckwood, interview with the author, 23.3.87
18. Richard Compton Hall *Submarine Warfare — Monsters and Midgets*
19. Mr C. F. Tuckwood, op cit
20. Mrs J. Harris, interview with the author, 6.2.87

Chapter 17   The sinking of the *Conte Rosso*

1. Captain M. L. C. Crawford *Profile Warship 16 — HM S/M Upholder*
2. Ibid
3. PRO ADM 236/48
4. Ibid
5. Ibid
6. Captain M. L. C. Crawford, interview with the author, 19.1.87
7. PRO ADM 236/48
8. Lt Cdr M. D. Wanklyn — Victoria Cross Citation
9. Captain M. L. C. Crawford, interview with the author, 19.1.87
10. Sydney Hart, op cit P79
11. Captain M. L. C. Crawford, interview with the author, 19.1.87
12. Captain M. L. C. Crawford *Profile Warship 16 — HM S/M Upholder*
13. Captain M. L. C. Crawford, interview with the author, 19.1.87
14. Sydney Hart, op cit P80
15. Mr G. Curnall, letter to the author, 31.1.87
16. Lt Cdr M. D. Wanklyn — Victoria Cross Citation
17. PRO ADM 236/48
18. Rear Admiral G. W. G. Simpson, op cit P142
19. Captain M. L. C. Crawford, interview with the author, 19.1.87
20. Captain C. P. Norman, op cit
21. Vice Admiral Sir Hugh Mackenzie, op cit
22. Vice Admiral Sir Arthur Hezlet, letter to the author, 25.3.87
23. Ibid
24. PRO ADM 236/48
25. Vice Admiral Sir Arthur Hezlet, op cit
26. PRO ADM 236/48
27. Vice Admiral Sir Arthur Hezlet, op cit
28. Rear Admiral G. W. G. Simpson, op cit, P150

Chapter 18   'One cigarette all round — and one only'

1. PRO ADM 236/48
2. Mr G. Curnall, op cit
3. Captain M. L. C. Crawford, interview with the author, 19.1.87
4. Captain C. P. Norman, op cit
5. Cdr A. Kimmins *Submarines in Action*, article in *The Listener* 26.2.42
6. Mr C. F. Tuckwood, op cit
7. Ibid

Chapter 19   'I could literally hear my knees knocking'

1. Rear Admiral G. W. G. Simpson, op cit, P150
2. Ibid P146
3. Ibid P150
4. Ibid P141
5. PRO ADM 236/48
6. Ibid
7. Cdr A. Kimmins, op cit
8. PRO ADM 236/48
9. Ibid
10. Ibid
11. Vice Admiral Sir Hugh Mackenzie, op cit
12. Sydney Hart, op cit P90
13. PRO ADM 236/48
14. Sydney Hart, op cit P96
15. Mr G. Curnall, op cit
16. PRO ADM 236/48
17. Mr G. Curnall, op cit
18. Ibid
19. Ibid

20. Ibid
21. Ibid

Chapter 20   'All the dogs in Sicily were barking'

1.   PRO ADM 236/48
2.   Ernle Bradford, op cit P89
3.   PRO ADM 236/48
4.   Mr B. Bird, letter to the author
5.   PRO ADM 236/48
6.   Ibid
7.   Mr B. Bird, op cit
8.   PRO ADM 236/48
9.   Mr B. Bird, op cit
10. Ibid
11. PRO ADM 236/48
12. Mr B. Bird, op cit
13. Ibid
14. Rear Admiral G. W. G. Simpson, op cit P145
15. Alistair Mars, op cit
16. Rear Admiral G. W. G. Simpson, op cit P145
17. Ibid P149

Chapter 21   'The most skilful attack ever made'

1.   Airey Neave *Nuremburg* Hodder and Stoughton, 1978, P220
2.   Cdr Richard Compton Hall *Cutting the Lifeline* article in *The Elite* Vol 8, P1739, Orbis Publishing Ltd, 1986
3.   PRO ADM 236/48
4.   Rear Admiral G. W. G. Simpson, op cit P151
5.   Ibid P151-2
6.   Ibid P166
7.   Ibid P152
8.   Mr C. F. Tuckwood, op cit
9.   Captain M. L. C. Crawford, interview with author, 19.1.87
10. Ibid
11. Ibid
12. PRO 236/48
13. Captain M. L. C. Crawford, interview with the author, 19.1.87
14. PRO ADM 236/48
15. Ibid
16. Ibid
17. Cdr F. W. Lipscomb, op cit
18. Rear Admiral G. W. G. Simpson, op cit P165
19. Ibid
20. Ibid
21. Ibid P163
22. Lt Cdr M. D. Wanklyn, letter to his wife, 6.11.41
23. Ibid
24. Ibid
25. Alistair Mars, op cit P174
26. Vice Admiral Sir Hugh Mackenzie, op cit

Chapter 22   'A sight granted to few submarine commanders'

1.   PRO ADM 236/48
2.   Ibid
3.   Ibid
4.   Ibid
5.   Ibid
6.   Ibid
7.   Sydney Hart, op cit P130
8.   PRO ADM 236/48
9.   Ibid
10. Ibid
11. Ibid
12. Sydney Hart, op cit P134
13. PRO ADM 236/48
14. Sydney Hart, op cit P134
15. PRO ADM 236/48

16. Sydney Hart, op cit P135

Chapter 23   'VC — but mother in tears'

1. Sydney Hart, op cit P136
2. Captain C. P. Norman, op cit
3. Ibid
4. Ibid
5. PRO ADM 236/48
6. Admiral Sir Max Horton, letter to Mrs E. Wanklyn, 10.12.41
7. Captain M. L. C. Crawford, letter to Mrs. E. Wanklyn, 15.12.41
8. Lt Cdr M. D. Wanklyn, telegram to his wife, 15.12.41
9. Mrs E. Wanklyn, op cit
10. Ibid
11. *The Daily Record*, 12.12.41
12. *The Daily Mirror*, 12.12.41
13. *The News Chronicle*, 12.12.41
14. *The Times of Malta*, 24.12.41
15. Rear Admiral G. W. G. Simpson, op cit P166
16. Cdr A. Kimmins, op cit
17. Cdr A. Kimmins *Half Time* William Heinemann, 1947, P93
18. Ibid P95

Chapter 24   'A pretty close call'

1. Captain C. P. Norman, op cit
2. Ibid
3. Ibid
4. Ibid
5. Graham Cook *Silent Marauders* Hart Davis, MacGibbon, 1976, P184
6. Rear Admiral G. W. G. Simpson, op cit
7. Ernle Bradford, op cit, P186

Chapter 25   'Second U-boat — the *Amiraglio St Bon*

1. PRO ADM 236/48
2. John Frayn Turner *VCs of the Royal Navy* George Harrap, 1956
3. PRO ADM 236/48
4. Ibid
5. Ibid
6. Ibid
7. Ibid
8. Ibid

Chapter 26   'A foul lake of wrecks'

1. George Hogan *Malta: The Triumphant Years* London, 1978
2. Bernard Gray, quoted by Ernle Bradford, op cit P140
3. George Hogan, op cit
4. Lt Cdr M. M. Wanklyn, letter to Mrs P. Thompson, 8.2.42
5. *The Times of Malta*, 25.2.42
6. Lt Cdr M. D. Wanklyn, letter to Mrs P. Thompson, 8.2.42
7. Sydney Hart, op cit P156
8. PRO ADM 236/48
9. Ibid
10. Ibid
11. Rear Admiral G. W. G. Simpson, op cit P198
12. Ibid
13. Ibid P199
14. Ibid P200
15. Lt Cdr M. D. Wanklyn, letter to his wife

Chapter 27   'Report farm casualties'

1. PRO ADM 236/48
2. Ibid
3. Ibid
4. Ibid
5. Ibid
6. Ibid
7. Ernle Bradford, op cit P149
8. Rear Admiral G. W. G. Simpson, op cit P210

9.   Ibid P209
10. Ibid

Chapter 28   'No mean achievement'
1.   PRO ADM 236/48
2.   Ibid
3.   Ibid
4.   Ibid
5.   Ibid
6.   Ibid
7.   Ibid
8.   Ibid
9.   Mrs J. Harris, op cit

Chapter 29   'Count the days, they are not so many'
1.   Mr G. Selby, op cit
2.   Mr C. F. Tuckwood, op cit
3.   Rex Woods *Special Commando*, William Kimber, 1985, P33
4.   Lt Col Robert Wilson, letter to the author, 20.7.87
5.   Rear Admiral G. W. G. Simpson, op cit P122
6.
7.   Mr B. Bird, op cit
8.   Sydney Hart, op cit P198
9.   Ibid P198
10. Rex Woods, op cit P52/53
11. Lt Cdr M. D. Wanklyn, letter to his wife, 10.4.42

Chapter 30   'A giant among us'
1.   Capitano di Vascello the Barone Francesco Acton, letter to the author
2.   Sydney Hart, op cit P201
3.   Vice Admiral Sir Hugh Mackenzie, op cit
4.   Cdr M. St John, op cit
5.   Captain M. L. C. Crawford, interview with the author, 19.1.87
6.   Vice Admiral Sir Arthur Hezlet, letter to the author, 25.3.87
7.   Mr C. F. Tuckwood, op cit
8.   Rear Admiral G. W. G. Simpson, op cit P228
9.   Ibid
10. Rear Admiral G. W. G. Simpson, letter to Mrs E. Wanklyn
11. Admiralty letter to Mrs E. Wanklyn
12. Ibid
13. Admiralty communique, 22.8.42
14. Captain M. L. C. Crawford, interview with the author, 19.1.87
15. Harry Morley, quoted in *The Daily Sketch* 30.4.43
16. Miss J. Wanklyn, op cit
17. Rear Admiral R. B. Darke, letter to Mrs E. Wanklyn
18. *The Daily Mirror*, 3.3.43
19. Captain M. L. C. Crawford, letter to E. Wanklyn
20. Mrs E. Wanklyn, op cit
21. Vice Admiral Sir Hugh Mackenzie, op cit
22. Vice Admiral Sir John Roxburgh, Foreword to *Periscope View* by Rear Admiral G. W. G. Simpson
23. Captain M. L. C. Crawford, interview with the author, 19.1.87
24. Ibid
25. Mr Alexander Tulloch, Academy of Graphology (see Appendix 2)
26. Ibid
27. Ibid
28. Ibid
29. Ibid
30. L. D. A. Hussey, letter to H. R. Mill, 22.10.22, Scott Polar Research Institute, Cambridge
31. Admiralty Communique, 22.8.42

Index